Suicidal Christians

SUICIDAL CHRISTIANS

Help for the Broken Hearted

Nita Tarr

SUICIDAL CHRISTIANS

Printed in the United Kingdom

ISBN: 978-1-78280-161-0

www.suicidalchristians.com

Contents

To

The Broken Hearted

How Can There Be Suicidal Christians?

My Child

It is healthy and good that you are questioning these things. Come, let's reason together.

You have been intricately made by me. I see your innermost being and understand you better than anyone else, including yourself. Together we can overcome anything. Nothing is too difficult for me.

I want you to have a balanced life, one that is rich and full. But, above all, I long for you: because I love you. I am eager to listen and ready to speak. So come, let us do this together.

Forever Yours

God

He was absolutely adamant that he was not going to accept Jesus as his Saviour. "Why would a loving God allow all this suffering?" he said, sitting across from me in my kitchen.

I had heard these arguments before - many times. My heart sank when I did because I knew that arguing was often futile. Sometimes, people are so busy complaining, that they don't want to listen to reason. So, while he was talking, I asked God to help me to say something that would cut through to the real issue. Instantly I knew exactly what to say: "You are going to give your life to Jesus today," I said, the assurance of God behind my words, "when you do, you will have two paths open to you and both are about freedom. You can learn the hard way, like I did, that freedom cannot be found in the things that the world offers you or you can find true freedom in Christ."

His eyebrows were raised at my presumption but it did not deter him: "How can all the religions of the world be wrong? How can you be so sure that Jesus is the truth?" he asked. I thought about all the

1

arguments I could answer to this, and picked one: "Never in my entire life have I found another religion where God is totally about love. Either Jesus was a madman, a liar or He was who He said He was." A pregnant silence followed, then: "Well! I'm convinced. Let's say the prayer."

He chose freedom that night, but I was still learning about freedom the hard way. The next time I saw him I too was celebrating – with a bottle of champagne. I was also on heavy painkillers and the liquor went straight to my head. Later, while my husband was in bed and my daughter and her newly saved friend were watching TV, I took an overdose of sleeping tablets and lost consciousness.

Had I died, people would have asked: "Why did she do it?" It is a good question. The Creator of the Universe is my personal friend, I live in the countryside of Ireland in a gothic house with my three beautiful children and my husband of twenty six years, I enjoy my job as a drama teacher – what could be wrong? It was true I had problems: crushing debt, debilitating chronic pain and a rocky marriage, but these weren't new hardships. So, why was I now shoving a fistful of pills down my throat? It made no sense.

As I lay vomiting violently the next day, I got a chance to think about this question. I was shocked by my action. I wasn't embarrassed and upset about being alive like I normally feel after a suicide attempt, I was flabbergasted because my action came out of the blue – I hadn't been feeling that bad! Claws of terror gripped me as I lay there, suddenly realising that I had not been in control of my actions at all.

How could this be? How can I have a deep quiet time in the morning with God and then be gulping down a handful of sleeping tablets on top of painkillers in the evening? It was like I had flicked on some kind of default button: "Drink, then kill yourself." The default button was probably there because of repetition – I had tried to take my own life many times before. The thought that I might have killed myself as some kind of automatic response, shook me to my core.

At the same time this event took place, I was running a support group. Even though the group was open to all, those who came were

2

mainly Christians. Many of them either had current thoughts of suicide or had contemplated it in the past. Some had survived a few attempts. The realisation that I was not the only Christian with suicidal thoughts led me on this quest to find answers – and so began the journey of writing this book.

"Suicidal Christians! How can this be?" you might ask. Perhaps you think this is an oxymoron – Christians are called to have the 'life abundant' and failing that they should at least be 'happy.' They are certainly not meant to be in a place where they feel they cannot continue to live anymore!

Perhaps you feel guilty about having had these thoughts. Maybe you doubt your salvation. Maybe you have, like me, reached a point where you see no way out. This book is written for you.

A modicum of relief may be gained by realising that we are not alone in having suicidal thoughts. We can read about many people in the Bible who were used and loved by God, but who were also deeply depressed to the point of wanting to die: David speaks about his 'downcast soul' many times in Psalms. Elijah wails "I have had enough, Lord...take my life."[1] Jonah was so distraught he said: "Take away my life, for it is better for me to die than to live."[2] We hear the anguish filled words that Jesus spoke before his death: "My soul is overwhelmed with sorrow to the point of death"[3]

According to the World Health Organisation, more people are killing themselves today than in any previous time in our history. More people die from their own hand than from war, natural disaster and murder combined. A million people across the globe die by suicide each year - that is an average of one every 40 seconds. Some statistics report that half of all those who kill themselves are Christians.

A hundred thousand adolescents die by suicide every year. More soldiers on active duty now die from suicide than are killed in

---

[1] 1 Kings 19 v 4
[2] Jonah 4 v 3
[3] Psalm 72 v 12 – 14.

combat. A 2012 study by the US Dept. of Veterans Affairs found that (on average) 22 veterans kill themselves each day, a total of more than 8,000 a year. We are our own greatest danger. In the last 45 years, suicide rates have increased by about 60% worldwide, with global suicide figures potentially reaching 1.5 million deaths by the year 2020. Suicide has reached pandemic proportions.

The word "suicide" comes from two Latin roots: sui ("of oneself") and cidium ("killing" or "slaying"). It is 'the action of killing oneself intentionally.'

The history of suicide is dealt with in depth towards the end of the book, with a view to answering the question: "Is suicide a sin?" People throughout the ages have killed themselves in an endless variety of ways. Some of the stranger methods include: swallowing poisonous spiders, ramming hot pokers down their throats, power-drilling holes in their skulls, injecting peanut butter into their veins, crushing their necks in vices and by jumping into vats of beer.

Each of these deaths leaves devastation in its wake. On average, between six and ten loved ones are left grappling with the loss and confusion that follows each death – husbands, wives, parents, children, siblings and friends. Each year churches grapple to deal with this tragedy. Everyone affected wants to know why it happened, if it was their fault and if there was anything they could have done to prevent it. Many ask why they did not see it coming.

Often, we are not seeking answers as much as we are seeking the comfort we believe the answers will bring us. We think that once we have an answer our pain and grief will be eased – perhaps so. These questions are always difficult and sometimes impossible to answer. However, God can and does comfort, heal and restore.

So, working on the basis that we cannot fix anything before we have admitted that it is broken, we need to admit that this phenomenon exists, that there are Christians among us who are suffering the torment of suicidal thoughts.

This book addresses these issues, but it is also a kind of autopsy with me as the 'body'. A medical autopsy determines the cause of death by looking at the physical condition of the body. A pathologist seeks to find out why a patient died by performing autopsies. A coroner, on the other hand, investigates the circumstances and evidence surrounding the person's death – why they did such alarming things to themselves in the first place. This book is less about the method and more about the causes. We will be looking beneath the surface in an attempt to dissect the reasons that lead to suicidal thought. This is a spiritual rather than the psychological autopsy. There are many good books that deal with the emotional and psychological components of suicidal behaviour. This one focuses on God and how He can help.

The major traumas I have experienced (kidnap, rape, abuse and even a suspected murder) are scrutinised in an effort to uncover truths. My frequent suicide attempts, and what triggered them, are laid bare in the hope that this will bring healing to others. I endeavour to speak candidly about how I have messed up and what I have learnt from the mess. My battles with alcohol, prescription medication, low self-esteem and chronic pain have been used to illustrate how it is possible to survive, overcome and triumph with God's help.

Insides are exposed to reveal if any vital organs are missing, how various parts relate to others, how the body malfunctioned and why the essential life-blood stopped flowing. Once the reasons for our demise have been discovered we will be better equipped to understand what motivates us to do the things we do.

The stories of my life are not written in chronological order, but serve rather to illustrate a point. I became a Christian at the age of fourteen and am now over fifty, so most of these harrowing events occurred after I had given my life to the Lord.

Each chapter concludes with a short prayer. Unwilling to dictate to you how you should speak to God, I have written these in the hope that they spark ideas about what to pray for, rather than dictate the exact way to pray. I leave it up to you to rearrange them, add to them and change them into your own personal way of praying. There are also prayers at the beginning of each chapter, where I imagine how God would speak to us.

While writing this book, I pictured myself on a ledge talking to a person wanting to jump. I knew that conversation, I'd had it before...

It was late and I was tired. Surely it was too late to phone someone, especially someone who I barely knew? But a persistent feeling told me to phone. I recognised the Voice and if I ignored it I would feel bad, so I called, unsure about what I would say. I learnt later that he had to take the barrel of a gun out of his mouth to answer that call. He came to know Jesus as His Saviour that night. His life was saved, his eternity secured. Months later when he invited me to watch him sky-dive I asked him why he wanted to jump out of a plane. His answer was a life-time away from the man with the barrel of a gun in his mouth: "I used to want to leave my whole life behind, but this jump symbolises me leaving my *old* life behind."

Overall, this book is a self-help book that teaches us what to do when life no longer feels worth living. It endeavours to point the reader to the 'life abundant' that Jesus promised: "The thief comes only to steal and kill and destroy; I have come that they may have life, and have it to the full."[1]

I pray that reading this will give you hope and peace or, at the very least, if you are teetering on the edge, that it will help you to see the purpose that God has in mind for you.

You are my God and King and I worship You.
Help me to keep my eyes on You.
Lord, intervene in my life.
Heal me in my innermost being.
Give me hope.
Teach me Lord.
Speak to me as I read this book.

---

[1] John 10: 10 (all Bible quotes are from the NIV unless otherwise stated)

Why do I feel like this?

Beloved

You have been searching for happiness all your life: in things, people and activities. I see your disappointment and heartbreak when these things are lost, stolen or have faded away. Come, you can find lasting joy in me!

I know you think there is no way out of your situation and that nothing will change. But there is a way - because nothing is impossible for me. So do not be afraid, I am with you.

Unlike the world, which is constantly changing, I will not be moved. You can rely on me. My love is constant. My forgiveness is forever. I am the living Rock on which you can build your life. When your foundation is in me you will not be shaken.

I know how tired you are and I see that life weighs heavily on your shoulders. So come to me, I will give you rest.

With love

Your Lord

Over the years, I have attempted suicide many times for many different reasons. Unfortunately, I cannot remember all of them, but I remember some: When I was in my early teens I took an overdose of tablets because I felt rejected, alone, misunderstood and scared. In my late teens, I was trying to get someone's attention. While I was being abused I did it because I wanted the fear and torture to stop. When I got married, crushing disappointment combined with feelings of being trapped led to another attempt. In my thirties medication for depression, combined with booze, caused me to want to die. Then, after childbirth and having just moved to a new country, the most insidious of all the reasons: depression set in. Its grip was gradual and I did not at first recognise it for what it was, but it led me to the brink.

When I was a child, I loved comic books. I had a mountain of them - Little Dot, Archie, Dennis the Menace, to name a few. One day I overheard my mother, a teacher, explaining to someone that she was concerned that I still wasn't reading 'real' books at the age of eight but that she thought comics might help. She was wise. But I thought she was crazy and that I would love them forever. But, quite gradually, something started to change. They began to lose their appeal. The pictures looked dull and the stories boring. I no longer cared about what happened to Betty or Little Dot.

This is how it felt when I got depressed: suddenly, everything changed. The things that had given me excitement and happiness before looked dull and boring now - the heaviness inside me stifled and paralysed. Whereas before, I had been able to change gear from first to second to third, now I was in neutral. It became difficult to motivate myself to get up in the morning and I slept at every opportunity.

At first I asked: "Why do I feel like this?" But gradually I began to feel nothing at all. I tried to make sense of it all by ascribing feelings to my lack of feeling, for example, if someone asked, I would say I was lonely or sad or unfulfilled. But I wasn't. I was just feeling nothing.

Whatever happened I remained in neutral gear: If something good happened...nothing; something bad...nothing. Everything meant nothing. Nothing on the outside changed anything on my inside. I had nothing to give and nothing to live for.

Not being able to feel anything led to mind-numbing boredom. I would see people laugh at jokes and wonder what was so funny. I didn't want to go anywhere or do anything. I would listen to others sing songs to God and wonder why. I heard sermons that left others challenged, but I couldn't get any meaning out of them. There was no meaning in anything.

Colours were duller. Music was sadder. Everyone looked desperate and unhappy. I found no purpose in work. I even began to avoid those I loved because they were too much effort.

I didn't want anyone to feel uncomfortable around me and I was scared of being judged, so I pretended. Having been trained as an actress helped. I would smile but it hurt. I would laugh and it would sound false to me. I couldn't cry. Well, not at first...

Some of those closest to me knew though, and they tried to fix me. I tried to fix me too: thinking happy thoughts, not thinking too much; eating better, not eating too much; getting exercise, not being obsessed with exercise; being good to me, not focusing on me; trying to be happy, not trying so much. I was left feeling like I had been put in a washing machine without any water – tossed and dry.

I started to feel like I was a shell with something dead inside. Thoughts of how to kill myself would lurk in my mind – drive into the wall, jump, if I took all these tablets would they do the job? I would catch myself thinking these things and try to reason: "It's not like I actually want to die. I just didn't want to exist anymore." What I really wanted to do was sleep – preferably forever.

I didn't tell others when I felt this way. There is no way to tell someone you want to kill yourself. There is no way to get the response you want from people. They either: make a hasty exit, begin to cry, tell you how selfish you are or get completely freaked-out and hover over the phone ready to dial emergency services. In all fairness, I don't know what the right response would have been.

Even though the word 'depression' does not appear in the Bible, there are many examples of people who have experienced it. David, the psalmist, wrote: "I am laid low in the dust,"[1] Elijah tells God: "I have had enough, Lord. Take my life."[2] Then there's Jonah, Jeremiah and Paul, all who felt the shroud of depression descend over them.

Today, depression is a leading cause of suicide: Over 60% of all people who take their lives are suffering from this illness. If one includes alcoholics (who are often depressed) this figure rises to over 75%. More Americans suffer from depression than coronary

---

[1] Psalm 119:25
[2] 1 Kings 19:3

heart disease, cancer and AIDS combined. It is believed that about 15% of the population will suffer from clinical depression at some time during their life. However, the good news is that it is the most treatable of psychiatric illnesses. Between 80% and 90% of people with depression respond positively to effective treatment.

The first thing to understand about depression is that it can be a serious medical illness and not something that you have made up in your head. You need to recognise it before it can be dealt with. It is more than sadness: a depressed person may feel guilty, hopeless, unloved, helpless, useless and worthless and is often riddled with shame. Here is a list of some of the **Symptoms of Depression**:

- disturbances in sleep patterns (either too much sleep or too little)
- feeling tired or run down
- a change in sex drive
- a loss of interest in things that used to bring pleasure
- 'low' feelings for most of the day
- a significant decrease or increase in appetite
- slowed behaviour or restlessness that can be noticed by others
- feelings of worthlessness or guilt
- trouble making decisions
- recurrent thoughts of suicide

If you have a number of these symptoms, persisting for more than two weeks, then you are most likely suffering from depression and should see a doctor. They may diagnose one of the many types of depression, for example: major depression, bipolar disorder, cyclothymia (a milder form of bipolar disorder), dysthymia (or chronic depression), postpartum depression or seasonal affective disorder (SAD). These can all be treated effectively by a healthcare professional once a root cause has been diagnosed, which may include: hormonal fluctuations, the nuances of our individual personalities, our genetic predispositions or a myriad of other roots. Trying to deal with our depression unrealistically or without the help of professionals can keep one trapped in misconceptions and unable to make any lasting changes.

Getting to the root of depression can be a major step to overcoming it and this may be simpler than you think. For example: it may be the result of a lack of sleep, or the side effect of a medication, or an imbalance in hormone levels. Even food allergies have been linked to depression. It is essential to have a full medical examination even if this is just to rule out the possibility of your depression having a physiological cause. Once you have been assessed by a doctor, you can decide on the best path to your healing – whether it is medication, talk therapy or behavioural changes.

There are some Christians who think that taking antidepressants and the like is wrong. Some believe that taking this medication shows a lack of faith in God. They also argue that it is a mood-altering substance and, like alcohol, is prohibited in the Bible. I disagree strongly. Firstly alcohol is not prohibited, in fact the Bible says: "Give beer to those who are perishing, wine to those who are in anguish; let them drink and forget their poverty and remember their misery no more."[1] Now before you reach for the bottle, remember that it also says that drunkards will not inherit the kingdom of God.[2] This by no means refers to people who get drunk occasionally; it is referring to habitual, unrepentant drinkers.

Secondly, antidepressants work by influencing how certain neurotransmitters (especially serotonin and norepinephrine) work in the brain. They balance the chemistry in our brains, which results in an improvement in mood. I would like to ask all those 'anti-antidepressants' if they take medication for a headache?

I do believe, however, that antidepressants are prescribed too readily. After a fifteen minute interview, without giving me any physical examination, knowing my medical history or telling me the side effects, I was given a prescription for antidepressants. A different doctor mistakenly diagnosed me with bi-polar disorder and sent me down a long spiral of confusion. The medication he gave me made me feel foggy, flat and fat. Thinking that this was to be expected, I persisted and became zombie-like. After a year of

---

[1] Proverbs 31:6,7
[2] 1 Corinthians 6:10

battling different medications I went off them all, suffering the horrors of withdrawal each time. My regular GP, who is a gem, correctly diagnosed thyroid problems, put me on the correct medication and all 'mood swings' disappeared. On a different occasion, I was prescribed antidepressants after being diagnosed with post-natal depression. They were an enormous help and after taking them for about five months I felt much better.

But what do you do when your 'physical' is clear and medication and talk therapy don't touch sides? Jesus does not ask that we just put up with depression, saying: "That is just the way it is." No, rather He said: "I have come that they may have life, and have it to the full."[1] If you have not managed to pick yourself up after calamity strikes or if you have sunken into a depression, don't settle for less and give up. We don't have to live 'lives of quiet desperation'. Depression can be overcome.

The 'solution' to depression is not found in the pursuit of happiness. Everyone wants to be happy. We pursue it by getting better and bigger things, searching for more exhilarating experiences and trying to find those perfect people who help us feel that way. But happiness is fleeting: when the experiences cease, things rust and the people leave, so does happiness; and often when it does, despair sets in. So there must be something more lasting - it is called joy. The original Hebrew word translates best as 'calm delight' and it runs much deeper than happiness. Rather than being dependent on circumstances, people and things, it is dependent on God and God alone.

This is a story of how God lifted me out of depression:

I never feel depressed while in the middle of the calamity. When the destructive dust of rape, abuse or the death of a loved one settled, it was then that depression set in. It was after one of these horrors (which I will discuss during the course of this book) that God showed me an amazing way to survive depression.

---

[1] John 10:10

He told me to hide. This verse stuck out one morning as I was beginning to feel the claws of depression closing around me: "My dove (I warmed, thinking this was how He thought of me), take cover in the clefts of the rock, in the hiding places on the mountainside, show me your face, let me hear your voice; for your voice is sweet and your face is lovely."[1] I knew He wanted me to be in 'The Cleft of the Rock.'

I lay in my bed and imagined myself looking at a towering mountain - an immovable fortress, safe against the storm of circumstance that raged around. Running down its surface, like a gigantic tear, was a perpendicular crack. I climbed a short distance up the mountain to a Cleft and took shelter.

At first, as I huddled there whimpering gulps of tears, I was more conscious of my own pain than of what was going on around me. But slowly I began to notice them, and as I did, the mere fact of their existence began to heal me. As the storm continued to howl outside, the solid, dependable, magnificent Rock seemed to hug me with reassurances of safety. The crack curved all the way up through the mountain to the sky, emphasising the sheer height and depth of the Rock. I was secure and warm.

At one stage, as I sat there, the storm picked up and screamed through the entrance, threatening to reach me. I was tempted to go out and fight against it once more, but I knew it was too big for me. This was not my battle. This battle had to be fought by One greater than I.

As I lay there, spent of all energy, I began to see my wounds. Some were little stings and cuts on the surface and some ran deep and needed long-term care. I knew that if I remained cradled by The Cleft, I would be healed in good time. Realising how secure I was, I became thankful and, as I did, the healing began. As it worked like an invisible nurse on my invisible wounds, I started to notice little things to be thankful for – the myriad of colours in a drop of water, a pretty little bird and the fresh breeze on my face.

---

[1] Songs of Solomon 2:14

I sat up and took a deep breath as words from the Lord gave me hope: "Now is your time of grief, but I will see you again and you will rejoice, and no one will take away your joy."[1] It felt good knowing that I was not alone. "So do not fear, for I am with you; do not be dismayed, for I am your God. I will strengthen you and help you; I will hold you with my righteous right hand."[2] I soaked in His Words: "The Lord is my strength and my shield: my heart trusts in him. And I am helped. My heart leaps for joy and I will give thanks to him in song."[3] As I rested and trusted, the words seemed to heal the deepest of my wounds: "He will wipe every tear from their eyes. There will be no more death or mourning or pain, for the old order of things has passed away."[4]

I stood and, as I did, I realised I was standing on The Rock: "The Lord is my rock. My fortress and my deliverer; my God is my rock, in whom I take refuge. He is my shield and the horn of my salvation; my stronghold. I call to the Lord, who is worthy of praise, and I am saved from my enemies."[5] While I stood there I knew I couldn't be shaken by anything.

With that assurance, I allowed some trusted friends into The Cleft. While others can be hurtful, there are still more who love and help. Their presence brought further healing. I ignored the sombre few who pointed out the storm. Eventually, in a state of expectant peace, I left The Cleft. As I walked out into the world again, the storm still raged, but there was a calm joy permeating my life because I knew The Cleft would always be there to shelter me.

While the Bible never mentions the word 'depression,' it sounds as though Jesus is referring to it when He says: "Come to me, all you who are weary and burdened and I will give you rest."[6] His solution is clear - rest. This is a different kind of rest to the one we are used to. The rest that Jesus offers is not the end to all hard work; it is a

---

[1] John 16:22
[2] Isaiah 41:10
[3] Psalm 28:7
[4] Revelation 21:4
[5] Psalm 18:2
[6] Matthew 11:28

deep inner healing all about love and peace with God and others. It is not battening down the hatches and shutting away from the world – that would be counterproductive. This kind of rest is a reliance on God rather than a reliance on your own efforts. For example, He may not take you out of a boring, seemingly meaningless job but He may make it productive and filled with purpose. This God-centred rest will break the back of your depression and, once you make it a life-style choice, it can see you through any storm.

Coming away into the Cleft of the Rock means being available to be completely moulded, nursed and loved by God. You rest while He does all the work. This is practical biblical resting, but if you want this kind of loving involvement in your life, you need to commit to making some choices – these are called **'The Cleft Choices'**:

- **Choose to recover** - Abraham Lincoln once said, "Most folks are as happy as they make up their minds to be." Decide that you can be happier because God said you can. Decide that you can enjoy your life. Decide that you want to get better.
- **Choose to get closer to God** - Making yourself aware of the fact that He is always present in your life should comfort you. Pray not only to be healed from depression, but also for a miracle in every area of your life.
- **Choose to trust** - Decide that no matter what your circumstances look like, you will trust that God is working. Decide that you do not need to understand what He is doing. Just understand that He will look after you and work everything out for the good.
- **Choose to be grateful** - Get into the habit of saying thank you to God for all sorts of things – both big and small. It is good for *you*. Misery and depression will not be able to spread in a grateful heart.
- **Choose to change** your thinking and rewire your mind
- **Choose to shift your focus** from yourself to God - Depressed people turn their focus inward. Turn your focus upward to God.
- **Choose to take care** of your body.
- **Choose to have time** when you don't do anything at all - Have down time. Be peaceful and learn about contentment.

- **Choose to show concern** for others.
- **Choose to think about positive, good things** - "Whatever is true, whatever is noble, whatever is right, whatever is pure, whatever is lovely, whatever is admirable – if anything is excellent or praiseworthy – think about such things."[1] Decide to monitor what you read and watch. Filling your mind with negative things will affect your thoughts.
- **Choose not to think**, ruminate and mull over hurtful and negative events in your past - You cannot change the past so there is no point in thinking about it. This kind of thinking will damage you.
- **Choose not to worry** about the future - Take one step at a time. Do what you can do today and leave the future in God's capable Hands.

Each day, resolve to make these choices until they become a habit of thought.

Depression takes time to heal, so be patient. Do not feel as though you have to put on a show of being cheerful and positive. Depression is nothing to be embarrassed about and it can be unhealthy to hide it from people or from God. He knows how you feel so you can turn to Him and be just the way you are while He works on your healing and restoration.

Lord I am feeling overwhelmed by depression.
Lift this depression from me.
Help me to draw near to you.
I trust you Lord. Only you!
I trust you with my past, present and future.
Lead me in obedience through this trial.
I am sorry Lord that I worry, please help me not to.
Help me to change. Change me.
Help me to stop reasoning and planning.
Show me how to enter your rest.
Show me how to be sheltered in The Cleft.
Show me how to hand things over to you to deal with.

---

[1] Philippians 4:8

I Feel Trapped

Dear Child

The world is full of things that promise to fulfil you and bring you happiness, but many of them have been designed by the devil to trap you. If you have become snared by one of these temptations, look to me and I will show you a way out.

As soon as they come into your life, run in the opposite direction and refuse to have anything to do with them. Then stay close to me. I will help you to resist them and you will find a complete, balanced life that is full of blessing.

Decide today that you only want what I have decided is good for you. I love you and know what is right for you.

Forever

Your Deliverer

One thing common to everyone who wants to take their own life is the feeling that they are trapped. They feel unable to find a way out: The daily sinking emptiness following the loss of a loved one; the clenching, breathless pain of feeling unloved; the inexplicable feelings of anxiety and hopelessness that don't seem to have any reason; the haunting, nagging memories of the past; the cycle of trying to feed your addiction and the crushing guilt that follows a fall into it; the terror of being with someone who hurts you; the desperation of debt; the emptiness of harming yourself and the confusion that follows; the rage and jealousy that blinds and engulfs and the anger and frustration of not getting what you need or want. Any of these may leave you thinking: "I feel trapped."

In all these scenarios, the person feels cornered, whether by an abuser, an addiction, those around them, a grief, a habit, the past, debt or themselves.

17

Perhaps when you heard: "It is for freedom that Christ has set us free"[1] or "if the Son sets you free you will be free indeed"[2] it left you asking: "If Jesus came to set us free why don't I feel free?"

Here is the key to answering that question: Jesus did not give us the freedom to do what we want, He gave us the freedom to be in a relationship with the Father and to follow Him. This sounds disheartening when one first hears it because we want to be free to do what we want with an assurance of there being no consequences. Following someone with blind faith does not sound like freedom, it sounds like slavery.

But we are not following just anyone. We are following someone who loves us more than we will ever understand and because of this love, we can be certain that whatever He has planned for us will be for our good. Therefore, in following we are free.

We've all spent time in the pit. It's a muddy, dirty place where we were slaves to sin and oblivious of this bondage. Then He came, reached down and lifted us out. Now he is walking with us and, as we walk and talk and get closer to Him, the mud is falling off and we are learning what it means to be free. As we look back we see how desperately stuck we were in the pit. Our sin shackled us around our ankles. It dictated to us what we should do with each waking moment, and perhaps worst of all, we could not even see these shackles or hear the relentless brainwashing. We simply obeyed. We didn't know who we really were and we had no idea what our true purpose for living was. We were trapped in every way.

Looking around for a rope to pull us out, we found none. We saw roots that looked like they could save but as soon as we tried to pull on them, or tried to rely on them, they snapped. In our desperation we called out to God for help and immediately a Strong Hand reached down into the mud and pulled us out. But even though we now stood, hand in hand with Him, each time we looked back at the mud we felt like we were sinking. We remembered the mud and

---

[1] Galatians 5:1
[2] John 8:36

tried to hide from Him that we missed it a little. We lost focus of His Strong Hand in ours.

But as we began to gaze up at His Face we were overcome by enormous relief because we saw His unconditional Love. Hope flooded our hearts. We had a future - with Him.

Suddenly we heard the bubble of the mud behind us and, as we half-turned to look back, we stumbled. No longer looking at Him, we noticed that we still had bits of mud on us. We tried to wipe it off, but it stuck fast. We asked Him to wipe it off and He reached down, smiling and the globules of mud fell off effortlessly. Delighted, we continued walking hand in hand, muddy but looking forward to the adventure ahead.

After I was saved, I did more than just look back at the mud. I jumped back in. I still thought there might be some freedom in that mud. My enticing little root was alcohol. I loved the feeling I got when I drank. I felt elated, happy with the world around me and 'the belle of the ball.' But more importantly it helped me to forget. So I returned to the mud, still hand in hand with God, planning to get just a little bit muddy. A little is fine right? The problem with dabbling in the mud is that you do not notice yourself sinking.

This time, though, the mud is not as enjoyable because you can see it. Also, He is still holding your hand. So even though you can decide to do the things the captives still do, you have Him right there as a reminder that what you are doing is not really what you should be doing. This is conviction, and when conviction is not addressed God allows the mud to stick until it begins to stink.

Also, the devil is now taking a deeper interest in you. He now knows that you are walking with God and he is looking for any opportunity to keep you from telling others about how you got free from the pit. As long as you look muddy, no one will ask you how you got free. He wants to keep everyone in the pit. That is where he is lord. But he has a problem: you can see the mud now that you have been saved.

So he disguises the mud. He covers it with a beautiful hand woven rug, especially made to mould to the specific contours of your body.

The comfort is a relief. Your pains are temporarily propped up and eased. The picnic begins and you feed yourself on whatever you want. You now no longer see or feel where you really are.

But the devil always dumps you. When you have suitably gorged yourself and sunken so deep into the rug that you begin to feel the mud beneath, he will rip it out from under you. That's when you feel the full weight of where you are. Having known freedom, your captivity feels that much more devastating.

Painful past memories begin to envelop and daily problems bombard. You scream to be satisfied but your loneliness continues to forge a gaping hole inside you. Hopelessness creeps in to devour. You feel like you are nothing and have nothing.

Then you feel a gentle squeeze on your hand and you remember that you were saved from all of this. So you cry out to God for help. Once again, you are lifted out of the mud. This time you find it harder to accept that He doesn't see the muck and you feel more ashamed than before. But He assures you that you look as clean as driven snow to Him and that He loves you. It is hard to believe. He says He will teach you how and shows you the path.

When you continue on that straight and narrow path you will come to the Living Rock. It is immovable, constant and solid. When you stand on it you realize that this undeserved favour towards you never ends, that this forgiveness is complete and that this love is unchanging. So you can build your life on it, trusting in it and relying on it in all circumstances. You will be able to withstand the darkest, fiercest storms in life. When the winds of adversity are howling and the rain feels like darts to your heart, the Rock on which you stand holds you steadfast. You have a firm foundation: "...who is the Rock except our God?"[1]

But you ignore the Living Rock, thinking that it looks too high and impossible to climb. Just ahead you see a fence; it looks like a good place to rest, a place where you won't have to make any decisions. So, dropping the Strong Hand, you run and jump onto the fence.

---

[1] Psalm 18:31

On the one side you see the Green Pasture where you were walking with the Strong Hand. You remember being here. It was great. You felt part of something important. You were proud that you were doing everything right and certain the Strong Hand was pleased with you. You had clever things to say to other people that made you feel good about yourself. You were told you were a blessing to people and you felt like you belonged. You thought that you had discovered perfect peace and felt sorry for anyone else who didn't want it. The birds were singing and the air was fresh.

Suddenly a storm breaks out and it rains on the Green Pasture. Aghast, you wonder what it is all about. When you read the Bible it just looks like empty words. You pray and it feels as though you are talking to yourself. You go to church and find it boring and the people start to look like hypocrites. After all, you reason, they cannot possibly be *feeling* the happiness they are showing on their dry, dull faces - they are living in a bubble and being false you conclude. You don't fit in anymore. The worship doesn't make any sense and it all leaves you cold and irritated. The message drones on. Maybe it's not even true. You begin to fear you made a mistake.

Wolves, sensing your fear, begin to circle. Some have been sitting in the pews all along, disguised as sheep. They snarl and growl and your fear increases. The sheep run around looking busy, but you realise they are just scared. Their well-meaning but callous bleating disillusions you even further. Either way, you feel this is not the place you thought it would be.

You hear the distant call of a voice you think you recognize from the past. It sounds beautiful - full of promise. You have been warned not to go over the fence but, you reason, you will just nip there...have a quick look...you won't touch anything...just a look...after all...everyone deserves a break.

You jump off the fence and stagger as you land. Without helping you to steady yourself, you are profusely welcomed. The lights are brighter, the music louder, the colours throbbing and persistent. Streets are lined with gold and neon signs drip with nectar so you take the promise of happiness. "Surely I am meant to be happy?" you reason. The pain in your body stops - gone in an instant. This, more than anything, is what keeps you coming back for more, over and over again.

But, each time you return, the glowing edge of things seems to be fading: the lights are dimmer, the music softer and the nectar has a nasty aftertaste. You persist, hoping to find that pain-deadening euphoria; instead you are left feeling worse than ever before.

Just as you are about to leave, you notice others who have come over from the Green Pasture. You are relieved: "So not all of them are boring! If they can do it, then it must be alright. I can have fun!" you reason again. Keeping close to them helps keep the guilt at bay. But you soon find that they are also making the trip back and forward to the Green Pasture trying to find that elusive initial high. When their hurt and frustration spills over and they lash out, you wander off frustrated and crushed.

The Fence looms ahead of you as you consider sitting on it again. You know where you should be, but that's not where you want to be. Both sides look false so you think: "Maybe 'on The Fence' is the right place?" It promises neutrality. If you sat there, you reason, you could avoid having to choose sides. "At least no one can say I am doing anything wrong if I sit there. I can say the right things to people on both sides of the fence and be acceptable to both. I can then enjoy each side whenever I feel like it."

As you sit there, trying to get comfortable, you realise you are not alone. Sitting next to you, grinning from ear to ear, is the devil. "Welcome! This is my fence," he says as he encircles you with his arm.

Our way to freedom, whether we are trapped in the pit or teetering on the fence, begins with making the right choice. The most important choice we will ever make is to decide who we will follow. We may have chosen to follow God when we first asked for forgiveness for our sins and accepted Jesus into our lives, but since then we may have chosen to follow a path that is not His, and if it is not His path then it is the devil's path. Maybe we chose to sit on the fence thinking that it was safe, neutral territory, only to discover it to be the most painful place of all. I know - because I have bounced on and off that fence more than a few times in my life. Most of the times I was suicidal was while I was sitting on the fence.

I'd like to say I had a whirlwind courtship with my husband Richard, but there was no space for a whirlwind and no time for a courtship – we married after only knowing each other for twenty five days. We both felt God wanted us to marry. But that didn't stop it from being a stormy marriage as we fought for power and tried to get our own way. Two years later, after the birth of our eldest daughter Sasha, I left my career as an actress and singer and moved to a farm where we thought we could build our relationship together, live off the land and get closer to God.

It became a crazy time of jumping back and forth over the fence. We went to a little church where I led worship and I enrolled at Bible College. I was also being given inspiration from God to compose, record and produce songs in our home studio. Soon afterwards I was asked to sing and give my testimony at various churches. As soon as I had enough songs I approached a Christian record company who agreed to sign me on as an artist. They were so pleased with the backing that I had produced for my album that they invited me to come into their studios to record. A date was set.

At the same time, desperately lonely and missing the glitzy world of filmmaking, I binge drank. Richard was often away and I would be left alone and scared. Farming can be dangerous in South Africa - a neighbour had been raped recently and we had received threatening messages from those who thought we overpaid our workers. On one occasion when Sasha and I were home alone, an Egyptian cobra slithered into the sitting room, trapping us in a corner. After what seemed like an eternity, we managed to make our way past it and phone for help.

I filled my days home-schooling and playing with my daughter, studying for Bible College, composing songs and doing all sorts of 'farm-wife' type things. But as soon as I had tucked her up in bed, I would drink to drown out the fear and try to make sense of the traumatic events in my not-so-distant past. I couldn't. Wild thoughts would race around my head with no end in sight. When I saw Richard we would inevitably argue. I didn't trust him during his frequent trips away, I resented him for getting us into a financial mess and I was deeply saddened that we were not getting on. So I drank. But the pain of hangovers would heighten my resolve to give up and I usually ended up recommitting my life to the Lord yet again...only to fall weeks later. This yo-yo lifestyle left me feeling trapped.

On the few occasions I travelled to the city I went overboard. I was so pleased to be away from the farm and so excited to be out, I inevitably drank too much. On one such occasion, I refused to leave with Richard because I wanted to carry on partying with the people I had met in the bar. My husband begged me to come home with him, but I wouldn't. He even tried to carry me out but when I went back he left me, with an assurance from those there, that I would get a lift home.

As soon as he left I started to feel scared and it dawned on me that the drive home was nearly two hours long and the women in the group had already left. In those days there were no mobile phones so I couldn't get in touch with Richard. I had no choice but to get a lift from one of the men.

My fear began to mount as he turned off onto a deserted, dirt road explaining that he needed to stop at his workplace to fetch something. Then, in the middle of nowhere he stopped the car and walked around to the rear. I took a deep breath, prayed silently and went into survival mode. As the Scary Guy called to me to come and see something in the trunk, I looked out the window. By the light of the moon I could make out low bush stretching out in every direction – too low to hide behind. But further on, the bush vanished into darkness; I presumed it was a valley. Taking off my stilettos I slung my handbag across my body and ran.

I could hear him yelling: "Come back! I'm not going to hurt you." But I knew. You can feel some types of evil. As I ran, the rough ground cut my feet but I didn't fall. My mind was crystal clear and a surge of energy pumped through me. The Scary Guy's voice faded as I ran further, down into the dark valley, towards the sound of rushing water.

It was only when I reached the bank of the river that I stopped and took stock of my situation. In the distance, on the other side of the river, there was a glow on the horizon that I thought may be a town. But I had to cross the river to get there. It looked like it was flowing fairly strongly but I reassured myself that I was a good swimmer. It was hard to tell the depth as moonlight skimmed off its rolling surface.

I slid down the bank and stepped in, shoes held above my head. Mud squelched between my toes as I waded deeper and deeper into the cold water. Reaching the halfway mark, I suddenly stopped dead. Just ahead and slightly to the side, I saw what looked like a rock appear and then disappear beneath the undulating water. "Crocodile!", I thought to myself, breathing through the panic that threatened to well up inside of me. The water was now well above my waist so I began to swim as fast and as silently as I could to the other side, keeping an eye on the 'rock' as I did. It never moved.

Once on the other side I scrambled up the bank, and to my disappointment, saw that the light from the town was no closer – the low scrub stretched as far as the eye could see - flat and unrelenting, offering no hope of rescue. I steeled myself for a long walk.

After about twenty minutes I came to a dirt road and began to walk down it, even though it was not heading toward the light. The gravel tore so badly into my feet that I sat down and, for the first time, I cried. As I sat there I noticed the lights of a car appearing in the distance and, as they grew closer, I worried that it may be the Scary Guy coming back to look for me. But I was too sore and too tired to run. The car stopped a little distance away and as soon as the person got out of the car I knew it wasn't the Scary Guy. The silhouette of this man loomed huge in the lights of the car and, as he walked towards me, I saw that he was a black man.

"Hey missus, what are you doing here?" He said identifying himself as a prison warden and explaining that I was inside the prison grounds. Nervous, but out of options, I accepted his offer of a lift. After a short drive I arrived at the low-security prison. They phoned Richard, who had by now arrived home, while I took a shower and rung out my dripping clothes to the best of my ability. As I waited to be fetched I told the wardens about the Scary Guy, but they became very defensive and said things like: "You should have gone home with your husband." I could do nothing but agree with them. No more light was ever shed on this event and I returned home, ashamed and full of guilt. But I also realised that I had narrowly missed being raped or murdered.

I told God and my husband how sorry I was and became even more determined to try harder. As the date for doing the final recording of my album approached, I threw myself into getting my voice into shape and working on the songs. Even while I was writing them with uplifting themes like: 'Soaring on the wings of eagles,' I was riddled by deep loneliness, shame, a growing fear of people and confusion about my faith.

When the record company called the day before the recording date and told me that building housing their studio had just burnt down, I wasn't particularly surprised. Deep down inside I believed that God had seen my sinful life and had decided that I wouldn't be a 'good witness' for Him. These feelings grew until I felt worthless and unloved and rejected – by Him.

During this time I took an overdose in an attempt to kill myself. I never told anyone or wrote any notes. While my husband was away and my daughter was visiting her grandmother, I simply took all my sleeping tablets and any other tablets that looked vaguely dangerous and lay in bed to wait for death. A sense of failure choked, fear paralysed and shear loneliness left me breathless. I was overwhelmed by an inability to change any of it. I felt trapped by my circumstances and cornered by my choices. Death was the only way out.

But God had another plan...again. I woke up the next morning. I don't think anyone even realised I had tried to kill myself and I wasn't going to tell them. It is easier that way.

As I look back at this story and try to make sense of what happened I realise I was cornered, not only by bad choices but also by the devil.

My choices opened doors for him to sneak in and "steal and kill and destroy."[1]

If you are bouncing between two sides of the fence you will be feeling trapped. The Bible explains that in order to gain freedom one needs to make a choice: "No one can serve two masters. Either he will hate the one and love the other, or he will be devoted to the one and despise the other." We need to decide who to serve: "...then choose for yourselves this day who you will serve..."[2]

Paul seems to understand our human nature so well: "You, my brothers, were called to be free. But do not use your freedom to indulge the sinful nature."[3] There is a danger that we might fall into: that because "Christ has set us free"[4] we think we can do whatever we want. But we cannot. Feeding those desires will lead to depression, anxiety, guilt and all those negative emotions that lead us to the brink. Instead, he adds, "...rather, serve one another in love...live by the Spirit and you will not gratify the desires of the sinful nature."

So, staying out of that muddy pit and settling on the right side of the fence rather than on it, will lead to freedom. You will no longer feel trapped when you decide where you want to stand. "It is for freedom that Christ has set us free. Stand firm, then and do not let yourselves be burdened again by a yoke of slavery."[5]

None of us are strangers to temptation, as Dante shows in this allegorical story: The Christian is on a journey up a winding mountain road. After climbing a short while a wolf of lust jumps out at the young man. When he climbs a little higher, during his middle age, the tiger of pride leaps out at him. Later, when he is an old man a scrawny looking lion, representing financial security, pounces out. His point being that no matter what stage of life you are in, temptation will come - it cannot be avoided, but it can be withstood.

---

[1] John 10:10
[2] Joshua 24:14
[3] Galatians 5:13
[4] Galatians 5:1
[5] Galatians 5:1

C.S. Lewis wrote: "No man knows how bad he is till he has tried very hard to be good. A silly idea is current that good people do not know what temptation means. This is an obvious lie. Only those who try to resist temptation know how strong it is. After all, you find out the strength of the German army by fighting against it, not by giving in. You find out the strength of a wind by trying to walk against it, not by lying down. A man who gives in to temptation after five minutes simply does not know what it would have been like an hour later. That is why bad people, in one sense, know very little about badness. They have lived a sheltered life by always giving in. We never find out the strength of the evil impulse inside us until we try to fight it: and Christ, because he was the only man who never yielded to temptation, is also the only man who knows to the full what temptation means – the only complete realist."

For many years I had the false belief that God was testing me through temptation to see if I would be obedient or not. For example, I thought that God surrounded me with people who drink to see if I would be able to resist. My thoughts even went so far as to think that God was tempting me to see if I really loved Him or not. The Bible is clear – God does not tempt us: "When tempted, no one should say, "God is tempting me." For God cannot be tempted by evil, nor does he tempt anyone." He does not tempt you by trying to get you to sin. Temptation comes from within our souls. It starts with an evil thought that, if dwelt on, can become a sinful action: "But each one is tempted by his own evil desire, he is dragged away and enticed. Then, after desire has conceived, it gives birth to sin; and sin, when it is full-grown, gives birth to death."[1]

I also believed, falsely, that it was a sin to be tempted. For example I felt that if I thought: "Oh, I'd love to have a drink," that thought was sin. It is not. Even Jesus was tempted by the devil in the desert. It is a sin to give in to temptation.

So often we try to lay the blame for our sins and even our sinful thoughts on something or someone else: "They made me do it" or "Everyone is doing it" or "nobody is perfect. I am just human after

---

[1] James 1:13-15

all" or "I couldn't help it. The devil made me do it" or we plead ignorance: "I didn't know it was wrong" or "I wasn't trying to be mean when I did it." These excuses prevent us from taking the responsibility of change on ourselves. We need to accept responsibility for our actions and reactions as a first step to standing firm against temptation.

At the moment my Achilles heel is oat cookies and flapjacks ...anything with oats and honey. I can eat them any time of day, even on top of a full meal. Once I get started I want more. Then after the initial euphoria of eating wears off, the regret sets in as I realise I will have to work-out longer or eat less the next day. I know the formula: eat more equals more calories equals putting on weight. So I start to make rules with myself: "I will only eat one" or "I will eat nothing after seven at night" or "I will stop for a week." But it doesn't seem to work. Even though I know what I want to do, I don't seem to be able to stick to my goals.

I have had to get over some seriously damaging addictions in the past, certainly more dangerous than oat cookies! These are dealt with in detail in a later chapter. However 'bad' your temptation may be, the principles behind resisting them remain the same.

Scientists have researched what goes on inside our brains when we are trying to resist temptation. In brief, every time I eat an oat cookie I am telling my brain that this is an important action – one that needs to be repeated. The more cookies I eat the more my brain thinks I need to eat cookies! When I stop eating cookies my brain begins to yell for cookies. The more cookies I eat the more intense and frequent the cravings. However, when I stop eating them for a few days, my brain will become 'rewired' into thinking it is no longer a vital necessity.

So how do we resist the 'oat cookies' in our lives?

The quicker you respond to temptation, the less likely it will take hold. Pray at the first sign of temptation. Jesus said: "Watch and pray so that you will not fall into temptation."[1]

---

[1] Mark 14:38

I have written **The Six R's to Resisting Temptation** so that you can remember them easily and they can be readily used: Recognise, rewire, remind, remember, remove and refocus.

- **Recognise it** - Some temptations are not as discernible as are others. For example, having envious thoughts can be less obvious than having sexual ones. We need to learn to detect the early stages of a temptation and say to ourselves: "There is that craving/urge/thought again."
- **Rewire** your brain by reminding yourself that your urge or thought is just a feeling. Refuse to be governed by your feelings. Remind yourself that the urge is simply coming from your brain because it has been trained to think that way by repetition. The best way to re-wire your brain into thinking 'right' is by quoting the scripture that relates to your particular temptation: "I have hidden your word in my heart that I might not sin against you."[1] Find the scripture that relates to your particular 'cookie' and repeat it when you are tempted. For example, if you are being tempted sexually, quote this scripture: "Flee from sexual immorality. All other sins a man commits are outside his body, but he who sins sexually sins against his own body. Do you not know that your body is a temple of the Holy Spirit?"[2] Or simply repeat a shortened version of this by praying: "Lord I know that my body is a temple." If you are tempted to worry say: "My God shall supply all my needs according to his glorious riches in Christ Jesus."[3] Find the scripture verse that correlates to your particular temptation and learn it by heart or stick a reminder note up in a prominent position.
- **Remind** - Think about the consequences you suffered the last time you gave into temptation. Maybe it was guilt, a hangover, a disruption at work, a prosecution or damage to a relationship. Maybe you need to look to the damage that particular action caused in someone else's life to help you not to give in to temptation.

---

[1] Psalm 119:11
[2] 1Corinthians 6:18
[3] Philippians 4:19

- **Remember** the reward that is waiting for you: not only now, as a result of not giving in, but your eternal reward in heaven. If Jesus actually appeared to you right now would you be doing the thing you are thinking of doing?
- **Remove** it or run from it. Take it out of your life in any way that you can. For example, if you are trying to diet then don't buy the foods that you are not allowed to eat and don't stop on the way home at the fast food restaurant. Head in the opposite direction to whatever is tempting you, towards God. Don't pause to rationalise your actions with the devil because he is a master of excuses and lies.
- **Refocus** - put your mind onto something else. For example, pray, phone a friend, get some exercise or go to the movies. Make a plan about how you can avoid temptation in the future. God has a way of escape for you: "God is faithful; he will not let you be tempted beyond what you can bear."[1] Pray to God to help you. He will show you the way out.

By God's Grace you can resist every temptation that comes your way, but if you do fall, then don't stay down. Don't give up and say: "that's it, I have blown it again. I will never be able to get over this. Everyone thinks that is the way I am and they don't think I can change so I may as well just give in." Don't let the devil whisper in your ear: "You are a hypocrite. If everyone could see you they would know it too. You are not even a Christian." Everybody falls, but it is how you pick yourself up that counts. Remember that God is right there waiting, with His arms open wide, having already forgiven you. Pick yourself up with His help, dust the dirt off and be determined to move forward again. Never give up giving up!

Dear Saviour,
I have fallen again.
I am so sorry Lord. Please forgive me.
Thank you for your forgiveness.
Please God give me Your Grace to resist temptation.
Help me to persevere.

---

[1] 1Corinthians 10:13

I Don't Feel Favoured

Favoured One

Sometimes you think that I have forgotten all about you, but I have not.

You are highly favoured. There is nothing you can do to achieve this favour, it is simply yours because I love you - I chose you to be my child before time began. You are wrapped in my arms and being showered with my love every minute of every day, because I am your Father.

Wake up each morning expecting my favour in your life.

You will be pleasantly surprised by what I can do.

Your Father

No one who is so depressed that they want to die feels favoured by God, but everyone wants to be. We want God to show us that He loves us, and we want Him to take us out of our situation and make everything better. But sometimes it doesn't look like He will and we begin thinking: "I don't feel favoured!"

I was off the fence, living in the green pasture and walking hand in hand with God and yet I was still so miserable deep down that I wanted to die. In my regular quiet times, in church and in books I read that the 'life abundant' was mine, that I was meant to be enjoying a life of victory and that I was meant to be prosperous and healthy. Instead I was deeply in debt, had a chronic illness and was battling with many of my closer relationships. I read and heard that all of this was mine if I followed God: blessings, success, protection, financial breakthrough, restoration, healing, peace, wholeness, contentment...the list went on. But no matter how much I followed the rules, crushing reality set in after some time – I didn't have any of those things.

Doubling up my efforts to try to find out why, I entered Bible College and was taught that it was really all quiet simple: my lack of faith was preventing these blessings from flowing. Step-by-step books told me how I could get my prayers answered by using the Word.

I embraced this teaching with great enthusiasm and, after making sure I had forgiven everyone I held a grudge against, and casting out every demon that I could imagine, I stood on the Word and spoke it over my life.

I would speak to my finances and to my painful body with this formula for success. But when little changed over the years, I was left seriously confused. When I approached the people 'in the know' I was told that it had to be my fault, because it couldn't be God's fault, right? I went away convinced of this and tried even harder to have an even deeper faith. However, the hardships in my life continued, and I eventually concluded that I was still doing something wrong. Consumed by agonizing guilt, I fell into one of the most suicidal periods of my life.

The logic of the teaching made sense to me: God wants to answer our prayers and bless us abundantly, after all He is Love. We are hampering those efforts of His to shower us with His blessings by not truly believing that He can do it all, will do it all and is doing it all. We were told to believe that even if we do not see that it is happening, even if we are in blinding pain in our bodies, we are to believe that He *has* healed us already. I was told to ignore the pain and to tell others, myself and even God that I believed I was healed. So I did. It felt odd but I was told that was natural, so I pressed through, persevering as they told me too and speaking 'words of faith' into my life.

One of my suicide attempts during this time was the one I mentioned in the last chapter – the one no one found out about. The other one was a little more dramatic. I took the blades off a razor and sliced into my wrists. It stung like a hive of bees, so I stopped trying, bandaged up my wrists and left the bathroom desperately embarrassed about having to face questions from anyone who might notice.

At the time we were meeting with a small group of believers, where I led worship, and some of the members had thoughts about planting a church. I was also touring churches and seminars giving my testimony and singing songs that I had composed. I prayed and confessed miracles and healings. But most of the time I felt enormously conflicted; not only about the yo-yo life I was living but also about my inability to make the teaching I was receiving 'work' in that life.

One of the most powerful aspects of this teaching is that there is no need for the manufacturers to have a complaints department:

It was an impulse buy. You were just browsing through the shelves of teaching, thinking that you didn't need to buy anything because you had it all already when an advertising slogan on one of the bottles catches your attention: "Unlock Heaven," it promises. The brightly coloured bottle that has the faint aroma of something pure is called "Demand."

"Sounds good," you think to yourself, "I could use a bit of power in my life!"

Once you have bought the Demand you rush home and read the label: "Follow these instructions carefully. Failure to do so will result in the product not working. This will not be the fault of the manufacturer. Decide what your need is. Choose area for application. Ensure that all surfaces are clean before application - if possible ask two or three others to help you with application. Apply liberally to the area. Remove any sources of heat from the immediate vicinity. Believe that the product is working before application. Then, in a loud and clear voice, name the problem and claim that the area has been repaired."

If Demand does not work you complain to the manufacturers and are told that it is your fault. You are told that you didn't apply the product correctly or you did not follow the instructions. They go on to suggest that you did not order it through the correct channels. "However," they continue with great certainty, "the biggest reason why Demand did not work is that you didn't believe it would work!"

You leave the complaints department assured of your own inadequacy and failure.

During the eighties there was broad recognition that this teaching was false. When the pastor of the church and bible college that I was attending confessed and denounced this 'word of faith' movement I felt cheated - I had been studying with them for years.

Confused, I tried to make sense of it all in my head. Even though I saw that it was an incorrect teaching, it was very difficult to stop thinking the way that I had been taught. I chided myself each time I 'confessed' something negative, like: "I am fed up" or "I cannot handle this anymore" or "I feel really sick." I had been taught that this type of thinking invites harm into your life. For example, if I used a fairly colloquial expression like: "I am dying of hunger," it could be inviting illness and even death into your life. I got into a total muddle trying to work out what I was allowed to say and what I wasn't allowed to say.

Slowly the core of the problem dawned on me: It had become all about my ministry, my healing, my vision, me, me, me. It was all about what I wanted. I was trying to manipulate God into doing what I wanted. I had been trying to back Him into a corner and throw His own Word at Him. I was demanding that He give me what I wanted because, after all, He is faithful to His Word. I had put myself in the driver's seat of my life. At the root of this thinking is pride.

But I didn't see it straight away. I felt immense shame that I had been teaching, singing and spreading this error for so many years. Where could I stand? What could I believe? What was the truth? How was I meant to think and to pray? I got no answers...so I threw out the baby with the bathwater. I stopped singing and writing songs and stopped trying to get closer to God – it was too dangerous and I felt too stupid to ever be able to understand the truth.

Thank God for God. He led us to a wonderful church where I slowly began to focus on Him again. It was just what I needed, though it took many years for me to be able to get a more balanced perspective.

The focus in the Word of Faith Movement mainly hinges around Mark 11 v 23 where Jesus uses an everyday Jewish metaphor to teach his disciples to believe in the Power of God. This passage has been distorted and used to build an entire belief system revolving around faith and words as a means to obtain health and wealth. They do not teach faith in God, they teach faith in faith and faith in words. Where Jesus preached suffering and humility, they preach success and prosperity.

The truth is that there is no potion that suits all our needs. We are individuals and God treats us and our problems with tailor-made packages. We cannot possibly know what we need or what is good for us. He sees what the future holds and he sees the myriad of possibilities in our present, and therefore only He is qualified to see what we need now. He takes everything into account whereas generally we only take ourselves into account. The only way to 'unlock' anything from God is to spend time with Him and get to know Him and His perfect, specific design for our lives. Then he will decide, in His inexplicable loving way, what we need and what will happen to us.

When I look back at the kind of thinking I had then, I realize much of it was borne out of my need to feel God's favour. If my prayers were answered then I would feel like He loved me and that I was doing everything right. This belief skims close to the truth and yet misses it entirely.

Honesty is one of the qualities I most value – in others and in myself - sometimes to a fault. About a year ago, I was telling the story of when I was in a crash landing to my hairdresser: Returning from Portugal and coming in to land at Johannesburg airport, during a Highveld thunder storm, we were circling the airport in a holding pattern. Suddenly there was a loud bang and the cabin lights went out. The plane started to shake violently. After what seemed like an hour of fervent prayer, interspersed with sheer terror, we landed hard. That's when I lied to my hairdresser. I have no idea why I did. I think I forgot the truth, or my mind had made up a false picture or perhaps I was just trying to make the story more exciting. I told her that we had come out of the aircraft on an escape slide, whereas we had actually used stairs. Then, I told the rest of the story of how we had looked back at the aircraft and the whole front of the fuselage had been covered in a tarpaulin. I paid her and went home. But the lie sat with me like a bad meal. So as I pulled my car into the yard, I turned around and went back to the salon, apologised for lying and told her the truth. She looked startled and bemused. Maybe I was being a bit of a stickler, but I am a stickler for the truth.

So what was the truth here? I still wanted to know how God favours us and whether there was anything I could do to get Him to 'open the floodgates of Heaven.' True, God loves us. True, He wants to bless us. These are powerful truths and truths that anyone feeling desperate enough to take their own life needs to hear. But the big question remained: "Will He?"

The first mistake that I had made was to think that I could earn God's favour.   I thought that God's blessings were based on my performance and good works. I needed to shift my thinking: God does not bless us because we are good. He blesses us because He is good.   Blessings are not to be achieved, they are to be received. There is a subtle but huge difference.

The reason why you are trying to be better so that God will work in your life may be because you do not believe that you are righteous in the eyes of God. That's what it means when Jesus cried out: "It is finished!" on the cross. The full weight of all our sins past, present and future were hanging there with Him on the cross. He is no longer angry with you. How can He be angry with you when He himself declares that He remembers your sins no more and He has separated your sins from Him as far as the East is from the West? So there is no need to carry guilt and condemnation around with you. That is what the devil wants you to feel. He wants you to believe the lie that God is angry with you.

When you realise that you are completely forgiven and stand righteous before God and it becomes a reality in your life that you have His undeserved favour (His Grace), you will experience victory over hardships, addictions and all sins in your life. The reality that God sees you as spotlessly clean of all sin needs to become fresh to you again. We need to rekindle a deeper appreciation for the value of the blood that was shed for us.

Maybe you feel that your sins are so bad that He cannot possibly forgive you. But the Bible says: "If we confess our sins, he is faithful and just and will forgive us our sins, and purify us from all unrighteousness."[1] When Jesus died on the cross you were not even born yet, so all the sins you were going to commit were in the future – they were all 'future sins'. So what Jesus accomplished on the cross was outside of time. He died for all the sins you have committed, are committing and will commit. You are already forgiven!

There is also a damaging belief that has crept into the church that God only forgives us after we have confessed our sins each time. Remember forgiveness is not based on what we do; it is based on what Jesus has already done. You cannot possibly remember or even know all the sins you have committed, so with this line of thinking, you stand in a state of un-forgiveness. You would need to be confessing your sins all the time. But you were forgiven, once and for all, when you gave your life to the Lord.

Once forgiven you become a child of God and as such, are welcomed into His Kingdom and the life abundant that it offers: "I have come that they may have life, and have it to the full."[2] However, it does not always feel like that. Why?

Life with Christ is lived on a higher plane. We have the assurance of knowing that we need not fear death because we are going to be with Him for eternity. We can live guilt-free because if God forgives us, then why should we worry about others not forgiving us or, even worse, why do we not forgive ourselves? We also have His guidance to see us around or through difficult times. As if this wasn't enough, we have His everlasting love which should assure us that He is working in our lives for our good.

His forgiveness, guidance and love are already available to us. These are the favours of God. But what do you do when, against all reason,

---

[1] 1John 1:9
[2] John 10:10

this just doesn't feel like enough? What do you do when you're saying: "Yea, I know I am forgiven and God loves me and is with me, but I am still in so much pain and I have no money and my relationships are in bits - Where is the favour I really need?"

The trouble with that thinking is that I was glossing over the keys to abundant life.

Imagine if when you gave your life to Jesus, He gave you a new house. You approach it, hand in hand with your new, smiling Lord, and you see that it is magnificent. It is bright; homely and welcoming, despite its size.

As you look up to thank Jesus, you see unbridled love in His face as He looks down to you. Suddenly you become painfully aware of the weight of the bag on your back. Jesus explains that you are carrying your sins and offers to take them from you. When you agree He reaches down and lifts the weight off your shoulders. You had never realised how heavy they were before. How light and free you feel without them!

Skipping towards your new house you see that it has a promising name: Plenty Palace. Then a thought occurs to you and you turn to Jesus: "What is this going to cost me?" you ask nervous of the reply. But, smile broadening, He answers: "It is free - totally free."

Overjoyed, you look around and notice that the house has a prime location overlooking the neighbourhood and city. This overview gives you better perspective and insight into the lives of your neighbours. You always knew Mr Johnson gardened a lot, but now as you look from your vantage point, you can see the love in his face as he tends to his flowers. You now realise why Wendy always looks sad as you see her being yelled at by her husband in the back yard. Jesus explains that you have been given this deeper insight into the lives of people around you so that you will be in a better position to help them.

As you reach the front door Jesus turns to you and with impeccable manners says: "Would you like to follow me? I can show you around your house." You agree to follow Him.

Walking over the threshold you notice the welcome mat that reads: "Come as you are." Hearing your delighted laugh, Jesus explains: "That is not just for you, it should also be your attitude towards others."

Immediately on entering you feel as though you have arrived home. It feels as though everything has been tailor-made to your exact specifications.

As you stand in the entrance and look around, you notice that Jesus has not closed the front door. Seeing your quizzical look He says: "It is better if the door stays open to all. This is a house to be enjoyed by everyone."

Alarmed you ask Jesus: "But what if someone comes in and tries to hurt me or steal something." His reply startles you: "If someone steals from you, love them, and know that there will be those who try to hurt you."[1]

"But Jesus!" you interrupt, "Wouldn't it be better if we just closed the door so no-one could come in?"

"No, that wouldn't be better," He replies simply, "you need people and they need you."

Seeing your fear, He gestures for you to go over to a little button the wall. "You have no reason to fear. This is the panic button." Jesus explains. "It will get an immediate response at any time, night or day. This house is constantly being patrolled by the best response team imaginable. All intruders can be swiftly and effectively dealt with."

Relieved and reassured you look around the large and welcoming entrance hall. Jesus explains that the house is designed for entertaining. With delight you see that He is not wrong – there is a huge pool, a large kitchen, comfy little corners for cosy chit-chats and a large garden. A fresh aroma, one you have never smelt before, permeates the house and peaceful, happy music plays continually.

---

[1] Luke 6:30

The kitchen is situated off the entertainment area for convenience. The cupboards and fridge are filled to the brim. "I have much more than I will ever need!" you say merrily to Jesus. "Exactly!" he replies, "Every time you give to someone else, more will be given to you!"[1]

"Really?" you reply doubtfully, not being used to such blatant generosity. "Why don't you test me in this?" Jesus suggests. Making a mental note to do exactly that, you move on to see the rest of the house.

The opulence and comfort is throughout. All your needs are catered for.

The main bedroom is dominated by the huge bed. As you fling yourself onto it you realise it is exceptionally comfortable. Jesus explains that He considers good sleep and rest to be a top priority.

Jumping up, you run to see the bathroom. It has everything needed for cleanliness: a shower for that quick clean, a bath for a good soak and a sauna to get a really deep cleanse. Jesus warns: "Don't walk around thinking about being dirty; walk around feeling clean." He walks over to the veranda as he speaks: "You have been favoured," he says, gesturing with one sweeping movement to the city beyond, "so that you can tell others the good news that I have come so that all can have life and life abundant."[2]

This is a picture of the favours of God that are already ours. We have these, and more, when we give our lives to the Him. We appropriate these favours simply by knowing that they are there. I call these **The Favours of Knowing**, because you are:

- **Chosen** since before time began to be His child - The fact that you have been especially chosen by the Creator of the Universe should instil in you an appreciation of your worth. Not only were you chosen, but you were created in His

---

[1] Luke 6:38
[2] John 10:10

image.[1] You are the pinnacle of God's creation on earth. When others treat you disrespectfully, you can be certain of your dignity and value.

- **Forgiven** - Becoming forgiveness-conscious rather than sin-conscious will allow healing to begin. You are constantly being washed in the cleansing blood of Jesus.   This is not a once-off occurrence, it is a continual washing.
- **In Communication** with the Creator - Prayer should be your panic button – your first response. If you knew, at a heart level, that He is always there to listen to your prayer, you would have peace.
- **Well provided for** – If you really believed this truth, you would cease to worry about the future.
- **Completely protected** - Knowing that the Almighty is guarding you should help you to feel completely secure.
- **At Rest** - Knowing that we can rest in Him, should give us comfort in the midst of our busy lives.
- **Powerful** - Knowing that we have the power of God in us should help us to accomplish anything in Jesus Christ's name.
- **Eternal** - Knowing that we will be forever in Heaven with Jesus should fill us with a confident hope and peace.

These truths, while not exhaustive, are discussed in later chapters.

Our cry to God that we want to be favoured has already been answered. We *are* favoured. But we don't feel that we are because we want things that we don't really need. We think we know what we need. These unfulfilled desires leave us feeling dissatisfied.

I have been living with chronic, excruciating pain for nearly four years. Since the pain began I knew what I needed – no more pain! I prayed, begging God for relief. But none came. I became despondent and eventually confused. Did God want me in this pain?

Eventually, even though I did not give up praying I gave up needing to know why. I gave up needing an answer to why God either allowed me to be in this pain or whether He even caused it. After all the theological arguments died down I was left with the same

---

[1] Genesis 1:27

conclusion – we don't know why God does or allows what He does. I decided to say, along with David: "Such knowledge is too wonderful for me, too lofty for me to attain."[1]

During this time the daughter of a friend, told me that she felt God wanted me to read the story about the woman with the issue of blood.[2] In this story, Jesus is making his way through the crushing crowd to get to someone's daughter who is dying, when a sick woman reaches out to touch him. She thinks that just one touch will change her life, and it did. She is instantly healed. As I read this story, with new insight, my heart sank. Her faith had healed her. The old confusion left by the 'Word of Faith' movement began to surface in my mind and with it came the guilt. My loved ones and I had been praying with faith for years for my healing. Was my faith too small?

Maybe not. I remember praying for a mountain to be moved...and it was. I was with my daughter, Georgie, on a skiing holiday in Switzerland. Sitting in a gondola, we began to talk about faith and began to discuss whether God literally meant that we could move mountains if we had enough faith? Jesus said: "I tell you the truth, if you have faith as small as a mustard seed, you can say to this mountain, 'Move from here to there' and it will move. Nothing will be impossible for you."[3] So, praying hard to God in my head, I suggested to Georgie that we try it. Excitedly we looked over the snow covered valley below, strewn with little villages to the magnificent peaks on the other side. We selected a peak (that had no villages below it) and prayed. When the gondola reached the top we got off and skied down, stopping every now and then to see if our mountain had moved, but the trees blocked out view. As I reached the base of the same gondola again I looked up, and to my amazement, saw a great white billow of snow rising up the mountain side. There had been an avalanche on the peak we had chosen! Needless to say we were amazed. Now it isn't exactly a whole mountain moving, but I think God was having a little bit of fun with us that day.

---

[1] Psalm 139:6
[2] Luke 8:43-48
[3] Matthew 17:20

So as I read the story about the woman reaching out in faith to touch Jesus' garment, I knew there must be something more that God was trying to say to me. Then as I read the end of the story, I saw three little words that changed my focus forever: "Go in peace."[1]

It confirmed what I had been discovering from the doctors. My ailment was seriously exacerbated by stress. Any stressful thoughts, no matter how small, seemed to hold my pelvis in a vice grip and sting. This pain had become an instant and real response to any stressor.

So began my pursuit for peace. Being mellow seems to come naturally to some, but not so for me. In the beginning I didn't think I was stressed at all, but with a constant reminder in my stomach, I became aware of just how wound up, tense and stressed out I was. I discuss stress in a later chapter, and mention it here by way of explaining that I would never have become aware of my need for peace had I received the answer to my prayer and been healed. Over the next few years I was healed of something far more dangerous and insidious – stress. I was taught something far more valuable than that which any miracle can bring – peace.

These years of pain have given me a fresh understanding that His ways are not our ways: "For my thoughts are not your thoughts, neither are your ways my ways, declares the Lord."[2] One of the greatest 'Favours of Knowing' is that He is in control and has a plan for our lives.

Sometimes we become preoccupied with problems when we should be looking for opportunities. Instead of focusing on the negative, develop an attitude of expectancy: "Lord, I know that you love me and that something good is going to happen." Then, while waiting in an attitude of expectancy, keep on the lookout for that good thing! *Know* God's favour, don't try to earn it. Live in hopeful expectancy. Wake up each morning expecting favour: He says he works all things

---

[1] Luke 8:48
[2] Isaiah 55:8

for good[1]... so wake up expecting good! Get your mind made up ahead of time about this: When you know something horrible is coming up, try think in advance about how you may see it joyfully. For example, rather than thinking: "Oh no I have to go for that procedure again," think: "When I go for that procedure I am going to look for moments to encourage someone else in the hospital." There is a well-known saying: "Attitude determines altitude."

The importance of our attitude is described beautifully in a book by Gary Vanderet: Two seriously ill men are lying in the same room in a hospital. The one has his bed next to the window and is able to sit up for an hour each afternoon; the other is flat on his back all the time. As part of their treatment, neither of them is allowed to do anything except talk. The poor man who is unable to move looks forward to the hour each afternoon when the man next to the window describes everything he sees outside: the beauty of the lake and the activities taking place on it, games of softball and young lovers walking hand in hand. As the man on his back listens, he imagines the beauty of the scene that is being described. But as time wears on the man becomes jealous of his friend with the view and broods about how unfair it is that he doesn't have the bed next to the window. One night, the man with the view dies and as soon as he could the other man asks if he can switch beds. As the nurses leaves the room he painstakingly props himself up in bed and looks out at the view – it is a blank wall.

The way we view our lives will change our attitude.

Thank you that I am favoured.
Thank you that You have chosen me.
Thank you for all Your favours.
Thank you that You are in control.
Thank you that You have a plan for my life.
Thank you for Your provision, protection and for peace.
I expect Your favour today.

---

[1] Romans 8:28

How Can I Call Myself A Christian?

My Righteous Child

You sometimes think that you know best and then you think you don't really understand at all. I see you struggle with trying to make sense of your past and understand your life. But you don't need to understand everything. I know all about you and I can see deep into your aching heart.

So, instead of constantly questioning why things happened the way they did and asking what I am doing in all of this, just know that I only want what is best for you.

I have sent my Holy Spirit to be your counsellor. Learn to hear His Voice and allow me to heal your deepest wounds.

Come to me and be honest with me.

With love

Your Wise Counsellor

Before I move to get out of bed, the awful, recognizable feeling hits me. It is a bit like the sinking feeling you get when you go over a bump in the road. I know it well. The memories of what I did begin to creep back in my mind and with it comes guilt and shame. I drank and made a fool of myself. I said things I didn't mean and did things I shouldn't have.

Then I try to move; a wave of nausea sweeps over me and my head throbs. I have felt this before – many times. I try to drink some water and it makes me vomit. I know what I am in for – a day of lying awake, in pain, while vomiting and mulling over what I have done wrong. "What is wrong with me?" I think over and over again. I try to answer but my head just pounds.

Why did I drink? As was my pattern, I had been without alcohol for months. Is it simply because I needed a break from all that is happening in my life? Is it because of my past abuse? I remember crying my eyes out about that in the early hours of the morning. Is it just a habit or a crutch? I live my life determined not to drink, trying to get closer to God, trying to help those around me; but a pressure builds up inside me and drink seems to be the only release. I try so hard to be a 'good little Christian'. What happened? Was it the argument? What was I thinking when I reached for the bottle? I didn't think. It was as though I was on automatic. I felt like I had absolutely no control over what I was doing. Or did I?

I wonder whether it could be some demon plaguing me. But I had been for deliverance prayer so many times before. Sometimes I had even felt relief. Or had I?

Maybe I was just really damaged by my past? Yet, I had been to psychologists, counsellors, therapists and elders in the church. I had even been to a retreat where I was pounded by scripture day and night and, when I wanted to sleep, my eyelids were literally held open while they prayed for demons to leave me and threw scriptures at me in the hopes that I would change. I didn't. I hadn't. What strange things Christians get up to sometimes.

I was lying there with a mind-numbing hangover and no answers to why. I was a prisoner in a self-built prison that I felt I would never be free from, because I could not work out why I felt like I did or did what I did.

Why was I this way? The jumble of what I had become and the reasons why I had become that way looked like a tangle of spaghetti in my mind. Would unravelling the mess help? Would uncovering the painful memories of the past make a difference to how I felt now? I would need to take each strand of spaghetti and see where it led, then lay it out flat and see how it fitted on the plate of my mind. I realised that I needed to get to the root of my problem if I was ever going to find a solution.

When my mother married my step-father I went to live on his vast pine plantation in the Natal midlands in South Africa. I watched the trees being cut down and made into furniture in the factory on the farm. We watched as workers cut discs from the tree trunks and saw the rings of the cross-sections rippling out from the centre. Each ring told the story of a single year, together they were a permanent history, a vista into the past.

We too, need to find what is in the past to be able to understand what we have become.

It is a bit like that with us. On the surface the bark of the tree is like the mask that we wear to protect the inner core of our being from the weather of life. It consists of subconscious behaviours built in an effort to protect our softer inner core. We set up carefully constructed walls that deny, distort or manipulate our view of reality in an attempt to protect and maintain our view of ourselves and prevent us from seeing the root cause of our problems. These fabricated barriers are defence mechanisms and we all have them.

I will mention a few here: 'Rationalization' is when we create 'false but plausible excuses to justify unacceptable behaviour'. The believer excuses an action they know is wrong. I have used this many times with comments like: "I'm only human."

'Displacement' is when we "divert emotional feelings (usually anger) from their original source to a substitute target." An example of this would be an overworked father who gets back home and takes out his anger on his wife, who in turn yells at her child, who then fights with his little sister, who takes it out on the dog who in turn takes it out on the cat!

'Projection' is defined as "Attributing one's own thoughts, feelings, or motives to another." When we feel angry, rejected or guilty about something, we think someone else is being angry or rejecting us, or we might think they are hiding something from us. For example, a man might be fiercely jealous towards his wife and be convinced that she is cheating on him because *he* is having an affair.

Christians often use the next defence mechanism, which is called 'sublimation'. This is when impulses are channelled to socially acceptable outlets. For example, a gossip might tell a secret about someone and say that it is 'just for the purposes of prayer.'

We also use 'denial', where we refuse to accept or recognise a threatening situation or thought. This false perception of reality is often found in the Christian world when, in an attempt to appear perfect to one another, all wrong-doing is denied. This self-righteousness prevents them from seeing that they need to change and repent.

We also use 'suppression' to defend ourselves against any thoughts, feelings or experiences we might find disturbing. This is one of the strongest defence mechanisms standing in the way of being healed.

These defence mechanisms keep out the good as well as the bad and prevent us seeing things for the way they really are. They prevent us from looking beneath the bark of the tree, and this stands in the way of us receiving healing for our emotional wounds. The mechanisms have been constructed to try to protect us from further hurt. A person might say: "I will never let anyone close to me again!" Defence mechanisms are designed to help bury one's true feelings and cover one's true motives so that the roots of one's problems are never discovered and never tended to. As a result the person remains trapped by anger, resentment and fear.

We need to learn to recognise our defence mechanisms. God wants us to come before Him, transparent and honest about ourselves so that the Holy Spirit can do His deep healing work in our hearts and lives.

Beneath this defensive covering lie the rings of our lives – each ring representing a year.

Looking at them closely you will see the scars of old, painful hurts: the year of drought, brought on by the loneliness and rejection that you felt after the break-up of an important relationship; the pale ring of lack that affected all subsequent rings; the thick, soot-black ring from a devastating fire (a calamity that burnt you to your core); a dirty, reddish-coloured ring that seems to pulsate, where a trusted grown-up took a little girl to a secret place and dirty things buried a lifetime to come of inexplicable confusion and hurt. They all lie within, constantly reminding.

These annual growth rings are also affected by seasonal cycles – those recurrent waves of other people's actions and one's own habits that have become settled and hard to saw through. Like the child who hears over and over how stupid they are, who grows up to be an adult who acts as though they are stupid and so never even attempts to achieve their dreams. Some rings are laid down by emulating those we grew up with. For example, parents who had angry outbursts often raise children who have poor tempers. We may say: "We will never be like that!" when we recognise those family characteristics, but in so denying them, we don't recognise that we need healing. Left unresolved, they become entrenched in our personalities.

We see in the width of the tree ring the amount of growth that has taken place during one year and from this we can see the growing conditions for that year. When the conditions are good the tree grows faster and so lays down more tissue in the year, resulting in a wider growth ring. Poor conditions mean slower growth, less tissue laid down and consequently a narrower ring.

So it is with us. Our past is laid down inside of us and affects our everyday life. We need to look at these rings and acknowledge them as our real self, as the way we are made up at the moment. Healing begins at the point of recognizing the pain for what it is. However this is not always easy.

A person who has reached the point of suicide may have looked at these painful rings of the past and been overwhelmed by their complexity and feel incapable of doing anything about them. They can see that their leaves are withered by depression, anxiety, financial problems and relationship difficulties but they cannot understand why. These leaves will not be restored to health until the root of the tree is healed.

When my son was eight he complained about his shoes being too tight, so I bought him another pair, surprised at how big he'd grown. A week later however, he was moaning that his shoes were still too tight. I put the new pair on him and felt that the toe was comfortably away from the sides but he insisted, so I bought him another pair. To my amazement he came to me yet again with the complaint that they still weren't big enough. But when he wore them for sports day and while running his shoe kicked off into the unsuspecting crowd, I began to think there was something else going on. I asked him if he maybe just wanted to look bigger, or maybe he was used to the comfort of his old shoes and merely needed to break these ones in – but to no avail. He insisted they were too small. Then a few days later, having found out the problem, he came to me and sheepishly explained – it was his socks that were too small!

This little story illustrates how important it is to find the real cause of our problems. Sometimes, our first reaction once we discover these roots, is to try and tackle them with will-power, discipline or even ordinary prayer. But while these things are necessary and useful, they are often not enough. These problems need a deeper kind of healing, a healing that only the Holy Spirit can do. Shallow changes might make a difference for a while but for real change to occur we need to be healed at the root of our problem. "But how do I get to the root of my problem?" you may well ask.

Sometimes I feel like I have spent my entire life looking for these roots. During this quest I have had some strange experiences. My mother sent me to a child psychologist when I was about eight years old because I was not achieving well at school. His entire method of treatment seemed to consist of playing games with me. We played cowboys and Indians and Barbie during my visits to his office. His diagnosis was that I lived in a fantasy world. I don't know how he got me to live in the 'real' world but after only a few appointments, I began to get the progress prizes at school. He had done an effective job.

My experience with psychologists have not always been good though: When I was in my teens, my grandmother took me to one who molested me. I was terribly nervous as I walked up to his house, but Granny reassured me that he was a good friend of hers and I would be fine. As she waited in an adjoining room, I went in to see him. To my surprise I saw a pale, little, fat man in a wheelchair. He told me to sit very close to him so that he could hold my hand. I was a bit startled by his request but reasoned that maybe he wanted to comfort me.

As an aside, I think I need to explain something that you, my reader, may query a few times while reading this book. Questions like: Why didn't I do anything? Why did I let those things happen to me? Why didn't I tell anybody? Reasons include: that in 'those days' children did not question grown-ups; we were not aware of sexual predators like children are these days; I was often scared of hurting my loved ones and sometimes I was threatened if I told anyone.

So when he held my hand I was uncomfortable but did not question it. As we spoke, mainly about God because he was a 'Christian' psychologist, his hand began to move up my leg. I was very conscious of my granny in the next room and didn't want to embarrass her, so I stayed. When I shifted my position he quickly shoved his hand inside my shirt. Heart pounding, and ready to throw up, I rushed out the room. My granny was never told. I was a little in awe of her and loved her dearly and so I didn't want to hurt her.

There was another 'Christian therapist' who made me sit on his lap, insisting that it was the way he performed deliverance because, he explained, I needed to 'feel the love of a father.'

Much to my dismay, a secular psychologist, after hearing my life story, burst out crying. On another occasion, a psychiatrist misdiagnosed me (after a twenty minute consultation) with bi-polar disorder and prescribed heavy medication that stupefied me. His diagnosis was proved incorrect after a year of what felt like hell. Later on in life, when I turned to a pastor for help, he meddled so badly that he ended up causing major damage and distress for my whole family.

I have of course received much invaluable help from other pastors and therapists over the years, but they never got to the root of my distress. So I decided to do my own study. I went back to university in my thirties and studied psychology and when that didn't shed any light on my 'issues', I took numerous counselling courses. But my problems and their roots remained until I stopped looking for a solution in the world and relied completely on God for my healing.

But, as I lay there with that hangover, my mind found it hard to focus on Him: "How can I even call myself a Christian? I lash out at those I am meant to love. I keep doing the things I know are sins. I have these constant thoughts of wanting to die when I am told I am meant to be joyful. Everything I do is a failure. I mess up all the time. If anyone could see into my heart they would know that I am a hypocrite."

You, like me, may have thought these things. This is condemnation and it is the voice of the devil. It acts as a type of red herring, designed to distract you from being able to honestly appraise your life and get to the root cause of your troubles.

The Hebrew root of the word Satan means 'accuser.' His prime objective is to continually condemn you by pointing out all your faults. The definition of condemnation is to 'judge to be totally wrong' and 'sentence to punishment' but it also includes the idea of 'utter rejection'. This barrage of blame will leave you with very low self-esteem, crippling feelings of worthlessness and a sense of inferiority.

Condemnation demands punishment and payment for all failures and sins. If you have done something wrong, it tells you that you will need to pay in some way. While we are finding a way to pay for this sin, we shy away from God, thinking that there is no way He would want to embrace us while we are so guilty. When you fail, condemnation and guilt will cause you to run from God instead of to Him making all possibility of real, deep healing difficult.

Condemnation breeds low self-esteem. If you loath yourself, your thoughts or your actions, you are probably suffering from low self-esteem, which may have its roots in self-condemnation. This will result in defeat in many areas of our lives. It damages our relationships: our feelings of inferiority prevent us from communicating freely with others and our focus on ourselves prevents us from reaching out to others in any deep way. We also feel worthless in our relationship with God, so when we approach

Him it is not boldly or openly. It paralyses our potential and leaves our dreams unfulfilled. We look back at our lives and see all the things we wanted to achieve and did not – simply because we deemed ourselves incapable. Many people who commit suicide are carrying out the punishment they believe they deserve – it is the ultimate self-condemnation.

So often we think it is God who is pointing out our faults. This is exactly what Satan wants you to think. In fact he wants you to believe that God thinks that you are so worthless that you don't deserve to live. Sometimes we even think this is humility. This is a lie. Humility is freedom from pride. Are we not being full of pride if we refuse to forgive ourselves for something when the Creator of the Universe has decided that we should be forgiven?

"Therefore, there is now no condemnation for those who are in Christ Jesus, because through Christ Jesus the law of the Spirit who gives life has set you free from the law of sin and death."[1] Because we have committed a crime against God's holy law we have been sentenced to death. We were on death row, hooked up to tubes that were about to deliver a lethal cocktail into our veins that would kill us. The telephone rings but it is not the governor; it is God who declares us not guilty because Jesus died on the cross. We are saved!

If you believe that Jesus died on the cross for your sins then you are forgiven by God for what you have done. Your sins are forgiven by God and you should forgive yourself as well.

Your tree is ailing because of a deep root of condemnation. It can become a constant drip in our minds trying to convince us that everything we do is useless and that all we are is worthless. The devil wants you to believe these lies. For us to know the difference between God's voice and the devils, we need to know the difference between **condemnation and conviction**:

- Condemnation comes from the devil and conviction from the Lord.

---

[1] Romans 8:1

- Condemnation says God is an angry judge looming over us to punish, while conviction sees Him as a loving Father disciplining his children.
- Condemnation points out what a failure you are whereas the voice of conviction is encouraging. Jesus said: "I did not come to condemn the world but to save it."[1]
- Condemnation points out the problem without a solution, whereas conviction is solution orientated. It shows you the problem and conviction shows you the answer.
- Condemnation shouts: "Look at your past and see what a failure you are!" whereas conviction, in a quiet voice reminds: "Look at the Lamb who washes away all your sins."
- Condemnation is a curse and conviction a blessing.
- Condemnation pushes us away from God and conviction draws us towards Him.
- Condemnation keeps us focused inward; wallowing in self-pity and conviction is God-focused and brings hope.
- Condemnation tries to make us think that we will never change, conviction says: "All things are possible with God."[2]

The Holy Spirit continually waters our tree with reminders of our righteousness in Christ. As we absorb these truths, the root of condemnation will begin to wither and eventually the reality of who we are in Christ, a saved child of God, will strengthen us and we will stand firm.

Continually remind yourself that you are not righteous because of what you have done, you are righteous because of what Jesus has done. It is hard for some of us to accept a 'free' gift; difficult to accept that there really are no strings attached. But this amazing free gift of love is the essence of the work of the cross. Believe that you are righteous, because you are.

Once the bark of self defence mechanisms has been stripped away and the poison of condemnation removed, you will be free to examine the rings laid down by your life experiences and this can help you get to the root of the problem. Of course, it would be

---

[1] John 12:47
[2] Matthew 19:26

impossible for me to know the specific root to your problem. However, a few of the major, common roots are discussed in some depth in this book, for example, fear, rejection, stress and pride.

The advice we often receive is: "We will help you to remember all your problems, and when you do, we will give you pills to help you forget them. In the meantime, get it together and straighten out your life by cleaning up your act."

But God accepts you just the way you are. You don't need to come to Him already cured and problem free. He comes in the form of Himself to live inside you and work from the inside out to 'heal and deal' at the pace and level that is perfect for you.

This is the work of the Holy Spirit and Jesus calls Him our Counsellor.[1] This is someone who guides during an ordeal or trial but it is also a legal term for one who will defend someone against an adversary. He is our Helper and Advocate.

- He helps us in our weakness.[2]
- He gives us strength for extraordinary tasks.[3]
- He brings deep and lasting peace.[4]
- He convicts the world of sin, righteousness and judgment.[5]
- He steers us away from harmful or wrong places.[6]
- He helps us pray.[7]
- He helps us to know God's thoughts.[8]
- He makes us completely new![9]
- He carries out God's work in us.[10]
- He helps us to produce good fruit.[11]

---

[1] John 15:26
[2] Romans 8:26
[3] Judges 3:10
[4] John 14:27
[5] John 16:8-11
[6] Acts 16:7-9
[7] Romans 8:26
[8] 1 Corinthians 2:15
[9] 2 Corinthians 5:17
[10] Philippians 1:6
[11] Galatians 5:22

- He transforms us.[1]

In short, He gives life! The same life that was breathed into the creation of the world can be breathed over your life today. If you want this supernatural, transforming power it is available to you today.

All you need to do is ask, believe, and receive!

It would be prudent to mention here that there is debate surrounding the issue of whether you receive the Holy Spirit at the point of your salvation, or if it is a separate act. I believe it is clear that the Spirit is received when you accept God as your Saviour, after all He is one with the Holy Spirit, and His work in you continues throughout your life.   But this is a question you may like to investigate yourself. The Holy Spirit washes you continually with His comfort and peace. Speaking from personal experience, I know that every morning when I say: "I welcome you Holy Spirit!" I get the same feeling of something arriving and filling me up.

Dear Lord Jesus

Thank you that Your Word says that You baptise us with Your Holy Spirit[2].
Thank you for dying on the cross so that my sins could be forgiven.
I ask Lord, for the power of Your Holy Spirit to come upon me now.
I receive Him by faith and thank you for answering this prayer and filling me with Your Holy Spirit.
Thank you Lord that You see my innermost being and that You know what the root of my problem is.
Thank you Lord, that you will heal me deep down inside.
Search me Lord and know my heart.
Help me Lord to discern Your Voice.
Help me not to listen to those voices that condemn.
My life is in Your Hands.

---

[1] 1 Thessalonians 1:5
[2] Luke 3:16

I Am So Scared and I Don't Know Why

My Brave Child

I know that you have many fears and that some of them are holding you captive. You fear man, you fear yourself and you fear me. Whatever form it takes, know that it is never from me, so you do not need to hold me at arm's length when you feel hurt by others. You only do this because you fear I will reject you, as they did. But know this, I will never reject you.

Your fears have hidden your talents and your love because you are too scared to express yourself. They make you try so hard to be acceptable to me and to others. Know that I accept you and love you as you are.

As you take shelter, know for certain that you are secure and rest in my Love and see your fears dissipate.

Take courage for I am with you.

Your Protector

I was in a hurry. The girl behind the counter was being infuriatingly slow. She counted out my change by picking each coin up and then placing it in a neat row in front of me. I resisted huffing to let her know I needed to go. My husband was double-parked outside and he was probably being yelled at to move by now. Downtown Johannesburg is not the ideal place to double-park. Finally, smiling up at me, she finished the transaction.

Admonishing myself for being irritated with someone who had done nothing wrong, I hurried out of the shop and stopped dead in my tracks. Two meters away, a gun was pointing straight at me. Everyone in the busy arcade had frozen, staring at the ragged, dirty, white man with the ragged, dirty, black gun. "Ipf arrey-won moofs, I'll shoot!" he screamed, drunk. In a heartbeat I assessed his drunkenness, the distance he was away from me and the angle of the gun...and ran...straight at him and his gun. I passed its barrel by an inch.

As I ran, I became incredibly conscious of my back, convinced that at any minute I would feel the heat of a bullet ripping through my flesh. It seemed as though I ran a marathon before I was able to round the corner.

On reaching the car, tears flowed as I explained to Richard what had just happened. We noticed a security guard leaning against a wall. As I approached him I thought to myself how odd it was for one so gentle looking to have such a job. As soon as he heard that a man with a gun was holding up shoppers, he ran round the corner. It was the last I saw of him.

We heard on the news that he had been shot dead by the gunman, who was apprehended and charged. No shoppers were killed that day. That gentle, brave security guard probably saved their lives.

I have often thought about my reaction. This experience left me with a big, guilty question: Should I have told the security guard? If I hadn't told him then the other shopper's lives may have remained in danger. On the other hand, telling him cost him his life. I have accepted that I will never know the answer because I cannot possibly know how things would have turned out. But there is one thing I do not question: Whether I should have run or not. Fear caused me to run. If I hadn't I might have been killed.

Walter Bradford Cannon, a professor of physiology, describes our reaction to fear as the 'fight-or-fight-or-freeze response.' When faced with a harmful event, attack or threat to our survival, we flee, stay and fight or freeze. The response is on a physiological level; our sympathetic nervous systems produce a cascade of chemicals and hormones that give us a boost of energy that enables us to respond quickly when threatened. Fear helped me run from danger that day.

But if this stress response is prolonged by an on-going threat or multiple threats, the continual barrage of chemicals becomes damaging to our minds and bodies. This is what happened to me. Living in continual fear for so many years had a cumulative effect.

Fear built upon fear and became so unbearable that it became the underlying emotion behind many of my suicide attempts. It is a deadly root, a crippling emotion, and I needed to learn how to eliminate it.

Easier said than done, because we live in a fear dominated world and it seems to permeate every area of our lives. Franklin D. Roosevelt said that there is "nothing to fear but fear itself." When you are scared of something, that object often becomes your primary focus. God is acutely aware of our penchant for fear.

He tells us to "Fear not!" throughout the Bible, some say 365 times - to cover each day of the year. It is a command rather than a request: "For I am the Lord, your God who takes hold of your right hand and says to you: *do not fear*; I will help you."[1]

Surely it stands to reason that if He tells us to do it then it must be possible. No matter how terrifying your memory or the situation you are facing, God can and will bring you to a place of peace.

Webster's Dictionary defines fear as "a distressing emotion aroused by impending danger, evil, pain, etc., whether the threat is real or imagined." You may find yourself saying: "I am just so scared and I don't know why!"

There are many types of fear and each has their own particular poison. Growing up in a country with many types of snakes, we knew that we needed to name the snake that had bitten us, or failing that, actually catch the snake and take it to the doctor for effective treatment to be possible. They needed to know what poisoned you before you could get treatment. So too with fear – if we can identify the underlying cause, it is easier to treat.

Some fears are deep-seated. These are known as phobias, which may be defined as: "Persistent and recurrent fears of a particular situation, object or activity that poses little or no danger. The person experiencing a phobia knows the fear is irrational, but they cannot help it."

---

[1] Isaiah 4:13

The following questions can determine whether you have a phobia:

- Does it disrupt your life mentally, socially or professionally?
- Does it create uncomfortable involuntary reactions – physically, emotionally, behaviourally or cognitively?
- Does it block your attainment of goals and objectives – personally, professionally, socially or financially?
- Does it drain your energy?

If you answered 'yes' to a number of these, you need to seek help. Health care professionals have a number of effective methods that may relieve and even cure phobias.

Less dramatic fears, like the fear of rejection or fear of pain, can also seriously disrupt our lives. Once we have found the cause of our fear we can apply its specific antidote. Even though the poisons causing the fears are different, the antidote remains the same. This Fear Antidote has two components: Love and Acceptance.

We read in the Bible that the perfect antidote to fear is love: "...perfect love drives out fear..."[1] When you are filled with God's perfect love, fear has no place. It leaves. This is not about trying to cover fear with a positive mental attitude; it is about opening up our lives so that the free flow of God's love can wash away all fears.

The other component in the Fear Antidote is Acceptance. To combat fear we need to learn to accept it. This does not mean accept it as a permanent fixture in our lives. It simply means that we are to acknowledge it for what it is - acknowledge the fact of its existence. There is an element of confrontation in this acceptance – we need to face up to it and learn to deal with it. Fear is something that will come and ignoring it will not make it go away. Whether we let it sink in and take root depends on our next response: We need to become vulnerable to it.

This may sound alarming, and could be better explained by using an old African story: The King of the jungle is old. His once proud mane

---

[1] 1 John 5:18

is matted and mangy, some teeth are missing and he has such bad arthritis in his joints that he can no longer move quickly. He still, however, plays a valuable role in the hunt.

As he stands to one side, the muscular younger lions go to the opposite side of the field and hide in the bush. When their prey appears, the old King lets out a series of ferocious roars. The frightened animal, seeing the King, rushes in the opposite direction right into the path of the waiting younger lions.

The animal would have been spared had he run towards the roar. The lesson here is: If you choose to run towards your fear its influence will be broken.

God does not want us to be irrational and run headlong into the jaws of hungry lions. For example, it was right for me to run from the gun and to run from the Scary Guy, but we are not to ignore the fear, or worse, embrace it by believing that it is a permanent part of our lives. We need to get real with ourselves and, having identified the fear, we can say: "I see ____ is causing fear in my life. I *can* stand up to it."

Psychologists have used the principle of running towards fear in the successful treatment of phobias. By confronting, accepting and dealing with the feared object or situation in a gradual way, people learn to control their reactions. Whether fears are imagined (as with phobias), or real; they can be overcome by accepting them. The Bible says: "For God didn't give us a spirit of fear, but of power and love and discipline."[1]

The Fear Antidote of love and acceptance will drive out fear. Let us apply it to specific examples:

Fear of Death

A fear of death haunts many people. This fear is extremely deep-seated and difficult to detect because people avoid thinking about it.

---

[1] 2 Timothy 1:7

One may think that when someone becomes a Christian and discovers that they will be spending eternity in heaven, this fear dissipates naturally. If you know that you are accepted by God because He loves you and that you therefore qualify for heaven, you should not be afraid of dying, because your future in eternity is secured. However, this is not always the case because some Christians continue to fear death. A fear of death has other fears that come alongside: Some fear no longer being here, others fear the unknown beyond the grave, still others fear that people will forget them and some the way that their death will take place.

I have had pangs of fearing death, but generally I don't. Perhaps that is why I have been so ready to take my own life. My assurance of a beautiful eternity with God has probably worked against me in a strange way. Even though I am looking forward to being with God in Heaven, I now know that God has exciting plans for my life and I want to stay here, with my loved ones, for as long as possible.

The Fear Antidote may be applied to the fear of dying by saying: "I love Him and know He loves me and I accept whenever He thinks it is my time to die." Your fear will be eased by accepting that it is inevitable, and by believing that He loves you and will be overseeing your death. He will be there to lead you home at the right time.

I wonder though, how many people kill themselves because they are too scared to face the potential pain that may be involved during the act of death? So they pre-empt it by taking their own lives. This has its root in another fear – the fear of pain.

Fear of Pain

While this fear is a necessary survival instinct because it warns us of something that could harm us, it is destructive if constant.

Most of us are afraid of physical pain to some extent. When someone faces chronic illness, this fear can become linked to the fear of losing one's freedom, as physical mobility becomes limited. Chronic pain sufferers avoid actions that increase their pain and in so doing they lose a certain amount of freedom. This can serve a good purpose by

63

letting us know that we are to stop doing whatever it was that we were doing, to prevent further damage to our bodies.

When I first felt the crippling pain in my pelvis and was diagnosed with a chronic pelvic disorder, I cried out: "What if this is the way it is going to be until the day I die?" The thought horrified me. I was working as a drama teacher, had three children to look after (one of which was a bouncy boy) and was in a new country without the support of extended family. I couldn't see how I was going to manage all of this while in debilitating pain.

Some loving Christian friends advised me to 'refuse to accept the pain', and I tried to banish it from my mind and body, but when the pain persisted, I was left deflated. Relief from this fear came when I ran towards it; when I allowed myself to consider the possibility that I may be in that pain forever. This by no means meant I had given up my belief in the power of God to heal and my hope that He would, but I no longer railed against the fact of its existence. I accepted the possibility of it continuing. Once I had done that, I was able to be at peace with whatever God had planned for me, rather than thinking I knew what His plans were and railing against them.

Fear of the Unknown

The fear of death is tightly linked to the fear of the unknown; we are not completely certain what will happen to us when we leave this world. But, in various scenarios throughout life, we believe that we need to know what can be expected before we go forward: "If I know what to expect then I can be prepared and control the situation, if I don't know what is happening then I will have no control over it." We are scared about the possibility of not being able to manipulate the situation to suit our needs and to avoid pain. This fear is what pushed us to needing the light on at night when we were children – we needed to see what was there.

The fear of the unknown prevents us from moving forward and discovering new things. If we fear the future, we will not be free to enjoy the present.

Applying the Fear Antidote (Love and Acceptance) to the fear of the unknown targets the root of this fear – the need to know. Accept that you do not need to see your future because your loving God not only sees it, but is working everything out for your good. This will give you the peace you need to face the unknown.

The Fear of Loneliness

The next fear, the fear of loneliness, stems from our basic need for survival. We feel we will be more likely to survive if we are in a group. We also don't want to be alone because we worry that we will do something and no one will be around to notice. We are also scared that we won't be able to manage things without help. Our lives gain meaning through interaction with others and without it we feel empty. God created us to share our lives with others and when we don't have that fellowship, a void is created. It can be a devastating time and many people have chosen to end their lives rather than have to face another day alone.

Applying the Fear Antidote can fill that void. First, we are not alone. God is with us and Jesus calls us friends.[1] Also, we have nothing to fear – if God created us for fellowship with others, then He will see to it that we get it. If you are alone, accept that it is God's will for you to have people in your life and keep praying for the right people to come into your life. Accept that, for now, you are alone but that this time will pass. This can be an opportunity to develop your love for Him as you learn more about His Love for you. There have been many times in my life when I have been lonely, but when I have applied Love and Acceptance these times have become precious moments with God.

Fear of Rejection

The fear of rejection is one of the main fears that we encounter. Many people reach the point of suicide with the nagging voice of rejection overseeing their every thought and action. It is closely linked to a fear of failure.

---

[1] John 15:15

Everyone has suffered from rejection at some point in their lives. It produces a wound in us that is often indistinguishable from its original cause and is therefore difficult to pinpoint. It governs the way we act.

If you have this gnawing fear you will, most likely, have a number of these **Rejection Traits**:

- **Perfectionism** - where such high standards are set that, when they are not reached, you become overly self-critical and depression sets in. You may appear highly motivated but you are being driven by extremely low self-esteem. Ask yourself: Do I get irritated with myself or others for not doing things perfectly?
- **Risk avoidance** – new and challenging endeavours are not tried because you fear failure. Ask yourself: What have I avoided doing because I am scared I may fail? What am I afraid may happen?
- **Anger and resentment** towards self and others - When failure comes, you are unable to accept responsibility and look for somewhere else to take the blame. This anger is often directed at God. Ask yourself: Am I blaming others for something that is my fault?
- **Depression** – Anger and rejection pointed towards oneself may lead to depression. Ask yourself: Am I showing signs of depression. (see earlier chapter)
- **Low motivation** and hopelessness – You think there is little chance of success and so don't even want to try. Ask yourself: Does my fear of failure prevent me from trying things.
- **Pride** – Do you say: "How dare they think that way about me?"
- **Easily manipulated** – If your self-worth is based on the approval of others you are likely to do anything to please others. Ask yourself: Is the approval of others a driving force in why I do things?
- **Controlling behaviours** - In an effort to avoid being hurt you try to dominate situations and are unwilling to let others be

themselves. Ask yourself: Have others complained about me being bossy or 'always trying to get my own way.'

- **Sexual dysfunction** – In an effort to avoid the pain of sexual failure you tend to avoid sex altogether or you blame your partner. Ask yourself if you avoid sex because of fear of failure.
- **Chemical dependency** – In an attempt to ease the pain of failure you self-medicate with drugs or alcohol. Ask yourself if you seek to ease a pain (emotional or physical) when you imbibe.
- An **addiction to success** – You never feel good about your achievements and so strive for more and more. Think about times that you have done well and ask yourself if you gave yourself a pat on the back.
- **Isolation** – You fear rejection and therefore avoid people to avoid being rejected. This can lead to loneliness. Ask yourself if you have been doing this.
- **Other general attitudes**, for example: self-pity, petulance, competitiveness, self-centredness, ridicule, jealousy, haughtiness, insecurity... to name a few.

This fear of rejection is a social fear that explains why many people act the way they do, for example, why we sometimes blindly follow the actions of others. We fear rejection from society because we justify our existence through the acceptance of others. We decide that they are 'normal' and that if we become more like them then we will be accepted by them. Pleasing people becomes a governing standard in our lives.

Fear of People

The greatest fear in my life, by far, has been my fear of people. Like most poison I did not realize that I had taken it until the deadly symptoms started to show themselves in my body.

Maybe the bottle of poison that I drank was labelled 'rejection', but I don't know. I don't think I gave it to myself, but I could have – I can't even remember when I took it. At first the symptoms were imperceptible. Whenever I was out in company I was concerned that I wasn't dressed correctly or saying the right things. This would cause me to watch what others were wearing and saying. If someone spoke to me I would carefully dissect anything they said to see if there was any threat or rejection in it. I would replay conversations in my head to see if I had said anything to hurt them or if I had missed some cue or other. I was hyper-vigilant at all times. This poison prevented me from enjoying other people. I am sure that this scrutiny was unpleasant for others because my focus was so 'me' orientated.

As a result, I would be excluded from their groups and this resulted in me feeling rejected. This would confirm all the fears I had about them in the first place and so the horrible cycle was set in place. Essentially my fears fed my fears.

At first this fear caused me to change my personality to try to 'fit in' and I lost my true self. I was often accused of 'not being myself' – I didn't even know what that meant! How could I not be myself when I was myself? Eventually the poison of this fear of people ran rampant through my veins and I got twinges of it when the telephone rang or the postman knocked. That was when I realized I had been poisoned – when I got others to answer the phone and door. I was shocked to realize I was scared of such everyday things.

This fear poisoned my career. As an actress, model and singer my job was to be in front of other people on the stage, television and cinema. Other people's opinions of me mattered. If others liked me I got more jobs, if they didn't I was rejected. I never got used to it. Their criticism stung. They were, no doubt, triggering a deep root of rejection inside of me. Rejection is dealt with in the next chapter.

Thanks to Joyce Meyer, one of the biggest lessons I learnt was not to be a people pleaser. She explains that we can become addicted to the approval of others: "Approval addiction happens when people need the approval of others so much that they are miserable anytime they feel they don't have it. They even make certain decisions to gain approval rather than to follow their hearts or to obey what they believe to be God's Will for their lives." I did not learn this lesson overnight. I need to be constantly on guard against needing the approval of others to reinforce my sense of well-being. I had to learn to search my motives for doing things and stop myself from blindly following someone else's ways.

Others don't necessarily know better than you, so why lean on their opinions? What do they know about you and your life that you don't know? The problem with basing our self-worth on the approval of others is that their opinion is often not correct and sometimes not in our best interests. This obsession with others is tiring and we need to be freed of this stress of obsessing about what others think about us.

When what others say about us has such a profound effect on the way we think about ourselves, we need to make an adjustment in our thinking. The Bible speaks clearly on the subject: "Am I now trying to win the approval of men or of God? Or am I trying to please men? If I were still trying to please men, I would not be a servant of Christ."[1] If we are living to please men we are not living to please God. We are to seek God's approval above all.

Within the definition of rejection, 'to refuse to accept', we can find the secret to healing from it. If rejection is a refusal to accept something then healing from it will come from an acceptance of something. That something that we need to accept is our own self-worth.

Healing from 'people pleasing' comes by increasing your self-worth. We do this by looking factually at what we are worth. We are made in the image of God.[2] The essence of us, our 'self', reflects the image of God. Accepting that we are made in God's image and that we share many of His characteristics should provide the basis of our self-worth. Not our comparisons with the 'success' and standards of the world. God loves us as we are and so should we.

In summary, most of these and other fears, will respond to the Fear Antidote of love and acceptance:

---

[1] Galatians 1:10
[2] Genesis 1:26

- Accept the fear by making yourself vulnerable to it, but don't let it remain a foothold in your life.
- Accept that God is with you to protect you and give you a wonderful future.
- Love and accept who you are - made in God's image.
- Accept that some people will not always love and accept you. Love them anyway. People will continue to hurt people. But we have somehow to become immune to these barrages of criticism and the ensuing rejection that we feel or we will be in danger of being paralysed and doing nothing.
- Accept whatever God has in store for you, knowing that it is good because He loves you.

There are some fears that you cannot make yourself vulnerable to and that cannot be accepted. These are fears that come as a result of demonic interference.

Many years ago, while we were still living in South Africa, I became aware that I was living in constant fear. There wasn't a particular thing that I was afraid of, I was scared of everything. It was such an all-encompassing fear that I knew in my spirit it was demonic oppression and I needed deliverance. As soon as my husband prayed for the evil spirit to leave, calm fell on me. How to deal with the demonic is discussed in depth in a later chapter.

Once you have asked God if you are being plagued by the demonic and after you have applied the Fear Antidote, there remains one more important step to take: "Be strong and courageous. Do not be afraid or terrified...for the Lord your God goes with you."[1]

My favourite description of courage comes from John Wayne, an actor famous for his roles in Westerns: "Courage is being scared to death, but saddling up anyway." Fear stops our forward motion, courage continues in the face of fear. Fear thinks: "What if?" and courage thinks: "I can!" Courage takes action and fear paralyses.

Interestingly, courage is more than a feeling, because it occurs on a physiological level. Our limbic brain signals danger and our neo-

---

[1] Deuteronomy 31:6

cortex reasons that the danger is not real. So when you decide to be courageous, the neo-cortex is taking control away from the emotional limbic brain. You feel the fear but you take action anyway. The brain can learn to become more courageous.

Each time you give in to fear you strengthen it. Every time you avoid facing a fearful event, and then feel relief, you are psychologically rewarding yourself. This reward reinforces your avoidance behaviour making it more difficult for you to face the fear in the future. For example, the more often you avoid meeting up with someone you have hurt and need to apologise to, the harder it becomes to see them.

When you fear, say with Paul: "I can do all things through God who strengthens me."[1] Jesus can give us the strength to face those fears. Say "I can" rather than "I can't". Look upward towards God rather than inward. If you look at yourself you will see limitations, whereas if you look at God there are no limitations. If God says you can, then you can.

Having looked 'fear in the face' many times throughout my life, I relate to what Eleanor Roosevelt said on the topic: "You gain strength, courage and confidence by every experience in which you really stop to look fear in the face. You are able to say to yourself, "I have lived through this horror. I can take the next thing that comes along."

Sorry Lord for being proud, controlling, manipulative, jealous, self-centred and people pleasing.
I am so scared Lord, help!
I don't want to live with this fear anymore.
Lift this fear from me.
Help me to know that you are with me so that I can be brave.
When fear comes, Lord, help me to look to You.
Thank you that I can do all things through You.
Thank you that my life and future are in Your Hands.

---

[1] Philippians 4:13

I Am Not Good Enough

My Child

The things others have done to you in the past have left you with deep wounds. You carry this pain with you today and it is affecting the way that you deal with others, and even the way you deal with me.

But why do you turn from me when you sin? I am not rejecting you. I knew you were going to sin when I chose you to be a child of mine, and I still chose you. I sent my beloved Son to die on the cross so that you would understand that you are reconciled to me. Why do you still try to do things to gain my acceptance? You are accepted...and loved...and cherished.

Stop allowing this root of rejection to govern our relationship and your relationships with others. I have sent my Word, which is the Truth, to combat what the devil is whispering to you. Saturate yourself with these Words so that you can guard against rejection.

I will show you how.

Loving you unconditionally always

Your God

When I gave my life to Jesus, I barely understood what I was doing. On my fourteenth birthday, I knelt at the fireside with my mum, confessed my sin and received Jesus into my life. There was not much love in me towards God when I did - I was driven by a need to belong.

Four years earlier, thousands of miles away, I had been living in one of the most beautiful places in the world, Camps Bay in Cape Town. It is a little village, hugged by mountains, with the Atlantic Ocean stretching out from its white beach to the front.

I lived in an apartment with my mother and my sister Lindy and visited my Dad on weekends. We were so poor that I had to share the bed with my mother, but I didn't mind; in fact it was a lot of fun. We lay on that bed and wrote poetry, read stories and sang songs. At night, when she saw a thunderstorm brewing, she would wake us and we would eat chocolate and watch as lightening lit up the ocean. I didn't realise how close my mum and I were, until one holiday everything changed.

A friend invited me to spend the holiday with her family, and on my return my mother announced her engagement. I was told we would be moving immediately to a farm far away. I had no time to say good-bye to my dad, Lindy or my dear friend Hazel. With my budgie cage on the seat next to me we drove inland, with a man I had never met before, to start a new life.

He told me to call him Tat, which means 'Dad' in Polish. He was large, sombre and scary. My new home was a sprawling pine plantation in Kwa-Zulu Natal. My mother, completely involved with her new man, had very little time for me. I desperately missed those I had left behind and I was lonely and scared.

The grown-ups would have weekend long tennis parties. When the festivities died down Tat's anger would flare up. Drunk, he would pound on our locked bedroom door and threaten to kill us ... or himself. He was convinced I was trying to get my mum back with my dad, but the thought had never occurred to me. I began to write a diary during that time and in it I recorded what he said on one of these occasions: "You bloody women. I came to see whether you (my mum) had gone back to your lover (my dad) in Cape Town, I don't see why I should have to pay for you anymore." I think, looking back on it now, he was riddled by unfounded jealousy. No one wanted my mum and dad to get back together again – their marriage had been a stormy one.

Probably out of desperation, my mother sent me away to boarding school. On the rare occasion I came home, the tension was palpable and the dramas frequent. Tat hated me and resented me being in their lives. My mother, in an effort to appease his jealousy, tried to get me to be extra nice to him. But my efforts were met with grunts and I was I left feeling more alone, unloved and rejected than ever before.

While at boarding school, I attempted to take my life. My mother later said that it was a cry for help. I went along with that when I saw it seemed to make her feel better, but I know that I wanted to die that day. I took all my diet tablets. They didn't even make me fall asleep, but I must have been acting strangely because the matron called my mother to come and fetch me. My mum, while obviously sad about what I had done, seemed very concerned about Tat finding out. I was sworn to secrecy and sent back to school.

While I was there they became re-born Christians. But I didn't see much change in Tat. The drunken rages continued, except now they were compounded by endless arguments about financial worries. I watched helpless, as my mother, so educated, beautiful and cultured, worked in his furniture factory. She would return to the house bone-weary and despondent. Her delicate hands covered in varnish and cuts. She had changed. While the sounds of her wonderful piano playing were seldom heard, her love for Jesus shone on her face as it still does to this day.

So, when I said the salvation prayer, it was in a confusion of desperately wanting to fit in, please my mother and hoping that God would indeed be a home for me. I was driven by my need to belong.

This is an excerpt from my Diary on the day I was converted: "Today is my birthday! I don't feel fourteen. But I guess I am because the world spins. I brought the subject of going to Vanessa up again. Mom had a tantrum and when she told Tat he said I was selfish and vain and showed my body to guys. It hurt me a span and I screamed that I hated the way he walked into our lives and took us away from Cape Town. I broke down asking God to help me. We prayed and I was converted, even though I had believed in God for years."

The traumatic, confused way that I gave my life to Jesus did not change the reality of what had happened: "Therefore, if anyone is in Christ, he is a new creation; the old has gone, the new has come!"[1]

---

[1] 2 Corinthians 5:17

74

We were all different, even though we couldn't see it at first. Tat changed too and, over the years, he grew to love me in his own way.

My grades at school improved dramatically. I felt full of life and purpose and started a healthy living day care centre for the children living on the farm. It sounds grander than it was. I simply decorated a room on the farm and invited mothers and their children to come for talks about hygiene and healthy living. My love for teaching was set as I made posters, handed out toiletries that I had bought with money I made from packing strawberries and taught everything I knew about how to be healthy. In the holiday I went to Christian Camp, helped lead worship and started to write songs about Jesus. I wrote a song entitled: "I have found a home with God." I no longer wanted to die.

Nevertheless the rejection I felt during this time had an accumulative effect over my life. The more significant the relationship from which the rejection comes, the deeper the rejection runs. It had long-term consequences. Even though my mother loved me deeply, I had felt rejected by her, and this had an adverse effect on many future relationships.

The mechanism of how the effect of rejection occurs is complicated and difficult to understand. It begins in childhood with our desire for acceptance. When the significant figure, normally a mother or father, fails to give us the acceptance we desire, we feel rejected. The child returns to the parent, searching for acceptance and if the rejection continues, the child will emotionally distance themselves. Very often, frustration, anger and a desire for revenge is set up in the young heart. Rejection propels us towards emotional instability and sets up a chain reaction of negative emotions and responses. I will attempt to explain the mechanism behind rejection and the effects that it has on individuals with an allegory...

A cataclysmic event was about to occur in the far reaches of the universe. Near the edge of a distant galaxy two planets danced around a Sun and around each other. Planet U-me, sparkling like an emerald, was attracted by the strong gravitational pull of Planet Else, a friendly giant that circled it protectively – dependable, reliable and steady.

At the centre of this cosmic whirl, like dancers around a maypole, a sun held them in orbit. Kept spinning by this almighty force, and not by any force of their own, they danced.

But now their union was about to be shattered. Hurtling through the universe, Comet Jection was on a collision course with Planet Else. Either both planets would collapse or they would be separated from each other forever. Or perhaps, after shifting position, stability could be regained. It all became dependant on the size of Comet Jection and how close it came to Planet Else. But the most determining factor was how close the planets were dancing around the Sun – the closer their orbit; the less likely they would be to be dislodged. If they were too distant from the sun, a large impact could throw them off into the galaxy where they would become unattached – wandering nomads forever.

As the comet approaches it gains momentum. Then, without warning, it hits Planet Else. At first, maybe from shock, it seems as if the universe is holding its breath. Then a cloud of debris gives way to a black dent, like Munch's painting 'Silent Scream', appearing on the surface of the devastated planet.

The relationship between both planets is destabilised as their gravitational pulls are disrupted. Like a domino effect, their turmoil ricochets through the galaxy.

Planet U-me, once so close, is now pushed away. On its surface, dust clouds blind and volcanoes erupt angrily. Lonely wastelands are injected by frightening electrical storms. Noxious gases make it difficult to breath. Earthquakes rip the planet to its core. The loss is enormous.

Rejection has catastrophic consequences and can affect us at any time during our lives. We seldom see rejection coming and when it does, it can knock us off course. It often comes from people who are being rejected themselves.

We all search for significance through love and acceptance from others, but when we fail to meet the standards of others or ourselves, rejection may result. Rejection causes us to say: "I am not good enough."

It can be real or imagined. The devil discovered real rejection when he failed to meet the standards of God and was banished from God's presence.[1]   Later, Adam and Eve, through disobedience, failed to maintain God's standards and were thrown out of the Garden of Eden.[2] All humans since have been separated from God: "But your iniquities have separated you from your God,"[3] because "all have sinned and fall short of the glory of God."[4] God did not reject Adam and Eve and he does not reject us, but our sins separate us from God until we accept the saving Grace of Jesus.

Imagined rejection, though not real, can be far more common than real rejection. This rejection is triggered when we believe we have been, or will be, rejected because of some failure that may or may not exist. For example we may believe: "If I tell them what I really think, they will never speak to me again." We think our thoughts are so bad or worthless that we imagine what others will say. We then proceed to compound the unfounded belief in our minds with justifications: "I was told how stupid I was all my life and now everyone will know it." Imagined rejection results in us having illogical and sometimes excessive reactions to the innocent words and deeds of others and situations. A self-defeating counter-attack is then mounted. For example: "I am not going to tell them how I feel. No one understands me." We are then left in a worse situation that before – we are isolated. This vulnerable position opens up doors for demonic attack.

Imagined rejection also affects the way we respond to people. For example, a person suffering from rejection may overreact to criticism. Their response would most likely be: "How dare you think that about me." They immediately spring into offensive mode and begin to attack the person who delivered the criticism. We make it clear that we reject their opinions and values. Hence the expression:

---

[1] Ezekiel 28:17
[2] Genesis 3:23
[3] Isaiah 59:2
[4] Romans 3:23

"Hurt people hurt people." Rejected people often hurt others because they are hurting. They often 'imagine' rejection by lashing out pre-emptively; before anything has even happened to them.

There are myriads of situations that can lead to a person feeling rejected, including: poverty, receiving criticism, internet bullying, favouritism, unemployment, the media, marital problems, parental illness, loneliness, problems at school, relatives living at home, feeing abandoned in an old age home or adoption.

The responses to these circumstances may include despair, inferiority, pessimism, negativity, fear of failure, sadness, defiance, fighting, criticism of others, hardness, self-centredness, envy, arrogance, self-pity, anger, confusion, shame, striving and perfectionism, isolation, feelings of loss, self-justification or manipulation.

Rejection can manifest in a number of ways. These vary from person to person, but may include:

- Rebellion – the rejected person (adults or children) rebel against authority.
- Fabrication of personality - they pretend to be someone that they are not.
- The rejected person becomes preoccupied with whether they are being rejected or whether they are rejecting others.
- They develop a chronic need to fit in and be part of whatever is going on.
- They have an inability to receive criticism.
- They appear proud and would say or think things like: "How dare you..."
- They fear confrontation because their identity is based on what others think of them.
- They reject others in an attempt to avoid being rejected first.

Needless to say, this barrage of negative emotions and endless self-talk leaves many feeing suicidal.

The emotional wounds of rejection, if left untreated, may grow and become spiritual. These can be set up as strongholds, as the devil seeks to invade us with negative feelings towards God, ourselves and others. Very often, rejection has become so deep-seated that it is demonic in nature and the individual needs deliverance (this is discussed in depth in a later chapter).

Therefore, before these strongholds are set up, we need to recognise rejection and root it out. As imagined rejection takes that which is non-existent and treats it as fact, there is only one cure – the relentless application of the truth - this is **The Truth Cure for Rejection**:

- You are not rejected by God.
- You have worth.
- You have a Friend.
- You have a Defender.
- You are not alone.
- You are talented.
- Christians are not perfect, they are saved!

You are not rejected by God

Maybe you feel that you have committed such a great sin that God will not forgive you? When Jesus died on the cross He took upon himself all sin. If you believe this and have told God that you believe it and have asked Him to live in you and be involved in your life – then your sins have been erased at the cross. You are eternally forgiven. He remembers your sins no more.

I realise that this is hard to accept, let alone understand. But it is true. No matter what sin you have done, you are saved. No sin is too great for God to forgive. How could sin be 'greater' than God? He says in the Bible that He remembers your sins no more. Go before Him and tell Him how you feel, say sorry for what you have done, thank Him for Jesus' sacrifice and tell Him you want to change that area of your life. Then you can say in faith: "The old has gone, the new has come!" It's the new you!

It is not about whether you *feel* forgiven or not, because feelings do not count in this matter. What counts is what *is*. He has forgiven you:

"If we confess our sins, he is faithful and just and will forgive us our sins and purify us from all unrighteousness."[1]

It is true that God rejected our sins but it is not true that He rejected us. It is written: "For the Lord will not reject his people."[2] God didn't reject Adam and Eve; it was their behaviour and attitudes that caused their expulsion from Eden and He still continued to be with them after that. He has brought us back to himself by blotting out our sins on Calvary and we have been reconciled to Him. Reconciliation means 'the re-establishing of relationship.' "God was reconciling the world to himself in Christ, not counting men's sins against them. And he has committed to us the message of reconciliation."[3] It is clear that we are not being rejected by God.

However, we fear that He will reject as others have rejected us, and this sets up dangerous behaviour - we begin to 'perform'. In a desperate attempt to try and gain His approval because we fear we have lost it, we try to make ourselves more acceptable. This is called the performance trap.

Here is a test for you to see if you are performance orientated: On a scale of 1 to 100, how sure are you that you are going to heaven? If you answer anything less than a hundred then you are trapped in a performance trap. You are trusting in your own efforts to get to heaven. But this is futile because you cannot do anything to earn your salvation. If you have accepted Jesus as your Saviour, then you are going to Heaven and can be a hundred percent assured: "But when the kindness of God our Saviour and His love for mankind appeared, He saved us, not on the basis of deeds which we have done in righteousness, but according to His mercy."[4] We can't earn our salvation by performance. So, let us give up our own efforts to achieve righteousness and believe rather that Christ's death and resurrection alone are sufficient to pay for our sin and separation from God. That does not mean that we give up our efforts to be good,

---

[1] 1 John 1:9
[2] Psalm 94:14
[3] 2 Corinthians 5:19
[4] Titus 3:4,5

merely that we do not rely on those attempts in order to be accepted by God.

You have worth

It is true that that we are not as good as some people at some things, but it is not true that we are no good at all. You are not a failure even though you might have failed at something.

God said: "Let us make man in our image."[1] This should give us a solid basis for self-worth. It should not be based on public acclaim, our achievements, attractiveness or possessions, but rather on the fact that we are made in the image of God.

Through Christ's death and the placing of all our guilt on His shoulders, God makes us, not better, but perfect in His eyes. We appear to Him as though we have no flaw or fault. It is as if we had never failed. It is hard to accept that God sees us that way, I know. But we need to keep our standards for judging ourselves in line with God's standard and he sees us as being perfect in Christ, so who are we to disagree? We are pleasing to God, despite our failures.

Bringing your relationship with God into proper perspective is a vital step in the process of overcoming strongholds of rejection. You are accepted, loved and appreciated by God.

You have a Friend

It is true that some people may not want to be our friend, but it is not true that we are friendless. Jesus says: "I have called you friends."[2]

When all others have rejected you, even if it is a really significant figure like a father or mother, then the Lord is standing by: "Though my father and my mother forsake me, the Lord will receive me."[3]

---

[1] Genesis 1:26
[2] John 15:14
[3] Psalm 27:10

You have a Defender

It is true that you may be attacked, but it is not true that you are defenceless: "But make up your mind not to worry beforehand how you will defend yourselves. For I will give you words and wisdom that none of your adversaries will be able to resist or contradict."[1]

You are not alone

It is true that you may be lonely but it is not true that you are alone: "God sets the lonely in families."[2] God is with us all the time.

You are talented

We each have our own unique, specific talents, but it is not true that we have the same talents. The Bible says that God gave talents, "Each according to his ability."[3]

Christians are not perfect, they are saved!

If we understand this truth we will become more understanding and tolerant of others and we will not be so hard on ourselves.

I have felt the deadly darts of rejection and criticism in the church. They often came when I was happily engrossed in some work in the Kingdom. When you are hurt by believers the pain seems to run extra deep. I think this is because we expect Christians to be better behaved than others. While this is often the case, it is not always so. Christians hurt other Christians – it is a sad fact.

The dart of criticism, fired by a believer, is often a lethal combination of truth mingled with lies as Scripture is read out of context to suit the needs of the moment. Malicious gossip fuels its course as other well-meaning Christians share information under the guise of 'just telling you so we can join together in prayer'. Innuendo plants

---

[1] Luke 21:14
[2] Psalm 68:6
[3] Matthew 25:15

disunity and veiled threats plant fear. They do not realize that they are not doing God's work at all. They do not realize that they are rather being used by the grand manipulator who has one goal – to make you feel rejected and offended just enough to give up the good work that you were doing. He accomplishes this by picking at your old scabs of rejection and opening new ones. We can end up doing what he wants us to do instead of continuing to do what God wants us to do.

Over the years of running house groups, we noticed many others who have been poisoned by this type of rejection. A steady stream of wounded Christians, disillusioned and hurt by fellow believers from established churches have come to our home to find healing. Some of them had left their church because they were disenfranchised by clerical abuse; others carry the fear of rejection, having felt its sting.

We have been shocked by the number of these 'walking wounded'. Those who now feel too scared to confess their sins one to another lest they be judged, too scared to voice their opinions lest they be shot down, too scared to volunteer lest they mess up, too wounded to help others because they are wounded themselves and too nervous to strive for excellence in case they are accused of 'showing off.' To our shame, it has become a common saying: "Christians shoot their wounded." We are shooting and we are being shot because of our misconceptions and deep-seated hurts.

This rejection would not cause such deep pain if we took each other off the pedestals of high expectations, stopped having pre-conceived ideas about how our fellow believers should behave and accepted each other for the way we were. We need to live with mercy and understand that others are in the process of being made more Christ-like, just as we are. This will stand us in good stead to avoid letting rejection take root when it comes.

Applying Bible truths to your life is essential for maintaining a rejection free environment in your heart. However, for rejection to be truly rooted out, it may be necessary to take the following steps:

- Identify
- Confess

- Forgive
- Love

Identify the relationship and event where rejection occurred, remembering that the rejection can be real or imagined. When you take this step, avoid questioning yourself about whether the rejection was real or imagined. Be satisfied with never knowing. For example, the rejection I felt when my mum married Tat, my step-father. Try to think of a time you felt rejected.

Now imagine the person with you. If you find this difficult try imagining something that they like to do or some aspect of their appearance or clothing. This often makes it easier to picture them in your mind. Imagine them sitting or standing near you. In my example, I imagined my mum sitting opposite me.

Now continue to identify the feelings that you had as a result of this event. I had feelings of rejection, loneliness, fear, grief, isolation, guilt, shame, frustration and confusion. Tell the person the way that you felt: "Mum I felt lonely, rejected and filled with guilt..."

Confess to the Lord the negative emotions that you felt as a result of this rejection. For example, I felt anger towards both my mum and step-dad and I rebelled against them. I also isolated myself and refused to ask for help in subsequent years. Ask God to forgive you for having these feelings and reactions and then thank Him that you are forgiven.

Now tell the person you are imagining how you felt about them and confess to them any negative feelings you had towards them and anything you might have done to them: "Mum I am sorry that I got angry with you and rebelled against you and refused to listen to your advice or follow your rules..."

Then decide that you are going to forgive the person who rejected you. Tell God that even if you cannot see how you will forgive, you are available to forgive. Imagine them standing or sitting with you, and tell them that you forgive them. This can be the hardest step of all. Remember that forgiving someone is not an act of condoning their behaviour; it is an act of letting go. Decide that you want to be free of this feeling of rejection, and understand that it is a vital step towards being free.

Now, tell God that you want to learn to love them. Remember that at this point you may not feel loving towards them. That is okay. Ask God to give you His Love for them. Tell Him that you are willing to love them.

As you imagine the person standing in front of you, tell them that you love them. For example: "Mum, I love you completely." This is sometimes extremely difficult, but it is the last and most important step towards your healing. You will benefit from no longer being a slave to rejection. As love becomes the plaster on this wound of rejection, you will begin to be healed with the help of God..

This entire process should be done in quiet prayer with God.

Thank you Lord that you give me the love that I need to love even those who have hurt me.
Thank you for accepting me as I am.
Help me to accept others as they are.
I am sorry Lord for putting unreal expectations on my fellow believers, help me to see them and love them as you do.
Help me to be on guard against feelings of rejection by applying the Truth of your Word every day.
Saturate me in this Truth and heal me.

Everything is Out of Control

My Dear Child

I know that life is difficult and I see you worrying so much about so many things, but you wouldn't if you just trusted me.

You find it hard to trust because you have been let down by others in the past. But I will not let you down. It may seem to you as though I am not answering your prayers and that I am not with you during these difficult times, but I am always with you and I hear all your prayers.

It is never easy to put your trust in another's hands. You worry that they will hurt and disappoint you. But I am not like others – I am faithful.

So, I am asking you today, to decide that you will trust me. Not just for a moment, and not in this circumstance alone and not only when you understand what I am doing, but trust me at all times. When you do, you will find contentment.

I am waiting to show you how worthy I am of your trust.

Faithfully yours

God

His teeth chatter so violently that he thinks they will break. His tongue feels like sandpaper against his dry palate and his stomach is gnawed by hunger. The incessant lapping of the waves against his life raft feels like some macabre, ancient, Chinese water torture. His head throbs. His skin lies loose on his bones, salt stings his open wounds, but more painful than all this is the void screaming inside - he misses those he loves.

As he lies there he thinks about the last person he saw: His wife had kissed him as she handed him a cooler box filled with snacks for his fishing trip, "I'll see you tonight. Catch something good for dinner," she had said. He wished now that he had said he loved her. But how was he to know that his engine would catch fire, his boat sink and he would be ship-wrecked? How was he meant to know that he would be washed into the open ocean by strong currents? As he lies in the life raft in the dark, lonely, he wishes he had known.

Peeping out from his foetal position, he gazes up at the stars. They look like millions of expressionless eyes observing him. That's when he begins to think about God for the first time in many years. Sitting up he clears his dry throat: "God please help!" He rasps at the laden sky. There is no reply. Dejected, he curls up again and falls asleep, crying.

The next morning he is awoken by a flappy-slapping noise in his boat. He begins to panic as soon as he sees the size of the huge fish flaying about in his boat. "It's too big! The boat is going to sink!" He shouts as he scoops it up and throws it overboard.

Exhausted he flops down. "God!" he yells up at the scorching sky, "I asked you to help me, so why did you try to sink my boat?"

Suddenly, he hears a whirring sound drowning out the noise of his tirade, and looking up he sees a huge black rescue helicopter. The waves are being whipped up by the force of the rotors and he becomes terrified that his flimsy craft will be blown away. "Go away! Go away!" he shouts, waving frantically. Terrified, he sees that they are ignoring him and releasing the ladder. "I don't need help. I am ok!" He yells. With that the helicopter leaves.

"I can do this on my own." He says getting out the one oar he has left, and beginning to row. Reaching to one side he dips the oar in and pulls, then reaching over to the other side he pulls through the water again. The raft begins to go in circles. No matter what he does, he cannot make headway.

Now, drained from his futile efforts, he huddles up, distressed. "God how can you do this to me? Do you want to kill me? The fish would have sunken my boat and that helicopter would have capsized it! What next?" His wailing nearly drowns out the deep rumble that is growing louder. Looking up he sees a trawler heading straight for him. As it approaches he can see the smiling fishermen on board waving to him.

"You stupid idiots!" he screams at them, "Go away! You're going to capsize my boat! His anxiety reaches tipping point as he sees them turning broadside. Frenzied and convinced that he is going to be killed, he jumps into the water. Blackness engulfs him as he is sucked under the boat.

In an instant he is in what appears to be a long tunnel, at the end of which is a bright light that seems to draw him closer. As he approaches the light he feels enormous waves of warmth and love washing over him. Realising that He is in the presence of God he blurts out: "God where were you? I was capsized and I cried out to you and you didn't answer my prayers?"

"I sent you a fish to eat and you threw it overboard, then you refused to go with the helicopter and boat that I sent you. I did answer you, but you couldn't see the help that I offered because you were so wrapped up in your fears and worry."

It is often like this for us: We get so anxious about our lives that we fail to see that what appear to be our troubles are often life-lines from God. So we resort to relying on our own efforts and reject the help offered by God. No longer trusting Him we become anxious. Stress stifles trust and kills contentment.

'Stress' is a word that has been bandied about so much that it has lost any impact. We use it to describe anything from the irritation we feel when our phones ring incessantly to feelings associated with the death of a loved one.

The widely accepted definition of stress is given by Richard S. Lazarus, a psychologist, who says that stress is a condition or feeling experienced when a person perceives that "demands exceed the personal and social resources the individual is able to mobilize." In layman terms: we feel stressed when we feel that "things are out of control." When our basic needs are not being met, our safety is threatened or we feel our lives are out of our control, we tend to get stressed. We worry about the past and stress about the future and we are rarely in the present. We are caught in a rut filled with negative thoughts, where our ruminations drag us down.

The word 'stress' is not mentioned in the Bible but trials, tribulations, troubles, hardships and ordeals are, with clear instructions about how to deal with them: "Be anxious for nothing,"[1] and "Do not be afraid,"[2] and "Do not let your hearts be troubled"[3] and "Do not worry about tomorrow."[4] These seem more like commands than requests, and we can surmise that if we are commanded to do it, then it is possible for us to achieve. These commands are even directed at those who say: "You don't know what I am going through. If you were in my situation you would be stressed too!"

Medical professionals have discovered that one of the major roots of many illnesses and diseases is stress.

People respond to stress in different ways. One person may respond with headaches, while another may suffer digestive problems. Stress makes us more prone to viral infections like influenza and the common cold.

Routine stress changes health so gradually that it is often difficult to notice. Those little, constant stressors in our everyday life keep the body heightened without allowing it to return to its normal functioning level. Over time the continued strain of routine stress can lead to serious health problems like: depression, anxiety disorders, diabetes, heart disease, sexual dysfunction and mental health problems that can lead to suicide.

The roots of fear and stress are linked. Every time we have a fear response, stress is produced in our bodies – it is the way we are wired - the greater the fear, the more dramatic the stress response. But this response is not only triggered when the fear is extreme, like

---

[1] Philippians 4:6
[2] Deuteronomy 31:6
[3] John 14:1
[4] Matthew 6:34

feeling terrified, it is also triggered when fear is moderate as in concern, agitation or worry. At any level, fear produces a stress response.

When I first heard about the damaging effects of stress I thought: "Yea, I am sure it makes you feel a little icky inside, but surely our thoughts can't have such drastic consequences!"

The British Heart Foundation published this list of **23 Warning Signs of Stress.** If you have five or more of these symptoms, you may be suffering from stress:

- Feeling sweaty or shivery
- Pounding heart or palpitations
- Needing to go to the toilet a lot more than normal
- Feeling sick in the stomach ('having butterflies')
- Dry mouth
- Exhaustion
- Odd aches and pains
- Smoking or drinking more
- Working to exhaustion
- Headaches
- No time for hobbies any more
- Being irritable at everything
- Thinking "I can't cope with this anymore"
- Loss of appetite for food, fun or sex
- Eating too much or too little
- Loss of sense of humour
- Loss of interest in personal appearance
- Loss of interest in people
- A feeling that everything is pointless
- Tearfulness
- Forgetfulness
- Feeling tired with no energy
- Difficulty in sleeping, disturbed sleep and waking up unusually early

There are a number of other ways to test if you are stressed: If you are unable to get to sleep before a half an hour of trying, if you wake up more than once a night or if your jaw hurts from grinding your teeth.

Once you realise that you are stressed, find out what triggers your stress. Identifying our stressors can go a long way towards dealing with them.   Make a note of what situations or people make you anxious and what negative thoughts trigger stress. Doing this will help you to begin to see which are real and which are not. Then think about which of these you can change and which you cannot. A little stress every now and then is not something to be concerned about. However, if you find you are suffering from many of these symptoms then you need to take measures to deal with it.

You may have noticed that one of your stressors is financial problems. Financial stress can cause unhealthy coping behaviour like over-eating, self-medication with drugs or alcohol or angry outbursts. These in turn may wreak havoc in your relationships.

Money issues can affect the rich and the poor. The poor may not be able to pay their debts or have money for their basic needs, but the rich can feel trapped by their belongings – working and never being able to enjoy the fruits of their labour because they are locked into keeping up the life-style they and those around them have become accustomed to.

These are some of the physical, emotional and intellectual signs that will indicate whether you are suffering from financial stress: headaches, fatigue, irregular heartbeat, digestive disorders, skin problems, disrupted sleep patterns, frequent anger and irritability, inability to relax, embarrassment, a sense of futility and depression. Your mind may also be affected by thoughts of running away, memory problems, difficulty making decisions, a short attention span and confusion. When stress affects many areas of your life, it becomes difficult to deal with the problems at hand and you can become locked in a vicious cycle. This can leave you feeling trapped and suicidal.

Some of the main stressors during my adult life have been financial, but many have had to do with my husband...

I had no idea what was wrong with him, but I knew something was. Shortly after getting married, I began to realise that I didn't know Richard at all.

I felt as though my life had become a chaotic circus - he bought things on a whim, whether we could afford them or not, booked holidays at a moment's notice with little planning and constantly had new business ideas. He didn't seem to be able to stick to anything for long and nothing he did was organised. His disorder railed against my need for order.

He had chronic forgetfulness. One such example came when my parents had been visiting us after the birth of our second daughter and we ran out of milk at breakfast. Richard offered to nip to the shop. He arrived home late that afternoon with a Coke and a packet of crisps, having totally forgotten all about his errand. He had met up with a friend, he explained.

The problem was larger than simply forgetting small things – He forgot to pay bills, forgot to do the usual things that come with running a home, forgot to run errands, forgot to pick up after himself, forgot to put petrol in the car, forgot to shave, forgot to check the time, forgot to take medicine, forgot to keep up with family and friends. It often felt as if he had forgotten about me.

In a frantic effort to avoid calamity, I became his secretary, mother and a compulsive list writer. But he forgot to read the lists. It became impossible to plan for the future or to set goals because he could not remember what the plans were.

Waiting for him became regular. So many romantic meals spoilt as I sat waiting, a new bride, feeling more and more rejected and lonely. His excuse "I forgot" no longer carried water – I felt that he didn't care about me. I felt he acted as though I didn't exist. When I spoke to him I could see that he was so wrapped up in what he wanted to say that he didn't listen to what I was saying. I felt lonely even when he was present.

I made endless excuses for him: that he was just behaving like an irresponsible little boy or that he was immature and trying to find himself. But excuses didn't help as, on a day to day basis, I tried to cope with the chaos his life brought. Who I used to be seemed to fade. No longer spontaneous, I became obsessed with order, and found none. As soon as I brought order to one area of our lives, another area would explode with some kind of drama – something wasn't paid so someone was suing us, someone was cross with us for not doing something we said we would, something had to be done that wasn't, someone felt affronted – the pandemonium went on and on…

For years I concluded that he was selfish and perhaps narcissistic, until I found out what was wrong: He had attention deficit disorder (ADD). A syndrome characterised by a persistent pattern of impulsiveness and a short attention span that interferes with academic, occupational, and social performance.

Once recognised, I could look at the many years of chaos that I had been living with and see its effect. Each day had been filled with stress as I worried constantly about what needed to be done, what I had not managed to see that needed to be done, what he had missed, what I had missed and whether there was anything that I could plan for in the future in case it was missed. The stress of not being in control of my life became constant and there seemed to be nothing I could do about it.

During the course of my marriage I have tried to kill myself many times. There were other reasons why, but this turmoil and the deep conviction that I could not leave someone who was fundamentally ill, left me feeling particularly trapped. I also felt anger and resentment towards him for what I thought was him not 'just growing up and taking responsibility'. My feelings of being unloved and neglected were eclipsed by the daily grind of stress to keep the bedlam at bay. It wore me down. I couldn't relax because I was always worried about something I might be missing that he was meant to be remembering to do. I only relaxed when I drank enough not to care anymore. But that didn't help with the wall of chaos that was constantly mounting.

This stress was compounded by financial stress. I have always had a yo-yo relationship with money – there have been years of plenty followed by years of famine repeated so many times in my life.

After my mother and father divorced we were so poor that we barely ever ate meat, except on Friday when my grandmother would bring us sausages - but I was happy. When my mother remarried, my rich step-father bought her a new bright red car. I can remember riding in the back and leaning out the window hoping that one of my friends would see me drive past. But money didn't lead to happiness as I entered the drama-laden life on the farm. I became so desperate I tried to kill myself when I was in my early teens.

I felt the sting of poverty once again when I went to college and struggled daily to find money for what I needed. But I was happy learning about the theatre and working as a model and singer. Later, when I got married to my husband who drove a Porsche and had a chauffeur driven Bentley, the happiness was short lived. We drank champagne nearly every day and went on long five-star holidays, but every day became fraught with heart-breaking arguments. I was miserable most of the time. Up to this point it seemed as though happiness went hand in hand with poverty. But that theory was soon tested. During the course of my marriage we reached a point where we owed twenty times more than the total cost of our first marital home. Unpaid bills mounted, threatening letters from creditors moaned and the constant drum of needs that remained unmet wore me down. Financial stress was constant.

It was during this time that doctors diagnosed me with a painful, chronic pelvic problem and explained to me that stress exacerbated the pain. This made sense to me because I had noticed that the slightest thing, like my son jumping out to tease me with a surprise fright, or even a stressful thought, led to hours of pain. This constant financial stress was causing real, immediate pain. I was forced to find a real solution - and as soon as I tried to stop being stressed, I realised just how stressed I was. It had become a life-style.

I had heard that the only way to be free from this type of crippling stress was to achieve freedom from financial difficulty: pay debts, spend less, stick to a budget and cut expenses. But this endeavour, albeit sound advice, caused me to feel even more stressed than before. A great sense of failure crept in every time I went over budget or spent money on something that I didn't need. I began to search for more ways to live stress-free.

I realised early on that I would need to implement some changes in my life, changes that would need to be practised daily for them to become entrenched. Realising I would need a reminder and having become a consummate list writer, I compiled a daily **Stress Check List**:

- Choose to eliminate stress
- Worry changes nothing
- Be a glass-half-full person
- Stop trying to fix people
- Drop Guilt
- Laugh
- Meditate
- Be good to your Body

Choose to Eliminate Stress

Make a decision to eliminate stress from your life. This might sound like an obvious step, but it isn't. We too often blame stress on everyone else or on our situation and even though they may be the cause, there is often nothing that can be done. So blame won't work, you can only change yourself. Decide to stop complaining about your stressors and take on the responsibility of doing something about them. In the story of Mary and Martha Jesus says (and I am paraphrasing): "You are worried and upset about many things, but only one thing is needed...choose what is better and it won't be taken away from you." He praised Mary for being less stressed: "Mary has chosen what is better,"[1] while Martha was probably slaving away, stressed-out, in the kitchen. We too need to decide to be more like Mary and choose a stress-free life.

---

[1] Luke 10:41

Worry Changes Nothing

If you like instant cures for things, this is your answer to stress: Worry achieves nothing. Once you really grasp this, you will be well on your way to getting rid of stress. Worry serves no purpose. We sometimes think we are making plans, when all we are doing is worrying. We don't gain any more control over the situation by worrying. We believe that if we keep thinking about things over and over again, we will somehow be able to change them, but worry changes nothing. In hindsight, has worry changed anything in your life to date?

The Bible gives us clear guidance about what we are to do with worry: "Therefore do not worry about tomorrow, for tomorrow will worry about itself. Each day has enough trouble of its own."[1]

In Matthew chapter six we are given five reasons why we are not to worry:

- While you are worrying about the future you are not focusing on today.
- It is harmful and not helpful.
- It shows a lack of faith and dependence on God.
- It keeps us from pursuing the real purpose that God has in mind for us.
- It implies that God is not concerned for us.

What is the point of spending today worrying about what might happen in the future? We need to stop our incessant questioning, "What am I going to do?" and be content with not knowing what the future holds.

Be a Glass-Half-Full Person

Proverbs says: "The cheerful heart has a continual feast."[2] Imagine that our actions are the outline of a drawing in a child's colouring in book and that our attitudes are the colouring in. Our attitudes

---

[1] Matthew 6:34
[2] Proverbs 10:15

colour in our day – dark, dismal colours will make your picture look miserable, bright, cheery colours will liven up your picture.

Our attitudes are so important that they actually determine our personality. Positive people are often referred to as glass-half-full kind of people and negative people, glass-half-empty.

Glass-half-empty people tend to set themselves up for stress with pre-emptive negative thoughts like, "I tell you if he does that one more time I am going to blow!" They have already decided to have a negative, stressful reaction.

They are also full of excuses for their negative behaviour: "I know I lose my temper...but..." or "I know I shouldn't complain...but..." or "I know I should hand this person/issue over to God to handle...but..." These people have settled into their negative way of thinking and a life filled with stress instead of a heart that will have 'continual feasts.'

But being a positive or a negative person is not something that is set in stone. I recently saw an interesting program on television about how we can reduce our negativity in six to eight weeks by looking at a few pictures. It is a cognitive bias modification technique developed by Professor Elaine Fox to increase a positive bias in people, thus improving their stress levels. While this is an experimental technique, the results have been good. The idea is that you can reduce your conscious negative bias by seeking out that which is positive. This technique seeks to break the habit of your brain towards negativity by getting it to focus on the positive. The way this is done is by showing you a page of faces, all of which are angry, except for one face that is happy. You simply click on the happy face and this action changes your bias. You can repeat this exercise a few times a week at home on your computer!

Even though we cannot choose what happens to us in life, how we respond to each and every situation is a choice. For example, when I emigrated from South Africa to Ireland with my family, the children could have been anxious about the uncertainty of the move to a new country, Instead, I made it an adventure for them. I noticed that as soon as I smiled and said: "Ok guys, we are off on a wonderful adventure," their whole attitudes changed and they became excited and happy about the upcoming move.

It is good news indeed that we can change from being a negative person; however it is not a new thought. The Bible tells us how to have healthy, right thinking : "Finally, brothers, whatever is true, whatever is noble, whatever is right, whatever is pure, whatever is lovely, whatever is admirable - if anything is excellent or praiseworthy - think about such things."[1] We need to examine ourselves and filter through what we allow ourselves to think and dwell on. Think about your thinking. This takes practice but, given time, it can be done.

Stop trying to fix people

We all have people in our lives who we feel are stressors. Mine was my husband, but nothing I did changed him and it was a waste of time trying. I had to learn to live with him the way he was. A lot of this stress comes from us trying to fix people and being frustrated by these efforts not yielding results. We feel it is our job to improve them - from children, spouses, colleagues and friends. These efforts can often leave us feeling frustrated and stressed.

Our children obviously need 'improving' in their formative years but when they are past the age of accountability; they are in God's hands not ours. At some point we need to decide to trust that God has them in His Hands. He is not only at work in your life, but He has those around you in His care as well – even if it doesn't look that way to you. If they have not come to know the Lord, continue in fervent prayer, but worrying about them will make no difference; in fact it could hinder your prayers for them. Someone said: "Nothing alters until you put it on the altar." So take the person who you are worried about to God in prayer and once you have done that, leave them with Him.

---

[1] Philippians 4:8

98

Drop Guilt

Guilt does not come from God – conviction does. Guilt leads to condemnation and conviction leads to healthy change. God may convict us through His Holy Spirit but it is the devil who takes us on a guilt trip. When you accuse yourself he stands by and eggs you on.

The pressure created by guilt and shame causes stress. But the nature of guilt and shame are to keep themselves hidden and it is therefore very difficult to get healing from them. Regrets, the precursors to guilt, linger and speak stress into our lives with "I should have done this or that" or "if only I had not done that."

Paul has the answer: "Forgetting what is behind and straining toward what is ahead, I press on."[1] Leave all your 'should haves' and 'if onlys' in the past where they belong. If God remembers your sins no more, why should you?

Then "Let us draw near to God with a sincere heart in full assurance of faith, having our hearts sprinkled to cleanse us from a guilty conscience and having our bodies washed with pure water."[2] Our conscience is sprinkled clean because He has incinerated our sins. Guilty feelings are not an appropriate response; they are counterproductive and cause stress.

Laugh

Figures vary, but it is generally believed that a six year old laughs on average 300 times a day whereas an adult laughs fewer than 20 times. This should speak volumes to us.

Scientists have demonstrated that our sense of humour is one of the most powerful tools in insuring a healthy emotional state and positive well-being. Laughter is strong medicine for mind and body and is a strong antidote to stress, pain, and conflict. Nothing works faster or more dependably to bring our mind and body back into

---

[1] Philippians 3:13
[2] Hebrews 10:22

balance than a good laugh. Humour lightens our burdens, inspires hopes, connects us to others, and keeps us grounded, focused, and alert.

Benefits of Laughter include:

- It is good for the health of your mind and body.
- It relaxes the whole body. A good, hearty laugh relieves physical tension and stress, leaving muscles relaxed for up to 45 minutes after.
- It boosts the immune system. Laughter decreases stress hormones and increases immune cells and infection-fighting antibodies, thus improving resistance to disease.
- It triggers the release of endorphins, the body's natural feel-good chemicals. Endorphins promote an overall sense of well-being and may even temporarily relieve pain.
- It protects the heart. Laughter improves the function of blood vessels and increases flow, which can help protect against heart attack and other cardiovascular problems.

With so much power to heal and renew, the ability to laugh easily and frequently is a tremendous resource. The more you laugh the happier you become. Why not set yourself the goal to learn a joke every week?

Meditate

Many outstanding Christians down through the centuries have practiced meditation regularly. It is also vitally important to healing.

Unfortunately, many have come to associate meditation with sitting cross-legged with your hands on your knees and have delegated it to the realms of other religions. But it simply means 'to ponder', 'to be in deep thought', 'to contemplate' or to have a quiet time. It is mentioned many times in the Bible and can be a form of prayer during which we attempt to become more aware of God.

It benefits us by focusing our feelings, steadying our thinking, making us more receptive and strengthening our communication with God. It helps us to assimilate deep truths that will change our attitudes and actions and lead us towards a place of complete healing from damaged emotions and distorted perceptions. Its purpose is to draw us closer to God.

Meditate in a quiet place, away from all distraction. Some people find it helpful to have gospel music playing while others prefer complete silence. Christ-centred guided meditations, which may be bought online and in some bookstores, can help you in the beginning. Once you are comfortably lying down or seated, welcome the Holy Spirit and make yourself ready to hear from Him and be moved by Him. Then begin to focus on a specific thought or Bible passage.

During this time soak in the presence of God as you become sponge-like; absorbing His Love, acceptance and joy. As you meditate more in His presence you will become more like Him, your restless thoughts will be calmed and you will slowly become sensitive to His Voice.

If you find meditation difficult on your own, you may join a Christian's meditation group.

Be Good to Your Body

Stress affects our bodies. So we need to combat it, not only on an emotional level, but on a physiological level as well. Regular medical examinations are essential for anyone suffering stress to determine if there are any underlying physical causes.

We need to ensure that we are getting enough sleep, exercising regularly and eating healthily. There is a definite link between sleep and stress. Lack of sleep does not cause stress, but it can make it worse. Getting between seven to nine hours of sleep a night is essential to your well-being. Sleep restores the body but when it is disrupted or you don't get enough, it can lead to feelings of irritability, anxiety and tension. When you are tired you exercise less and this inactivity can disturb your sleep, and so a vicious cycle of inactivity and lack of sleep develops.

There is another cycle that is at play here: If you are depressed you might have overwhelming feelings of hopelessness, sadness, worthlessness and guilt. You might feel as though your mind is in a loop, reasoning constantly about issues in your life over which you have no control. This reasoning leads to anxiety that makes sleep difficult.

Talk to your doctor about any problems you may have with sleep, because there can be many other causes. They may refer you to a sleep clinic, a therapist or prescribe medication.

Avoid stress eating. When you are stressed your body reacts as if it is in famine mode and stores what you eat as belly fat. While not a cure in themselves, there are supplements and foods that can combat stress: For example, omega 3 that can come in the form of supplements or you can get it from eating fish twice a week. Pistachios contain good cholesterols that help combat stress and doctors recommend that stressed people take Vitamins B and C to help reduce cortisol.

Cardiovascular exercise is essential for a healthy body and a stress-free life. Professionals recommend 'stepping' which involves walking on and off an elevated platform. It not only burns fat, but helps promote restful sleep and reduces stress.

Think about things to do that may help you relax: watching a sunrise or sunset, having a picnic, reading a good book or simply lying on the grass and looking at the stars on a cloudless night.

Having implemented my Stress Checklist, I still felt that something was missing. I was better, but not completely stress free. When I learnt what was lacking, it sent me on a journey that changed my life – I discovered the importance of contentment.

Contentment should not be confused with complacency - it is not being happy about doing nothing. We should also not make the mistake of thinking that if we are content we will be in danger of becoming apathetic and will no longer be driven to achieve our best. This couldn't be further from the truth. Contentment is synonymous with satisfaction. It will bring you peace of mind that will give you clarity that, in turn, will make the possibility of achieving what you want more possible. Stress cripples whereas contentment carries.

Paul discovered the 'secret' to contentment: "I have learned to be content whatever the circumstances. I know what it is to be in need, and I know what it is to have plenty. I have learned the secret of being content in any and every situation, whether well fed or hungry, whether living in plenty or in want. I can do everything through him who gives me strength."[1] He had learnt to be content during drought or storm, feast or famine and so can we. But what was Paul's 'secret'?

Contentment is not something that you will find at the end of your journey. Contentment is something you practice along the way. It is the scenic route. Contentment will allow you to enjoy the journey of your life, but it is something that needs to be practiced; it is not something that can be automatically achieved. I have a gadget that may help you practice contentment...

Imagine that you are holding a Contentometer - this contraption looks a lot like a barometer but instead of measuring atmospheric pressure, it measures your levels of contentment. A high reading on the dial indicates that you are feeling very content whereas a low reading could indicate that you are far from satisfied and feeling low. Attached to the Contentometer is a lens that can be focused on anything. Everything you do in your life is viewed through this lens. The choice of what to focus on is yours, and this choice directly impacts your levels of contentment. For example, if you focus on a horrendous accident, your levels of contentment may read low, whereas they may shoot up after a comforting meal.

The Contentometer also has a built in memory card. It becomes trained, over time, towards either being prone to high levels or low levels - the more you focus on the things that bring contentment the more it will tend towards higher readings. The choice is yours and depends on your overall focus. Here are some tips:

Philippians 4:11

Your Contentometer needs to be checked often, especially when you experience change in your life or you find yourself wanting something that someone else has, like their looks, possessions, life-style, peace of mind or bank account. These desires can cause your Contentometer to fall and you need to make adjustments to your focus to restore it. Shifting focus from what they have to what you have will cause your levels to rise.

Focus on what you can see not on what you cannot see. You may be looking at something through the lens but be thinking about something completely different. I call this phenomenon Life Dysmorphia. Sufferers of this disorder cannot see their life realistically; rather they fabricate what they think they see. For example, you see that you have food in your cupboard but act as though the cupboard is empty. This disorder will increase levels of stress and drive all readings on the meter down.

Try not to focus on more than one problem at a time because you might get confused and despondency may set in, resulting in the belief that that nothing can be done about your situation. Remember the old adage that asks: "How do you eat an elephant?" The answer: "One mouthful at a time!"

Don't focus on the wrong thing. There have been occasions where people focus on others, thinking that they are to blame for what has gone wrong, when in fact they themselves are the cause. Blaming others for anything is pointless because it will not sort out the problem and it will only add to your negative feelings and make your Contentometer dial fall.

Take your focus off money. That does not mean that you give up balancing your books or, if you are wealthy, that you need to give all your money to the poor. It means that you simply need to stop focusing exclusively on money. There is a Bible verse that warns us not to place our value in money: "...though your riches increase, do not set your heart on them."[1]

---

[1] Psalm 62:10

Focus, not on what you think you should have, but on what you have already. Benjamin Franklin said, "Contentment makes poor men rich and discontent makes rich men poor." Nowhere have I seen this illustrated more than in reality programs about rich and powerful women. The camera follows their glamorous lives as they get polished and pampered and wined and dined. It looks like they have everything and lack nothing. But as you watch, they begin to bicker with each other, envy each other and beneath their Botox smiles you can detect a deep dissatisfaction for life. Continually focusing on what you lack will leave you wanting more and more.

Focus on what you can be grateful for rather than on that which causes you to complain. It may be difficult, at first, but start with small things, like your bed being comfortable, a nice cup of coffee or fresh air to breath.

Focus on the needs of others and it will take the focus off your own problems. One of the reasons why the rich ladies in the reality programs are often not content is because they tend to be exclusively focused on themselves. We all need to focus more on others and less on ourselves because it is what we were made to do!

Do not operate this Contentometer while using drugs or alcohol. It may appear at first to make you feel more content, but your view of reality has in fact been distorted and contentment cannot come where there is a lack of focus.

Focus on what you can do and not on what you cannot do. For example: You *can* reduce the emotional and physical impact of money shortages by carefully analysing your money situation, creating an action plan for more prosperity and deciding to change your spending habits to ensure a better quality of life. Perhaps you *cannot* make your debt vanish overnight or get a job instantly. Maybe you *can* make a long-term plan on how you can work less so that you can spend more time with your family, but maybe you *cannot* spend all your time with them. Maybe you *cannot* do anything about your spouse who is spending too much money but maybe you *can* talk to them gently about what they are doing. Whatever the problem, once you have decided on a course of action, set it in motion and then rest content with what you have done.

The next focus is the 'secret' that Paul found to contentment - focus on the Power of God. After discussing contentment, he wrote: "I can do everything through him who gives me strength." His secret is that he gained strength by learning to draw on the power of God. There is no lack that He cannot fulfil and no need that He cannot meet. He sent manna from heaven for the Israelites, made a rock sprout water, sent ravens to feed Elijah and fed thousands from only five loaves of bread. He is asking us: "Is anything too hard for me?"[1]

Trusting Him to provide, heal and restore will bring contentment. Paul promised: "And my God will meet all your needs according to his glorious riches in Christ Jesus."[2] While he promises to 'meet all our needs', he doesn't necessarily give us all we want. But we can trust Him to know what will be good for us.

If you find that you are constantly preoccupied with your problems, try to shift your focus to God. When it looks as though there is no way out of your situation or when it feels as though you have reached rock bottom, take your focus off those things and pray more, read the Bible more and think more about all things to do with God.

Often, it is when our lives appear most out of control that God is hardest at work. What looks like a calamity to us, may be God at work, with us simply being unable to see the outcome. Aristotle Onassis, once one of the richest men in the world, said: "It is during our darkest moments that we must focus to see the light."

M. Scott Peck begins The Road Less Travelled with the statement: "Life is difficult." He continues: "This is a great truth, one of the greatest truths. It is a great truth because once we truly see this truth, we transcend it. Once we truly know that life is difficult—once we truly understand and accept it—then life is no longer difficult. Because once it has been accepted, the fact that life is difficult no longer matters." We find it difficult to accept that life will be troubled; instead we moan and complain incessantly about what we have or don't have. God knows that life is difficult and stressful

---

[1] Jeremiah 32:27
[2] Philippians 4:19

because He experienced it himself, and he has a simple solution: Trust Him.

Faith is a decision about where we are going to put our trust, it is not a feeling. Too often we put our trust in ourselves, others or even our circumstances rather than in God. Someone once said: "God is not limited by our circumstances, just our unbelief." Receiving answers to our prayers can often be hindered by our lack of trust in God.

We need to stop wafting between "I believe" and "I don't believe." These two contrary positions seem to waver depending on the circumstances we face. James says: "He who doubts is like a wave of the sea, blown and tossed by the wind. That man should not think he will receive anything from the Lord; he is a double-minded man, unstable in all he does."[1] Why? We know that God can do anything, so why would one problem be harder for Him to deal with than another? The answer is simple: it isn't. Nothing is too difficult for God;[2] therefore our trust in Him is well-founded.

There is a story about a mountain climber who was scaling a sheer cliff. He had underestimated the time it would take him to summit and it became dark. Clouds veiled the moon and, as he was nearing the top, his visibility was zero.

Suddenly he slipped and fell, plummeting to the earth below. But, like any good climber he had secured a long rope around his waist. With a jolt he came to a halt and hung suspended off the side of the mountain – too far away to be able to get a grip on the rocks. Unable to climb up or down he cried out to God: "Help me please!"

Out of the blackness of the night he heard a reply: "Cut the rope." But the climber, convinced he would plummet to his death, held on tighter.

After a few days, the rescue team discovered his lifeless body hanging from the end of the rope...two feet off the ground.

---

[1] James 1:6
[2] Jeremiah 32:17

Let us not be like that mountain climber, deciding that we know better than God. Let us be content in the knowledge that He is our strength, that His Power is available to us today and that He is in control. There is a promise attached to trusting God and not trying to rely on ourselves: "Trust in the Lord with all your heart and lean not on your own understanding; in all your ways acknowledge him, and he will make your paths straight."[1]

Lord you say when we are weak then you are strong. I am weak Lord, please strengthen me.

Forgive me for grumbling and for my worry and fear. I am sorry Lord that I have shown by my actions and words that I don't trust you.

I take responsibility for the way I think. I take responsibility for my attitudes.

Father I know that I have tried to fix my husband / wife / children. Lord I give _____ to You. I know that they are in Your Hands.

Lord I lay my finances at Your feet. I am sorry for....

Thank you that You supply all my needs according to your riches in glory in Jesus Christ, so I don't have to worry anymore. Thank you that You delight in blessing me.

Take my focus off the things that cause me stress and rather help me to be grateful, have a balanced mind, look after the needs of others and focus on all things that are lovely.

Fill me with faith instead of fear and teach me to trust You and not to 'lean on my own understanding.'

God, grant me the serenity to accept the things I cannot change; courage to change the things I can; and wisdom to know the difference.

---

[1] Proverbs 3:5,6

I Don't Know Who I Am

My Chosen One

You seem to be on a continual quest to try to find out who you are. You have listened to those who spew lies about your identity and they have left you feeling despondent. Do not listen to them. My values are not the same as those of this world, who hold physical beauty and success in high esteem. I don't. I look at your heart, and what I see, is that you are beautiful.

Don't let your self-esteem be governed by what others say about you. It is what I say about you that matters, and I see my Wonderful Child when I look at you.

Come to me now, and learn who you are by listening to who I say you are. Then, when the fiery darts of the evil one come, you will be able to stand your ground, knowing that I am here to defend you.

Always near

Your Defender

I cannot remember when he first hit me. Maybe my brain has blanked out some of the horror of this period of my life, or maybe it's because it was such a long time ago or maybe it's because so much was happening at the time. But I remember this part well because I had to tell the police about it so many times:

Having finally found my *forté* in life, I was flourishing at Drama College. To make ends meet I had landed the role of lead singer in an extravaganza at a five star hotel in the evenings, supplementing this income by modelling. It was glamorous, with twelve stunning costume changes, back-up dancers, a five piece band and a grand entrance on a divan, carried by two glistening muscle men like an Egyptian princess. But it was hard work, with two shows on a Saturday night and another five shows during the week. My days consisted of college, study, modelling and the cabaret, and I would eventually flop, frazzled into bed well after midnight.

Looking back, I cannot find any reason why I agreed to a date – he wasn't my type at all – intense, sullen and rough around the edges. Maybe it was my habit of picking up strays and I felt sorry for him or maybe I was drawn to the lost look I detected under his mucho exterior. Maybe it was because I was prone, in those days, to dating guys simply because I did not want to hurt them. I probably agreed to the next couple of dates for the same reason or perhaps because I thought I could change him. By that time I had heard about how he had been tied to the dining room table and whipped by his father – that would have clinched another date because I was always looking for someone to fix. I don't remember the exact reasons now, but I eventually told him I didn't want to date him anymore and I thought that would be the last I would see of him.

But that Saturday evening, after I had performed in the usual shows at ten and twelve, I headed for my car in the hotel garage. He was waiting for me. He begged me to continue seeing him and told me to get into his car so that we could go somewhere to talk. When I refused, he forced me in and drove off. Maybe that was when he first hit me. I remember the guitar I was holding being smashed.

I was scared but alert. His face was maniacal and he was ranting: "If I can't have you then no-one can!" As the car turned onto the highway and headed out of town, I became terrified, thinking that he would take me to some deserted place and kill me. So, as the car slowed slightly, I jumped out.

Crawling into a bush, by the light of the street lamp, I waited. One would think I would pray at this point, but I didn't. Even though I had received Christ as my Saviour when I was fourteen, my atheist Dad's arguments against my beliefs had cast enough shadows that I had pushed God to the back of my mind. I cowered in the bushes at the side of the road, wishing someone would rescue me. There was no way to contact anyone; mobile phones had yet to be invented.

I was no match for him when he doubled back, found me and dragged me into the car again. Most South Africans were armed during those years of apartheid, and even though he hadn't pulled his gun out, I knew he carried one in the back of his jeans. I also knew he liked knives. He worked out regularly and was tall and big. But then everyone looks tall and big when one is only five foot two.

He took me to a room in a building. I presumed it was his apartment but it had no personal effects and looked more like a deserted bed and breakfast - a room with two beds...

For two days I was beaten and raped. It was then that I saw the gun. He threatened to use it if I made any noise at all, and I believed him. When he was done with me, or maybe because of my pleas, or maybe I played some clever game about loving him...I don't know why, but he dropped me back at my apartment. I do remember a strange thing though: he left me there, bloodied and bruised, with a packet of marijuana, and threatened that if I called the police they would find it in my house. But I didn't listen to him.

I called my mother. While waiting for her, I bathed and scrubbed myself for hours. The dirt felt like it was inside of me and no matter how hard I scrubbed, I couldn't get it off. As soon as she arrived she called the police who told us to go to the station. Their interrogation of me was perfunctory and they admonished me for having taken a shower. I felt like I was a sausage being processed on a conveyor belt - I got the impression they did this often. We heard later that he had been arrested, but he didn't stay in jail for long.

Close to passing out, I was then taken to an attorney's office where I endured a barrage of insults. He insinuated that, because I was an actress and a singer, I was 'asking for it.' This cut me to my core and reminded me of the names my step-father had called me a few years earlier. Somewhere inside, on some deep level, I believed my attorney and his comments added fuel to what was already lurking in my heart – I deserved this.

He explained to me that he was merely giving me a taste of what I would be facing in court. "It doesn't look good," he continued, "with you being an actress and the way you dress with all that makeup on and being out late at night...you know," he said, in a manner that suggested we would obviously agree with him. It horrified me to think that I would have to face this wall of criticism again, in front of other people, in court. My inner voice was beginning to panic: "Then everyone will know what you really are!" it yelled. He continued his scare tactics and gave me the statistics for rape convictions in South Africa and told me the perpetrator would, most likely, walk free because I had known him prior to the offence.

So I dropped the charges and he walked.

It was decided that I would be safer at my mother's house because he was now free to attack me again. I remember sitting in the back seat on that drive – cut, bruised, and shattered. Tat had said very little during the entire ordeal. But his silence was loaded and spoke volumes to me. I knew he thought I deserved it. I wasn't certain he was wrong.

Embarrassed because I had always believed 'the show must go on', I phoned the producers and told them I would not be able to perform for a while. It was heart-breaking to hear that we had just been booked to be the main act at a new casino that had just opened – the largest casino in Africa. But no amount of persuasion could get me to perform, no make-up could hide the damage to my face and body, and nothing could heal the gaping hole that was left when the 'me' was ripped from my core. One reporter had called me 'a petite little spark plug', but now not even a flicker remained.

For my protection I was sent to stay with my sister who lived five hours drive away. I think the deeper truth is that Tat blamed me, and my mum thought his attitude would hurt me. But I knew, and it hurt me anyway. At the time when I most needed to be in my mum's loving arms, I left.

With no studies, modelling or performing, my entire life changed. Everyone seemed to think "Nita is such a drama queen, she got into an argument with her boyfriend," and I began to believe it too. I began to believe that I was the problem and, in an effort to escape myself, I drank. Things went from bad to worse.

One day he found me.

The next part of my story would best be read without judgment. But if you do judge, then I understand, I judged myself and found myself guilty for years.

I went with him.

Maybe it was because I was not thinking clearly, maybe he threatened to kill my sister's children or maybe it was that syndrome I have heard about where people return to their abusers... I have asked myself why I did so many times and I have no answer. I think the buried reason was that I didn't know who I was anymore.

For the next year I lived with him in an apartment many miles away from my family. He watched me like a hawk and guarded me jealousy. I remember trying to escape but he got to the lift before the doors closed and, as I huddled in the corner of the lift, he burnt me with his cigarette on my back, over and over again. I can remember hiding in a small space under the kitchen sink for hours, convinced he would not find me. I can't remember why I was hiding there or what my plan was, but I remember the smell of mould and the clench of raw fear. I was beaten regularly, but never enough to have to go to the hospital.

Except on one occasion - Thinking that he was away for the day, I slashed my wrists. As the blade sliced through the skin, it stung intensely, but judging from the trickle of blood I knew I hadn't cut deep enough. I panicked, terrified at the thought about what he would do to me if he discovered me half-dead. I had to cut deeper. I was crying so much that I couldn't see what I was doing, so I closed my eyes and with everything I could muster I sliced deeper, and lay there, in the empty bath, waiting to die. But he came back after a short time and found me unconscious, and took me to hospital. He was pretending to be my concerned boyfriend when I came around in the hospital and I was released into his 'care' promising that I would go to see a psychologist soon. I was so doped up on medication I followed silently.

I cannot remember the reprisals. When you are being regularly beaten, individual episodes merge. But during this time I found a semblance of respite. I completed the last few months remaining of my studies and, through correspondence, I became qualified as a speech and drama teacher. It was hard though, because every day was filled with pain.

He became even more vigilant and violent. His gun came out now...often. I knew he would kill me if I stepped out of line. He didn't need it though, I was now fully convinced that this was just the way things were meant to be – this was my lot. My mind had become more trapped than my body. I had learnt to avoid being hurt, for the large part, by not fighting anymore. I could get away, but I didn't. I believed I was in a relationship, everyone did.

We like to label things. It helps us to make sense of the world around us - people who have heard this story, like to categorise it either as an abusive relationship or as a kidnapping. I think it was much more complex than either of those two labels. I still struggle to package this period of my life into a neat, easy to explain box – maybe labels are not necessary for healing. Maybe they can sometimes hinder healing.

But I do know that during this ordeal one thought plagued: "I don't know who I am."

My identity had been stolen.

Today there is a different type of identity theft in the world, and it is big business. The Federal Trade Commission in the US reports an annual average of 266,000 cases since 2004. They believe this is not the real figure though because most people do not make a report. Rape often goes unreported too, but the similarities do not stop there.

Identity theft occurs when an imposter takes the victim's personal information without their knowledge and uses it to steal something from that person. This had happened to me on an emotional level – the real me had been stolen. There had been many imposters in my life; he was just the one who managed to complete the transaction in me.

One may well ask what had happened to my faith since giving my life to Jesus eight years previously.

Identity theft is carried out in many different ways. The imposter digs to find the weak spot in your private life. That is what happened to me when my father came up for the holidays to take me on one of our annual trips together. He, a staunch atheist, asked me some questions that started to shake my foundation of faith. Questions that I now welcome and can argue, but then, a young fourteen year old Christian, I couldn't: "If God is love then why does He allow so much suffering in the world?" was one such question I could not answer.

He dug in the rubbish bin of my life. When he heard about my conversion he hid his anger behind a mask of sarcastic criticism of my mother and her marriage. He pointed out all the rubbish in their lives; the 'horrible' things that went on in her home and said that if they were Christians then why would I want to be one. I argued, but his words lingered and doubt crept in.

I reasoned that if those around me called themselves Christians, then I didn't really want to be one. I looked at the way they were behaving and decided that God probably didn't exist and even if He did, I didn't want to know Him because He wasn't doing anything to make my life better. My Dad had found the account of my life in the bin and the theft of my identity had begun. I began to forget who I really was – a child of God. How could God love me?

Any time I thought about God, which became less and less often, I would think more like a servant than a child. A servant is accepted in the household on the basis of what he does rather than because of who he is. I thought that what I did determined my acceptance by everyone, including God. The concept of unconditional love was completely foreign to me. By the time I reached eighteen, I was spiritually off balance.

Each time I did something I thought was wrong, there would be a flurry of trying to get my life 'right' again so that I could work my way back into God's good book, just as I had done with the significant male figures in my life. It was years before I realized that my life should not be focused on 'doing' as much as on 'being'. Just as a servant would be continually preoccupied with what he could do to please his master, I too, became focused on trying to do good things to get God to be pleased with me.

Having never felt the unconditional love of an earthly father, it never occurred to me that this was how God felt about me. I never realized that it was not my performance that God was interested in, as with a master and servant, but that He was interested in a real relationship. He loved the essence of who I was, and I didn't have to do anything to earn that Love.

Just as a servant can lose his job, I felt that if I failed He would leave me. I imagined that His presence departed from me depending on the severity of my sin: if I was a little bit naughty then His presence would be withdrawn from me for a while, and if I was particularly 'bad' then His hand of protection would be lifted from me completely. Just as a servant would fear punishment, I too was convinced that everything that happened to me was a result of God's wrath against me. Instead of resting with the assurance that all my sins had been forgiven, I constantly reminded myself of them. Forgiving myself for what I had done was a foreign concept to me. The guilt and shame piled on as I became stripped of all self-worth.

My identity as God's child, had been stolen and I was living and thinking like a servant. Whereas a child feels secure in the knowledge that they always have a home, I felt that my relationship with God teetered on tenuous ground and that if I carried on sinning He would leave me altogether. I knew it said in the Bible that He would 'never leave me nor forsake me' but the more I sinned the more I thought I was the exception. I was quick to take on board all the things the Bible said we should not do, but when I failed to stick to the rules, I condemned myself and felt that I deserved the nightmares I'd suffered.

It took years of healing before I realised that we have no reason to feel condemned and shamed and no reason to heed people who tell us that we are worthless. It was years before I could say: "The Creator of the Universe has chosen me!"

He has chosen you too. He knew all the bad stuff you were going to do in your life before you even did it, and He *still* chose you. Now he sees you as blameless, consecrated and holy. Do not let voices from your past or other negative words said about you drown out the reality of who God says you are. We are joint heirs of God in Jesus Christ – we have inherited everything that Jesus has received from the Father through His death and sacrifice. In ourselves we are imperfect and we cannot do anything to earn this, but in Christ all these things are possible.

We need to protect against our identities being stolen. One way to guard against identity theft is to check continually the accuracy of personal documents and deal promptly with any discrepancies. By staying in a close relationship with God, we will be able to recognize the lies about who we are when they come.

Those fiery darts of the devil can be combatted by the truth of God's Word. This is the **Who I Am List**:

- **A Child of God** - When you feel bad about any situation in your life, rest assured that you have been adopted into God's family[1] and are a child of God.[2]
- **God's workmanship** - If you feel bad about yourself, remember that you are made by God.[3]
- **Strong in the Lord** - If you feel like a loser, see that God "chose the weak things of the world to shame the strong"[4].
- **A friend of Jesus** - If you feel as though no one wants to be around you, read that you are a friend of Jesus.[5]
- **Christ-like** - When you feel stupid or intellectually inferior, read how you have the 'mind of Christ'.[6]
- **Forgiven** - When you feel the weight of your guilt, read how you stand blameless in His sight.[7]

---

[1] 1 John 3:1
[2] John 1:12,13
[3] Ephesians 2:10
[4] 1Corinthians 1:27
[5] John 15:15
[6] 1 Corinthians 2:16
[7] Ephesians 1:14

- **Defended** - When you are scared, remember that He is your rock, your strong tower, your fortress, your defender and your deliverer.[1]
- **Not Condemned** - When those around you are criticizing and judging you, say this: "There is no condemnation for those who are in Christ Jesus."[2]
- **Powerful** with God's Power - When you are frightened, remember that you have authority over all evil.[3]
- **Blessed** - No matter what it looks like, believe that you are blessed with every spiritual blessing.[4]
- **Righteous** - Know that you are righteous in the eyes of God and so you don't need to run and hide from Him or try to work your way into His favour.[5] You have a clear conscience before God.[6] He no longer remembers your failures.[7]
- **Holy** - You belong to God and are holy.[8] You are holy because when God looks at you He sees the completed work of the cross.

These descriptions of your identity appear all over the Bible, because God wants you to know who you are in Him, so that you will be able to enjoy the wonderful plan He has to 'prosper you and to give you hope and a future.'[9] Don't ever forget who you *really* are.

I didn't know anything about my identity in Christ when I was being held captive by a psychopath and by my own befuddled mind. I had lost hope, when one day my mum and my uncle John knocked at the door of the apartment where I was a virtual prisoner. They had been waiting until my abuser left, and once he did, they ran upstairs quickly and knocked on the door. It was startlingly simple - I just walked out with them. The lady living next door told my mother how grateful she was that someone had come to rescue me, because

---

[1] 2 Samuel 22:2 and Psalm 18:1 GNT
[2] Romans 8:1
[3] 1John 4:4
[4] Ephesians 1:3
[5] Romans 3:22
[6] Hebrews 10:22
[7] Hebrews 8:12
[8] 1 Peter 2:9
[9] Psalm 138:8

she had heard my recurrent screams. I am eternally grateful to my brave mother and Uncle John.

This time I didn't bother going to an attorney or the police.

But that is not the Hollywood ending that we like to hear. We want vindication. Sometimes we hide this simmering emotion because we are told that vindication is wrong: "Do not take revenge, my friends, but leave room for God's wrath, for it is written: "It is mine to avenge; I will repay," says the Lord."

And He did.

Years passed after this terrible abuse. Then one day, while my husband and I were listening to the news on the car radio, a particular story caught our attention: A man had been attacked while sleeping in his home. He had been tortured, stabbed many times, shot repeatedly in the chest, burnt with a hot iron and had received over thirty blows to his head. Then the announcer gave his name. I recognized it immediately as the name of my abuser. We listened further and heard that his life was hanging in the balance in hospital.

After prayer, I felt I needed to write him a note by email. I wanted him to know that, not only had I forgiven him, but that I had moved on. It was a 'full stop' at the end of the chapter and a final declaration to myself, to others and to God that I had forgiven. After much agonising, I wrote: "I am praying for your complete healing." Then I quoted Matthew: "For if you forgive men when they sin against you, your heavenly Father will also forgive you."[1] At my request my husband, a computer-wiz, carefully ensured that there would be no details about my location on the email and no possible way that he could contact me. This, seemingly weird response, was borne, not only out of prayer, but also my deep need to move on. Forgiveness does that. It allows us to move on. The email was sent and the matter closed.

---

[1] Matthew 6:14

His attack became 'the country's best-publicised crime of brutality' in recent history. Even though he survived, he needed extensive long-term care and remained in a wheelchair.

When I have shared this story with friends some have called it 'poetic justice' and said 'what goes around comes around'. But I have avoided telling the story, on a large scale before now, because I have been worried that people who hear this will desire to have vindication in their own lives. Jesus never acted in vengeance, even though he was spat on and beaten and could have called down the wrath of heaven. He chose instead to forgive. We think that by not retaliating we become doormats, but God does not want that for us. He wants us to act when He tells us to act and that is always in a way that shows love to our fellow man...even the really bad fellowmen.

As time went on, I became aware that God was more offended by what happened to me than I could ever be. Our job is to pray for mercy for the people who harm us – so that they don't get what they deserve because, after all, we didn't get what we deserved from God.

We are called to "live in harmony with one another; be sympathetic, love as brothers, be compassionate and humble. Do not repay evil with evil or insult with insult, but with blessing, because to this you were called so that you may inherit a blessing."[1]

Many people ask me: "Where was God in all of this?" There is no simple answer, but I believe: "He reached down from on high and took hold of me; he drew me out of deep waters. He rescued me from my powerful enemy, from my foes, who were too strong for me. They confronted me in the day of my disaster, but the Lord was my support. He brought me out into a spacious place; he rescued me because he delighted in me."[2]

Real healing came when I learnt that I was who God said I was. I no longer needed to 'look for myself.' I was secure in the knowledge of who I was and the reality of my position in the universe.

---

[1] 1 Peter 3:9
[2] 2 Samuel 22:17-20

I was free to be me.

Thank you for showing me who I really am.
Give me the wisdom to hold onto my new identity.
Help me not to be affected by what others say about me.
Heal me from wounds inflicted by others.
Help me not to be vindictive, but rather, to forgive.
Show me how to be free to be me.

Why Should I Forgive?

Precious One

I know you find it very difficult to believe that I could forgive all your sins. But know this: nothing you do can separate you from me. I knew all the sins you would do before I created you, and I still made you. I sent my one and only Son to die for your sins. Now when I look at you I don't see them anymore. So don't hide from me.

In the same way that I forgave all your sins, I want you to forgive those who have wronged you. Do this quickly before a root of bitterness takes hold. Don't wait for them to recognise that what they did to you was wrong, just forgive them and move on. Forgive them as I have forgiven you. I know it will be difficult, but I will help you.

Forever

Your Forgiving Father

Marco was terrified. He was certain Don and Dino, the massive lumps of muscle standing on either side of the door, could see the sweat pouring down His trembling body. As he waited to be seen he thought about what his future held – his feet in a bucket of cement and thrown in the river, a bullet to the head? He hoped it was the bullet.

"Big Al will see you now," his dark thoughts were interrupted by Don, or maybe it was Dino – he couldn't tell the difference between the solid walls of man, as they shoved him into the office.

Through the haze of cigar smoke sat Big Al. His legend had not done him justice – he was bigger and shinier than Marco thought he would be - a man who knew things, you could tell. Lean, with slicked back hair and dressed in an impeccable Armani suit, Big Al sat behind his gigantic desk.

"Right, who do we have here?" He said looking down at a ledger in front of him, "Ah, Marco. Yes... yes... I see you have gambled yourself into a tight spot!"

"Um, yes, I know," Marco was struggling to keep his thoughts together as his fear mounted.

"A million dollars, you owe me a million dollars." Big Al said, in a matter-of-fact kind of way. The number made Marco reel – he knew he couldn't pay that back in ten lifetimes.

"I know. I don't know what to do. I am so sorry!" Marco said, falling to his knees, "Please forgive me! Maybe I can pay you back sometime soon? Please, let me pay it off. Please...please..." his voice trailed off into a wail of sobbing.

"Ok, Marco, you don't have to pay."

Marco, convinced he had misheard stopped sobbing and shrieked: "What?"

"You don't have to pay. Your debt with me is all clear. You can go." Big Al dismissed him with a flicker of a smile and a wave of his hand.

Stunned, Marco left the building. Walking along the busy city sidewalk, he tried to make sense of what had just happened. "Who does that? This can't be real. It's a con." His doubts seemed to be confirmed when he thought he got a glimpse of Don and Dino. Was his mind playing tricks on him?

Just then he spotted Little Luigi coming out of the Bookmaker. "What's he think he's doing gambling?" Marco thought indignantly, "he owes me money!" Hurrying over to him Marco pulled him by the scruff of his neck. "Hey Luigi, where's that five bucks you owe me?"

Luigi, hopelessness dripping from his eyes, looked up at the man towering over him: "Ah Marco, please, I cannot pay! I don't have the money."

Without hesitation Marco clenched his fist and with as much force as he could muster, he punched Little Luigi in the stomach. Winded, Luigi doubled over and fell to the ground.

Suddenly Marco felt himself being lifted off the ground. Hanging, he found himself looking straight into the black eyes of Don, or maybe it was Dino. "The Boss has a message for you - he said he is not pleased. He said you owe him nothing and then you go and put the squeeze on Little Luigi! Boss said you have to come with us." With that Marco, wailing loudly is led off to a fate that could possibly be worse than death.

This story is inspired by the Parable of the Unmerciful Servant,[1] where the debtor is "turned over to the jailers to be tortured, until he should pay back all he owed." It then, rather shockingly, goes on to say: "This is how my heavenly Father will treat each of you unless you forgive your brother from your heart."[2] Marco had not forgiven poor little Luigi even though he had been forgiven. There is a clear warning in this parable for those who refuse to forgive others.

The size of the debt is also worthy of note. Big Al, who represents God in my allegory, gives Marco far more than he even asked for; instead of being released from some of his debts, he is released from them all. Likewise, God forgives the 'debt' accrued from all our sins through Jesus' sacrifice on the cross. In the original story the enormity of the debt is stressed because the servant has to pay 10 000 talents, which was an impossible sum for him. Likewise, we cannot possibly pay anything back to God for our sins. Jesus however can, and does, on our behalf. The size of this sum also indicates the degree to which we are to forgive others.

However Marco couldn't believe such generosity existed. His disbelief in his freedom kept him in bondage to his feelings, which led him to act as if he was still in debt – he tried to collect money. Marco resented Luigi continuing to gamble and took out his revenge on him. That is how it is when we are unforgiving – we are plagued by guilt and resentment that leads us to seek retribution for

---

[1] Matthew 18:21
[2] Matthew 18:35

perceived wrongs. His unwillingness to forgive others when he had been forgiven led to his downfall. We too become tortured by a myriad of emotional conflicts, and leave a trail of broken relationships if we continue to have unforgiving hearts.

We have all felt the ravages of resentment, bitterness, indignation and unforgiveness at some time in our lives: being hurt by a parent when you were growing up, favouritism shown towards a sibling, friends who failed you, someone who cheated on you or a marriage partner who offered to love, respect and honour you and instead caused you pain. But we have not been called to sink into the feelings that result; instead we are told to forgive as God forgave us. C.S. Lewis writes, "To be a Christian means to forgive the inexcusable because God has forgiven the inexcusable in you."

So what is this illusive feeling called unforgiveness that we are warned not to entertain? Maybe if we understand what unforgiveness is, we will be better equipped to deal with it? Psychologists generally define it as a deliberate, conscious decision to show feelings of resentment or vengeance toward a person or group who have caused you harm, regardless of whether they actually deserve your forgiveness. In easier terms: Forgiveness occurs when you no longer hold grudges and grievances against a person or group – all blame is lifted.

Someone once said: "Forgiveness is me giving up my right to hurt you for hurting me." Poetically, Mark Twain wrote: "Forgiveness is the fragrance a violet sheds on the heel that has crushed it."

We should forgive for three reasons: The Bible says so, it shows love to others and it is good for us.

The Bible says: "If anyone has caused you grief...you ought to forgive and comfort him, so that he will not be overwhelmed by excessive sorrow."[1] The instructions are clear: "Bear with each other and forgive whatever grievances you may have against one another. Forgive as the Lord forgave you."[2] Jesus gives this alarming warning:

---

[1] 2 Corinthians 2:5-7
[2] Colossians 3:13

"For if you forgive men when they sin against you, your heavenly Father will also forgive you. But if you do not forgive men their sins, your Father will not forgive your sins."[1] It is clear that if we do not forgive others then God will not forgive us because that would mean that we are denying that we too, like them, are sinners in need of God's forgiveness. It then goes on to tell us to do what seems like the impossible: "I urge you therefore to reaffirm your love for him."

As with most things in the Bible, it backs up what science is discovering: Research has shown that people who forgive are healthier than those who don't forgive. Studies have shown that the cardio-vascular system comes under increased pressure when people rehearse grudges and grievances in their mind. On the other hand, through thoughts of forgiveness, the pressure decreases.

However, as we all know, it is not always easy. There are many **factors influencing how difficult it is to forgive**:

- The significance of the relationship - The closer the person is, the harder it is to forgive.
- The severity of the offence - The more severe the offence, whether real or imagined, the more difficult to forgive.
- The frequency with which the offence occurs - An on-going infringement can be harder to forgive.
- The length of time that has elapsed since the offence was caused – An offence that took place many years ago may seem like it is having less impact but one needs to be careful because the depth of the hurt could run deep.
- Being able to make excuses for the person who caused the hurt can lessen pain caused - Someone once wrote: "The more we know, the better we forgive.
- Whether the offended parties can communicate with each other - Forgiveness is more likely when things can be hashed out.
- Whether the person has apologised - Forgiveness seems easier when the person apologises, however this should not

---

[1] Matthew 6:14

be a prerequisite. We should forgive whether the other person takes responsibility of not.

- Various circumstances and personalities of individuals concerned - these affect not only the speed at which we forgive, but also the things we get offended over and the depth of hurt we feel.

In 1993 my ability to forgive was tested to the limit when my father died amidst suspicious circumstances.

He came, with his long standing girlfriend and nurse, to visit my husband and I on our farm. Even though he had recently suffered a stroke he was in fine form, charming and witty as always. He was well-known for telling tall stories, but when anyone approached him on the subject, he shrugged his shoulders and simply said: "It makes the stories far more interesting!" That was that – we continued to hear about his cat that fended off a lion, the magnitude of his appeal to the opposite sex and other figments of his imagination. The best example of one of these tall tales was his one about hunting in the forests of Northern Rhodesia (now known as Zimbabwe). He explained that he reached a river that was so wide he was unable to cross. But he noticed rocks, conveniently placed in the water to help him, and deftly prancing from one to the other, he reached the other side. When he turned back he realised that he had been skipping across the backs of hippopotamuses!

That night at our farm, as he was getting ready for bed, he sounded like he was panicking. My husband Richard overheard him arguing with his girlfriend in the bathroom – he didn't want to take the extra tablets she was giving him, and she was reassuring him that it was necessary. Richard was concerned, knowing that he was on some potent medications, but reasoned that she was a nurse and knew better. We all went to bed, blissfully unaware of the mayhem that would erupt the following morning.

It was common knowledge that my dad would have preferred if I had been born a boy, and he seldom told me that he loved me, but I loved him nonetheless. So, earlier that evening, it had touched me deeply when he had told me how proud he was of me. Having never heard it before, it filled an old void that I had been unsuccessfully trying to satiate with the love of others. As we sat together that night it was as though he had changed. He spoke about how much he loved my sister and me and that we were never going to have to worry about money for the rest of our lives, because he had taken care of us in his will. I was surprised - we had all suspected that my dad became a wealthy man when his parents passed away and through his work as an architect, but none of us were sure because he was such a skinflint. I went to bed feeling loved and secure that night.

The next morning we were called to his bedside. His girlfriend said that he was ill. On entering my guest room I saw his half-naked body lying on the bed and realised he was already dead. While she phoned the rescue helicopter, my husband gave him mouth to mouth resuscitation and I prayed for God to bring him back to life. But he was no longer there - my father was gone. We heard later that he had been dead for some hours.

The days after his death were spent in a haze. During this time, much to our concern, his girlfriend brought up the subject of his will with my husband. She said that she had no idea what was in the will and asked if we had any inclination as to what it contained. Richard replied that we didn't.

When my father's attorney phoned, alarm bells began to ring. He explained that a few weeks earlier, my dad's girlfriend had phoned him and instructed him to prepare documentation to change the settlement of my father's trust. He said that the signed document was then returned by her a few days later. This information, in light of her earlier denial as to any knowledge of the settlement of his affairs, raised grave suspicions and prompted us to request an autopsy. The strong objection expressed at this request made us all the more determined to proceed. The pathologist was so alarmed by the results that he phoned my husband immediately. He confirmed that the toxicology report indicated a lethal combination of prescription medication.

That was when we heard about the will - my sister and I had been all but nominally cut out of the new one written only weeks before his death. It was a blow. My first reaction was to question whether I had done something to offend my father, but then I remembered what he had said to me the night before he died – that he loved us and that we would be financially secure.

A handwriting expert was employed to analyse the new will. He concluded that it was forged. Then the pathologist died – before writing up his report. By this time my father's body had been cremated and we decided to drop the matter.

The whirlwind of events surrounding the death of my dad left us all shattered. I was unable to simply grieve his death because I had so many other conflicting emotions and I went on a downward spiral that left me physically and emotionally drained.

It took years before I realised I needed to forgive, because so many other emotions clouded my thinking. The lack of closure about his death made me unsure about whom I was to forgive: had he rejected me or had he been killed? I thought that maybe I had disappointed him so much in my life that he had decided to disinherit me. I felt utterly rejected.

But then another voice would tell me that it had not been his decision to die. At those times, I would remember that he told me my sister and I would be well provided for and I would feel better about myself. But I was never sure. At the end of the day, I had no closure and didn't know who to forgive. Even if I had worked out who to forgive I didn't see forgiveness as necessary to me: "Why should I forgive? It's not going to help me."

The secret to being free from so many of the hurts in our lives is forgiveness. But for us to be able to forgive, we first need to understand what it is. As you read through these lists about what forgiveness is and what it isn't, think about someone who you feel particularly unforgiving towards:

Forgiveness is...

- A step towards your healing. It is the first step in your healing process.

- A movement forward - It is as though you are saying: "I don't like what happened but I am choosing to move forward despite the hurt."
- A choice - It is a conscious decision to no longer blame the person for what they did to you.
- Letting go of your right to get even and take revenge - "Forgiveness is above all a personal choice; a decision of the heart to go against the natural instinct to pay back evil with evil" - Pope John Paul II
- Dropping the grudge – By doing this you will release all resentment and bitterness.
- An opportunity to walk in love by showing grace and mercy.
- Restoration of relationships with others, God and ourselves.

Forgiveness is not...

- Weakness - "The weak can never forgive. Forgiveness is the attribute of the strong" - Mahatma Gandhi.
- Forgetting - You are not called to gloss over or deny the offence. You will not suddenly forget what was done to you. There is no such thing as 'forgive and forget.' Even while you still remember what was done, it can stop hurting you.
- Making an excuse or ignoring the offence - Acting as if the offence never happened or that it wasn't 'that bad' will only fuel anger and resentment.
- An obligation to reconcile with the person - You can forgive a person without having to reconcile with them or release them from legal accountability.
- A mechanism whereby trust is automatically regained - Trust is earned and as such it will take time.
- Absolving the person of a crime – You are relieving yourself of the position of victim not taking the responsibility for the offence or crime away from the person.
- Instant healing - Sometimes forgiveness brings great relief but at other times it takes a little longer.
- Giving the injured party power over the person who is being forgiven - It cannot be used as some sort of 'you owe me' stand because this would violate the whole principle of forgiveness.

- An action whereby the consequences of the person's behaviour are taken away - even though you have forgiven someone they still need to face the results of their actions.

When we are affronted we become angry. This is one of the most potent of all feelings, and it has a goal - to keep our other feelings at bay. Anger aids our natural efforts to protect ourselves. We say: "No one is ever going to hurt me like that again," and in so doing, we build a Dam Wall of Anger. All that can be seen on its concrete surface is bitterness, resentment and indignation. Behind this massive wall grace, mercy and forgiveness are blocked up, unable to flow to bring healing and growth.

This Dam Wall of Anger represents a massive grudge that we have held on to for so long that it has become part of us. The idea of getting rid of it is terrifying so we remain in the misery because it is more familiar ground. We are not sure who we would be without it. Anger needs to be blasted away for life to flow.

Even though not all anger is sin, we must not allow anger to take root in our lives and we must avoid venting it in improper ways that cause us to sin. I have been angry about the abuse and hardships I have suffered, but the Lord has shown me that bitterness and anger were only making me rot from the inside out and preventing me from healing. When I decided to face my anger and deal with it in God's way, I began to heal.

Anger can be dealt with by:

- getting to its root
- understanding that the devil is trying to goad you to sin
- deciding not to give in to it
- choosing to forgive
- blessing those who have hurt us

Once anger is dealt with, forgiveness will become easier to achieve.

Forgiveness begins with a decision. "But," you might say, "Why should I forgive?" Here are **Some Good Reasons to Forgive**:

- It is good for you! We think that by holding on to a grudge, we will be teaching someone else a lesson, but it is having the opposite effect – it is hurting you. Thomas Chalmers wrote: "Unforgiveness is the poison we drink hoping another will die."
- When you relinquish past hurts you free yourself up to embrace the future.
- When you are not spending all your time feeding your grudge, you will be free to enjoy your life.
- You are giving the offender power in your life by allowing them to continually hurt you as you hold on to these negative thoughts - no longer give them any power in your life!
- You think that you have control when you are nursing a grudge, but that is a lie, you are in fact still being controlled by your offender and by the pain of the offence.
- Indignation might be making you feel good for the moment, but getting rid of it will make you feel better in the long run.
- While your defences are up you will be unable to love to the full.
- Once you get rid of the wall of anger and unforgiveness you will be free to be you.

Some people get instantly healed of unforgiveness once they confess it to the Lord and ask Him to help them. But for others, it takes time. Letting go of the resentment and bitterness that unforgiveness creates means:

- Making a choice to forgive, followed by a series of choices about what to think and do each day. This will become easier the more times you make a decision towards forgiveness.
- Releasing old relationships and situations where your toxic thinking was kept alive.
- Controlling all your thoughts. As soon as you find yourself thinking about the person or the situation, then recommit to forgiveness.
- Asking the Holy Spirit to take up residency in the space that was formally occupied by the grudge.

Genuine forgiveness, however, cannot come simply by our own efforts. We need to do all that we can do, and then we need to rely on God to complete the work in us. He does this by His Grace, a word for which Joyce Meyer has a wonderful definition: "It is the power of the Holy Spirit coming to us free of charge to enable us to do with ease what we could never do on our own". We cannot forgive on our own. The free gift of Grace can come and blast that Dam Wall of Anger to smithereens. We only need ask our Father for His help.

It's a collaborative effort. We have a job to do and God has His part. Doing each other's jobs is impossible. Our part is to come to a place where we sincerely want to forgive and to make the committed decision to forgive. God's part is to change our hearts on a deep level so that our feelings come in line with our intentions. This is a process and takes time. We need to be willing to allow God to take away our old memories and attitudes towards the offence. This can only be done if we constantly 'drop' any thoughts about it, stem any desires to discuss it with others or mull over it constantly. The offence needs to be dropped and we need to resist any temptation to pick it up again. As we keep re-affirming our decision to forgive, God will work a deep healing in us.

You will know that you have forgiven when:

- The first thought you have about them is not about what they did to harm you.
- You can pray for them to be blessed. God's idea of blessing is not the same as ours, He may or may not decide to bless the person by pointing out their wrongs – and when you get to a point where you really want them to be blessed you can be rest assured that you have forgiven.
- You no longer wish them harm and stop delighting in thoughts or news of their hardships or failures.
- You no longer have the memory of the offence playing in an endless loop in your head.

This thought, more than any other, helped me to forgive: "Forgiveness has nothing to do with absolving a criminal of his crime. It has everything to do with relieving oneself of the burden of being a victim - letting go of the pain and transforming oneself from victim to survivor." - C.R. Strahan. So decide not to stay a victim any longer and forgive.

Having forgiven my rapist and abuser, I was shocked to discover that I was still a victim. Even though I knew I had done and said what I needed to in order to survive, I felt enormous guilt, shame and self-loathing. I would replay everything I did and didn't do over and over in my mind, and when I saw ways that I could have escaped, I kicked myself for my stupidity for not having taken them. I felt deep guilt when I remembered times that I was nice to him because as the stinking, dark memories began to fade, I forgot how I had needed to struggle for life. I forgot the driving force of fear, the constant battle for calm and the relentless cycle of growing tension, explosions and attempts at reconciliation. I forgot all that, and what remained was guilt. 'I should have', 'could have' and 'would have' thoughts played endlessly in my mind.

This had a strange effect on my later life. Every so often I would go out to bars in the middle of the night. Even though I knew it was a potentially lethal thing to do in South Africa, I was driven by an unseen force so deep inside me that I could not even tell it existed. Later, I realised what it was: I wanted to prove myself to me. The question about whether I could have done something to escape my abuser churned and I set out, in a vain effort, to set the record straight: I could escape the lust of men. So I put myself in danger. Sitting in those bars, I pushed men away. Each time I did, I felt satisfied that I was in control. I felt invincible. No-one would be able to do that to me again. I had proved that I could take care of myself.

But it was a Band-Aid on an amputation. I was trying to heal my severed self. I had found myself guilty of not doing more to escape and, in so doing I rejected the essence of who I was. I couldn't forgive me.

There is no reference to 'forgiving yourself' in the Bible because we cannot forgive ourselves. It is God who forgives us and frees us from the guilt of sin. When we realise this, we will cease trying to constantly dissect our faults. Some situations are just too complex to analyse meaningfully and all attempts to do so will only leave one feeling confused. But God sees our sin. If we are unsure about our culpability in a situation we can go before God and ask him to make it clear to us. He may tell you. But if you remain unclear about your fault, don't continue to mull over events, simply accept that He sees and He forgives and this knowledge should be enough for you.

Then we can choose either to wallow in what we have done wrong or we can believe that Jesus died to set us free. The Bible says: "See to it that...no bitter root grows up to cause trouble and defile many."[1] Even though we cannot forgive ourselves, we can stop beating ourselves over the head about things we have done wrong. This root of bitterness can be about us not dropping the issue, not only with ourselves but with others, and it needs to be cut off before it becomes a tree that will overshadow your whole life.

But we often confuse forgiving ourselves with excusing ourselves. We think that if we forgive ourselves we will be condoning what we did. But if we remember that it is not up to us to forgive ourselves, then we are absolved of this responsibility. Our job is to ask to be forgiven and then believe that we are.

If you still feel ashamed of your past and you are still holding yourself guilty, then you need to ask: "Am I denying what God has done for me on the cross?" If your sins have been forgiven then you are separated from them. You may not think that you deserve forgiveness but that does not change the fact that God loves you so much that He has forgiven you anyway.

Holding onto your guilt is like refusing a gift. God gave you the gift of taking your sins away. Are you refusing to accept it? If someone gives you a present and you reject it, doesn't it leave you feeling affronted, belittled and unappreciated? Is that how God feels when we continue to beat ourselves up for the very sins that he suffered and died for? At the heart of holding on to our sin is pride. We declare ourselves guilty even though the Creator of the Universe remembers our sins no more.[2]

Regardless of what we've done in the past, God has forgiven us and the guilt that was rightfully ours, has been removed. If God says we are forgiven, then we are. Let's believe that and be free.

---

[1] Hebrews 12:16
[2] Hebrew 8:12

Lord I am sorry that I have held onto guilt and shame.
I know that You have forgiven me and I accept this now and believe it.
Thank you for forgiving me.
I am sorry that I have held onto grudges towards others.
Lord I want to forgive but I feel as though I cannot.
Blast my Dam Wall of Anger to smithereens!
Refresh me with forgiveness every day.
Help my unforgiveness.

Don't Blame Me!

My Friend

I know that sometimes you question what happened in your life to get you to where you are today, and in an effort to make sense of it all, you look around for someone to blame.

But blaming will not help; in fact it will stop you from growing.

So take responsibility for whatever is your fault and leave the faults of others up to me to deal with.

I have shown you my character traits. Study them so that you can become more like me.

Your Servant

Jesus

"You don't understand at all!" Jane stomped her foot, "they hit me first." It seemed to Jane as if her father was not listening at all: "Dad! Listen! They have been calling me names for ages. Ann told Cynthia who told Jack about what I did at the party and then the boys posted pictures up on the Internet about me and now the whole school knows!"

Her father, who had been sitting opposite her and listening intently, gently replied: "Don't worry, Jane, my Love. Now what did you do when they hit you?" Jane found it infuriating when he quizzed her. "Well...um...I hit back!" What else am I meant to do? Just roll over and let them beat me to a pulp?" she said defensively. Looking at her with love her father asked: "You need help?" Jane was amazed that she hadn't thought of that before. It was so obvious to her now, of course she needed help. "Yes, Dad I do," she said running over to sit at his feet "what are you going to do?" As she looked up into his strong face he asked: "Do you believe I can help you Jane?" Jane replied: "Yes, I believe in you Dad. But that is not going to change anything. They are being so mean. Ann used to be my best friend and she started all these rumours! It's not my fault that she got hit. Anyone would have done that."

While Jane continued telling her Dad all the things that had happened to her, he reached down to the side of his chair and picked up a huge Golden Box that Jane had never noticed before. "This is my gift to you." Her father said, handing her the box. Jane took it and making herself comfortable she began to study it more closely. Its beauty was breath-taking. It was made of pure, beaten gold. On it she could make out the word: Salvation.

As she ran her fingers over the intricate patterns on its surface she felt a delicate power surge through her. "It has supernatural powers," her father explained to Jane's delight. Thanking her father, and picking up the box, she ran out the door to go and tell anyone she could find about her incredible gift. As she reached the door she could hear her father shouting after her: "Tell everyone that I have one for them too!"

Walking through her neighbourhood, Jane hoped that people would see her walking along with her beautiful Golden Box. As soon as she met anyone, unable to contain herself, she showed it to them, adding: "And he says you can have one too. It is free of charge!" People seemed pleased for her at first, but as soon as she said 'free of charge' it was like a cloud came over their faces and they left. Some even looked angry.

Jane remembered a corner, near the fountain, where people often stood on a soapbox and told everyone anything that was on their minds. She had seen some strange characters ranting and raving there before. "But maybe if I tell everyone my story and show them my box, they will listen," she thought, heading for the fountain.

There were so many people milling around that Jane found it hard to get to the soapbox. Someone was already standing on it, shouting about something in a gruff voice. The crowd was booing so loudly that the man, yelling abuse at them, backed down.

Jane, seizing the opportunity, took his place. At first no one was interested as she started to talk about her father, some even jeered. But when she held the Golden Box above her head and shouted: "Here it is. See!" a few people seemed to grow more interested. At first, Jane told them all about how her dad had given her the box, but that only took a little while and, enjoying the limelight, she began to tell them all about the bullies at school. As she moaned on and on about what Ann had done to her the crowds began to leave. But Jane felt good. "Hah! That will teach them!" Jane thought. She noticed one old lady sitting with her fingers in her ears. "How rude!" Jane thought. But she was not deterred; she continued to complain. Seeing that people were leaving, she shouted: "You can have one too and it's free!" Some stopped, with a quizzical look on their faces, but then they raised their hands, scoffed in disbelief and moved on. She was soon left, standing with her Golden Box, alone.

Embarrassed, disheartened and a little angry Jane sat down and cried. To her relief her father was suddenly at her side. After holding her in his arms until her tears ceased, he dried her eyes, sat down next to her and said: "Jane, you haven't opened the box yet."

All signs of crying now past, Jane quickly opened the box. The first thing she noticed was the most exquisite aroma she had ever smelt, wafting up from the contents of the box. Looking, she saw a mysterious mist covering whatever was inside. On closer inspection she saw various objects vibrating very gently in the mist. They began to float out of the box. She looked at her father for reassurance: "I told you it was supernatural," he said smiling.

When she turned back to the box the objects were floating above it. Each one was a container of some sort, with writing on its side. She lent closer and saw that each container was different to the other and each one had an inscription written on its side. She read: "Love, joy, peace, patience, kindness, goodness, faithfulness, humility and self-control."[1] When she looked quizzically at her father, he explained: "These are my personality traits that I want to pass on to you. They are yours now, but you need to learn about them and then practice using them. It will take time for them to sink in."

---

[1] Galatians 5:22 GNT

Excitedly, Jane picked the biggest one out of the mist – Love. It was the most elegant perfume bottle she had ever seen and its aroma was intoxicating. She sprayed it on herself and then on her father, who was delighted, and laughed. As she did so, a strange feeling came over her and she immediately wanted to get up on the soapbox again and tell everyone about her magnificent present. But this time she wanted to tell them so that *they* too could have this wonderful experience. Before she began speaking she scanned the crowd and for the first time really saw them. It was as if she could see through them in some way, right into their hearts. She saw that some were afraid, some felt rejected, some were in anguish and some were even on the brink of giving up.

The concern she felt for them drove her speech. She started by telling them she understood how they felt. As she continued to speak, the tears began to well up and the rejection she felt poured out and, as it did, the crowd leaned a little closer. By way of explanation, she reached into the box and drew out the clear bottle labelled 'Humility' and rubbed some on her arms and mouth. Suddenly her story began to change. No longer was she full of complaining and blaming, but rather she spoke about how sad she felt that she had hit her best friend. She wept as she spoke about her love for Ann. As she dried her eyes she saw the tear-stained faces in front of her. Everyone was hanging onto her every word. "There is a gift that my father has for you, that is free of charge, if you will only believe," she said, pointing to her father standing in the crowd.

With that, she invited people to go speak to her father. As she did so, a pleasant pandemonium broke out. Everyone seemed to need to tell their stories too and everyone wanted a Golden Box of their own.

Jane and her father stayed with the people for hours. As the night wore on Jane constantly returned to the box. She sprayed Kindness onto her and as she did so she became aware of what people were *really* saying and her answers seemed to make a difference, she used Patience when the stories she heard went on and on and she discovered that Self-control helped all the other ointments and lotions to have a long-lasting effect. As the night wore on she became tired and used the small, pink bottle of Joy. She felt instantly stronger. By the time the sun was coming up, she had used all the little containers in one way or another.

As the sunlight began to rise over her little village, Jane noticed Ann standing in the crowd. She was crying. Just then her father caught her eye and gestured to her to rub some Humility on herself. Following his instruction and enveloped in the aroma of Love, Jane cautiously approached Ann and taking her hand she said: "I am so sorry I hit you."

To Jane's surprise Ann cried and told her all about the hardships she was enduring at home – Ann was being physically abused nearly every day. Jane felt deep compassion for her friend, and even though Ann never apologised to her, she took her to her father. That night Ann got her own Golden Box.

It wasn't long before Jane's town changed. So many people got the Golden Box that the next town could smell the exquisite aroma and when they came to find out what had happened, they too wanted Golden Boxes, and so the story continued from town to town to town….

Like Jane, when things go wrong in our lives, we are quick to lay the blame on others and cry out: "Don't blame me!" Even though others may indeed be wrong, our blaming them can have dire consequences. Jane discovered one of these immediately: in an attempt to vindicate herself and shame Ann, she began to complain, but no one was interested in hearing about her gift when she did. Our complaining and blaming prevents the message of hope from reaching others. It also prevents us from moving on with our lives – we cannot heal as long as we are in a state of complaining and blaming. This is partly because while we have this attitude we cannot accept responsibility for our actions.

Our modern world seems to be focused on convincing us that we don't have to take responsibility because we are entitled to blame someone else. The world of psychology has taught us that what happens to us during childhood pre-determines how we will think and behave as an adult. We have taken this observation a step further by ascribing blame. We not only recognise that certain aspects of our past have influenced us, but we blame our upbringing for any personality deficits we see in ourselves and in so doing we often absolve ourselves of all responsibility.

I know this, because I did it for years. I blamed the rejection I felt in every relationship I was in on the rejection I suffered as a child. I blamed my drinking and smoking on the fact that I had grown up around drinkers and smokers. The abuse I suffered explained my mood swings and fears. I had settled into an uncomfortable place called Complain and Blame saying: "I am this way (or my situation is this way) because of what they did to me."

In fact, I distinctly remember my reasoning before one of my suicide attempts: "This will show them! They will realise that they drove me to this when they discover my body!" I blamed so fiercely, that my death was going to be a final act of revenge! Of course there were other reasons governing why I wanted to die, but this was a distinct, fleeting thought.

We can also settle into this uncomfortable place called blame because of things that are happening to us now: We seek oblivion in our addictions because someone drove us to it, or we are miserable in our marriages because our partners are impossible to live with or we are over-weight because of the fast-food industry.

You may well say: "But you don't know my problem. If you did, you would know that it *is* their fault!" This may be so. You may well have had some very real events that happened in your life that many would agree are not your fault. You might even have had a ruling in court that clearly found you to be the victim. But the problem with settling into Complain and Blame is that you get stuck. While you stay there, you will go nowhere. It feels great at first, quite exhilarating really, when you first get the news of your vindication. The relief you feel comes from having the responsibility taken off your shoulders. You are relieved to find out that who you have become and what you do is not your fault: you have something or someone else to blame.

So you get fooled into thinking you have reached the root of the problem – it was someone else's fault and there is nothing you can do about it - you have 'closure'. But it is not over. That issue is still sitting inside you and it is causing havoc with your emotions. All sorts of negative feelings are gaining strength – bitterness, resentment, anger, fear. They are going unchecked as your focus remains outward. We need to turn the focus inward.

This can only be done by opening the Golden Box which contains the fruits of the Holy Spirit. Before we begin to avail of these fruits of the Spirit, we need to learn about humility. Andrew Murray said: "It is the root of every virtue." The lack of humility is also at the root of every evil.

Many are driven to suicide because of pride. We feel our rights have been infringed: "No one has a right to treat me that way; how could they have taken that away from me; how could God take that away from me; no one understands me; no one loves me." We blame others for not delivering what we feel we are entitled to. This false sense of entitlement has its basis in pride.

There is a lot of talk about entitlement mentality. It is a rigidly held belief that the individual has a right to some particular reward or benefit. An example of this would be a relative, seeing that you are educated and have a good job, thinking that you should take over the education of his children. Another example would be a beggar, looking at your smart car, believing that you should give him something for a meal. There is nothing intrinsically wrong with the desires of those individuals – however, the bottom line is that it is up to the person with the 'reward or benefit' to decide whether they want to share it or not.

Pride masks our real motives for why we are doing things, sometimes by claiming it is our right to do them: "I can buy this, after all I work hard for my money," or "If it wasn't for me selling these drugs, someone else would," or "It's a free country, if I want to do this I can," or "the banks have robbed us blind so I can cheat on my taxes" and "I can cheat because I deserve to pass this" and "this is by body, I can do whatever I like with it!" The reasons may sound okay, but at the core of all these thoughts is arrogance, which is rooted in pride.

At the heart of entitlement mentality is blaming and complaining. Blamers find it hard not to spread it around. They love to tell everyone else about the wrong that has been done to them. We all know that person who cannot stop moaning about others. But maybe we do it too because we like to find someone who can relate to our misery. So we blame: "Oh, I know how you feel, everyone has a problem with him." We blame others and it makes us feel justified. But this very justification traps us into remaining with negative feelings like anger. It even fuels it. We start to find that it is easier to complain than to resolve the disagreement.

If you are blaming others you have labelled yourself a victim. By believing that someone else is responsible for your circumstances you are taking the power to change things out of your own hands and putting it into theirs. You believe they will have to change. Normally you say this to yourself with thoughts like: "This could all be over if they would only apologise." You have placed your fate in their hands. Change will only come when you realize that you can only change yourself.

I do not mean to make light of the enormous hurt that others can inflict on us. What others do to us can wound us terribly, but holding on to resentment and bitterness will keep us hurting - over and over again.

It is logical. Since we cannot change the past or someone else, the only thing we can change is ourselves. The problem with blame is that it encourages you into the futility of thinking that maybe something else can and will change – and they may or may not change - but the one thing you can definitely change is *you*.

We need to change because God holds us responsible for our decisions and actions.[1] Of course other people are guilty for the harmful and cruel things they do to us, but that is their responsibility and it is between them and God. When one *really knows* this fact it is strangely freeing: "I cannot change anyone else; I can only change me." This lesson has been one of the hardest ones for me to learn and I am still not certain that it has become engrained.

---

[1] Romans 2:6

144

Quite recently I was going through a really rough patch. So many things seemed to be going wrong at the same time in my life. Resisting the urge to shut myself away from the world and throw a pillow over my head, I accepted an invitation to go to tea with a long standing friend. Towards the end of the tea, I poured out my heart to her and immediately realised my mistake. I don't know if she was having a bad day, but she lashed out at me. It wasn't like she was giving me advice, she was attacking my character. She called it tough love.

After listening and not retaliating at all, I went home feeling more miserable than ever. I blamed her fully for the way that I felt; after all, I had gone to her in expectance of sympathy and comfort. Instead I had been on the receiving end of an unprovoked, unkind, hurtful barrage. Now, not only did I have my original problems to deal with, but I was also facing a new one – a broken friendship. How, I reasoned, could I continue in a relationship with someone who thought those things about me?

I ran to God in floods of tears and He, in His ever more mysterious way, sent me to study up on humility. I couldn't see why this would be relevant to me at first, but later I would be driving home in my car, joy flooding my heart, having just seen the very friend who had hurt me only a few weeks previously.

But it took a few weeks for me to put humility into practice. At first, I whined to my husband, who wisely said: "Humility is a servant heart and pride is a master heart." But I didn't want to hear that: "It's not me! Why do I always have to be the one to change? She is the one who hurt me. All I was looking for was a little bit of sympathy!" My indignation and anger only grew hotter. But during my quiet times when I moaned to God, He continued to say that it was an issue of pride – but I needed to be convinced. So I wrote an inventory to check on whether I was guilty of pride. I call it **The Pride Questionnaire**:

- Do you have a problem asking for help? Do you say: "No one can do it as well as me" or "If I want something done properly I need to do it myself"? We not only need to let others do some things for us, but we need to let them do it their way. Humility is a dependence on God and others.

- Do you get angry easily when things don't go the way you think they should go or when people don't behave the way you think they should?
- Do you think too highly of yourself?
- Do you: "Bear with the failings of the weak."[1] It may help to realise that you are not in their shoes and don't know how they feel, so expecting them to act like you do is unrealistic.
- Do you talk too much and often want to be the centre of attention? Do you tell everyone the 'victory' stories about your life or do you share some of the times you messed up?
- Are you rigid and demanding? Do you put pressure on people to be perfect or to do things your way?
- Are you sarcastic and demeaning? This is usually a manner of speech for people who have this problem. There are even some families that have 'that way' of talking to each other e.g. "fine...see if I care" or "trust you to do that" or "that is so typical of you!" People who think like this act as though they always have the right answer and continually look down on others. This attitude hurts those around them.
- Are you defensive and blame shifting? Do you have a critical spirit? Are you blame orientated and judgemental? If so, then you will come across that way to others. "Let us stop passing judgement on one another."[2] To avoid blaming and judging you have to stop analysing why people do what they do. You should stop asking who is to blame, or making comments like: "What's wrong with them?" If you do this, your focus is on a problem you cannot fix and not on God, who has the solution. You are saying that others have it wrong and you have it right.
- Are you easily offended by criticism? Do you say things like: "How dare they think that about me?" or "I can't believe she would say that about me." Do you take offence before you have found out the facts of the matter? The Bible says that one of the signs of the end times is that many will be

---

[1] Romans 15:1
[2] Romans 14:13

offended and fall away.[1] Being mad at someone torments us, so we need to be quick to forgive and difficult to offend. It is possible to remain unoffended even while you are in the midst of the attack: "A wise person stays calm when insulted."[2]

- Do you have a hard time being excited for other people's success? Think: has someone recently told you something great that has happened to them and you have said all the right things, but in your heart you were thinking jealous or spiteful thoughts? Or perhaps you have turned the conversation around to boast about your own similar achievements. We all have different gifts and different lives. Learn to enjoy other people's blessings and be genuinely pleased for them.

- Do you see yourself as better than others? The Bible says: "In humility consider others better than yourselves."[3] This should not be manifest merely by what we say; it should be something that we genuinely feel. This becomes possible when we see the value in each person we meet. When we take time to really listen to them and see their strengths and abilities.

- Do you try to impress others? Pride tries to impress others with clothes, houses, cars, our jobs or even success stories about children. Do you flaunt your successes? If you are trying to impress people all the time, you will find it very difficult to admit that you are wrong about things, either to yourself or to others.

- Are you insecure? Some people confuse humility with insecurity. They tell others about how awful they feel about themselves in an effort to show how in touch they are with their failings. But they are really boasting about their humility. This is false humility and it camouflages pride. These people act humble in order to get praise and affirmation from others or God. The problem with humility is that it is easy to get proud about being humble. We need to be humbly confident and not 'pridefully' insecure.

---

[1] Matthew 24:10
[2] Proverbs 12:16
[3] Philippians 2:3

- Do you grumble and complain a lot? We complain because we feel that we do not deserve what someone is doing to us or what is happening to us. We think we deserve better. If we are unhappy with our 'lot' we are essentially implying that we have a better plan about how things should be
- Do you look at life expecting to be served or do you look for opportunities to serve? Christ was humble, willing to give up his rights in order to obey God and serve people. We too should have a servant attitude.

As I learnt more about humility I realised just how much pride I was feeling towards my friend. I had wanted her to respond a certain way and when she didn't I had been offended. CS Lewis wrote: "Humility is not thinking less of yourself, but thinking of yourself less." I had been wrapped up in my own feelings. As soon as I realised this, I ran to God and said sorry. Fearing that I might change my mind, I immediately phoned her and asked her if we could meet for a cup of tea. She readily accepted.

Overcoming my fear, I entered the restaurant. Her reception was warm and we began to talk about general things. I prayed, in my head, at every opportunity and felt that God did not want me to bring up the 'issue.' She didn't bring it up either. I didn't feel that I had to apologise for anything because I had not done anything wrong to her – my 'wrongness' was the pride I had felt. That had been taken care of between God and I. But, as I sat there, I guarded every word I said and made sure that I was acting out of love. I tried to exercise all the fruits of the Spirit to the best of my ability. On the way home I felt elated - God's Way had worked.

As believers, we should lay aside our false rights and surrender to God and His Will which is to "be completely humble and gentle" and to "be patient, bearing with one another in love. Make every effort to keep the unity of the Spirit through the bond of peace."[1] Humility is inevitable for every Christian: either humble yourself or you will be humbled by God. We cannot simply get these qualities by trying, because they are the work of the Holy Spirit when we come to know God. It is God working in us, but we need to make ourselves ready to

---

[1] Ephesians 4:2

be worked on: "Humble yourself before the Lord and He will lift you up."[1] As we know God more, the nature of Christ increases in us.

God instructs us to 'clothe' ourselves in humility.[2] It is as if we are called to put on humility like a garment. Here are some **Suggestions for Remaining Humble**:

- Guard your thoughts
- Forgive quickly
- Decide to be difficult to offend
- Realise that people don't owe you anything
- Stop comparing yourself with others
- Be glad for the success of others
- Be content with yourself
- Learn to keep your opinions to yourself
- Renew your mind by reading the Word
- Do not interfere in other people's business
- Be good-natured about little irritations
- Fight the assumption that you are better than anyone else
- Talk less
- Don't try to control people, they don't have to be like you
- Accept the help of others and let them do things their way
- Surrender your will to God's will
- Realise that you don't exist for your own ends, you exist to serve God and others

Mother Teresa, generally accepted as the quintessential humble person, said: "It is in being humble that our love becomes real, devoted and ardent. If you are humble nothing will touch you, neither praise nor disgrace, because you know what you are. If you are blamed you will not be discouraged. If they call you a saint you will not put yourself on a pedestal."

Our journey towards humility begins with surrender to the will of God.

I am sorry that I have blamed others and been arrogant and proud.

---

[1] James 4:10
[2] 1 Peter 5:5

Help me to see myself as I really am.
Help me to give up my demands and false expectations.
Lord, I surrender to Your Will for me. I don't need to get my own way;
I am fine with doing things Your Way.
I put on humility like a garment today.
Set a guard over my mouth.
Help me to stop blaming people.
Lord, what can I do for someone else today?

How Can God Love Me?

Dear Love

Even before you were conceived, I knew all about you. I formed you and made you perfectly. There is no need for you to complain about my design and wish it was some other way. You are my creation and I am pleased with you. So don't criticise the way you were made. Rather look at yourself and be thankful for the way that you are. I think you are beautiful.

I know that there are unkind, selfish people in your life but I want you to love them. I know it is hard but I will be with you to help you. It is easy to love those who are kind to you, but it is the difficult, broken people that I want you to love so that they can see me through you. The more you love others the better you will feel.

I also want you to love me because then you will see how much I love you. When you love me, you will want to be with me and who I am will rub off on you.

I love you with an unconditional love that is so deep I will be revealing it to you for eternity.

With love

Your Father

Early morning cuddles with my little boy, Greg, are all about love. I reach out to him and draw him closer, and as he snuggles in I mould my body to fit his. I caress his forehead and that familiar dreamy look comes over his face. As he moves his elbow, it wedges in my chest, but I think he has fallen asleep so I don't move it. I want to stay here forever, but I am torn between getting up and doing the many things I need to do, and knowing that these times lay down beautiful memories for the future. I nestle into the euphoric mist that has enveloped me...

This is what love is all about: It is an action. The warm fuzzy feeling may come, but it follows choice and action - reaching out, drawing closer, seeing things from someone else's perspective, doing things for their sake to make them happy and bearing with any of the 'hard elbows' that may needle you. In short: "Love is patient, love is kind."[1]

But that is not all love is about. The Bible mentions a whole list of things that love is not: "It does not envy, it does not boast, it is not proud. It does not dishonour others, it is not self-seeking, it is not easily angered, it keeps no record of wrongs. Love does not delight in evil but rejoices in the truth." Some of its attributes are expressed: "It always protects, always trusts, always hopes, always perseveres."[2]

This can all sound daunting. I probably struggled with the concept of love because of my abuse. I wondered if I loved as others did. I wondered if I loved the 'right way' or enough. Love was an enigma to me. How do we trust when so many have betrayed us? How do we 'always hope' when things just keep going wrong? How do we persevere when we just don't have the willpower? How do we love when we are so low that it feels like the last thing we are capable of? We want to be loved, but, subconsciously, we have settled into thinking: "Others don't love me so why should I love them?"

To understand this emotion, one that is so intrinsic to the human experience, we need to understand where love operates. This can be explained by imagining three Hula Hoops. Each represents God, others and self. They are interlocking and in constant motion: God loves us and we love Him; we love others and they love us; we love ourselves and we love God; we love ourselves and we love others....and so on.

Now the task looks even more daunting: Why should we bother to love when others don't seem to love us? How can we love others if we don't love ourselves? How can we love God when we cannot see Him?

---

[1] 1 Corinthians 13:4
[2] 1 Corinthians 13

The Bible has the answers: "...love comes from God. Whoever does not love does not know God, because God is love. Whoever lives in love lives in God, and God in him. In this way, love is made complete among us... perfect love casts out fear ... we love because he first loved us. If anyone says, "I love God," yet hates his brother, he is a liar. For anyone who does not love his brother, whom he has seen, cannot love God, whom he has not seen."[1] We are told to love "so that your love may abound more and more in knowledge and depth of insight, so that you may be able to discern what is best and may be pure and blameless until the day of Christ."[2]

So from these passages we know that love comes from God; it can quell our fears and give us what we need to deal with those around us. It is a process, and as it grows it will help us gain insight and understanding. It is certainly worthy of further investigation. First then, let us consider how we are to love ourselves:

Imagine looking at yourself in the mirror. Can you honestly say: "I love you."? Not in a vain, proud, self-centred, 'worship yourself' kind of way. But rather a healthy self-love: where you respect yourself, care about yourself and appreciate the essence of who you are.

Loving yourself is not only biblical, it is a command. "He who gets wisdom loves his own soul"[3] and: "Love your neighbour as yourself."[4] No instruction exists anywhere in the Bible for being 'against yourself' or 'hating yourself.'

I could not comprehend loving myself. When I read those sections in the Bible I would think: "I don't love myself at all! Why would Jesus instruct me to do this when He knows how messed up I am? Others are much more together than I am, so it must be easier for them to love themselves. In fact, I find it easier to love them than I do to love myself." I felt that if others could see the 'real me' they would be

---

[1] 1 John 4:7-21
[2] Philippians 1:9,10
[3] Proverbs 19:8
[4] Mark 12:31

disgusted. So, I fobbed the whole concept of loving myself off as something I would never understand, let alone be able to do.

A nagging feeling that I was to blame for what had happened to me, combined with the reality of the wrong things I had done in my life left me with gnawing self-loathing. I found it difficult to look at myself in the mirror. The result of this self-hatred was devastating. I was constantly beating myself up with criticism and rejecting the essence of who I was. I became extremely insecure. The few people, who I told about my insecurity, didn't believe me because I came across as effervescent and bouncy. But my exuberant exterior was covering the insecurity beneath. I held unforgiveness against myself and it was turning into bitterness and self-loathing. I became hard on myself and, as a result, hard on others. I pushed to be better and do better in a vain attempt to feel good about myself. But no matter what I achieved, I always saw myself as a failure in comparison to others.

It is still with a twinge of regret that I look at photographs of myself taken during my modelling days and realise that, when those photos were taken, I felt ugly. In those days, I thought that one day the agency would find out what I was really like under all my makeup. I lived in constant fear that I would be found out as being a fraud. What a pity I felt that way when I could have been enjoying my youth.

Part of my problem was that I was making assessments of myself and my worth by what others had said and done to me. Their opinions determined my worth. It was years later that I learnt to listen to what God said about me and not what others had to say.

When I was pregnant with my second child I went back to university and studied psychology. I came top of the class out of over seven hundred students. But I was so convinced that I would somehow be found out to be a fraud, that I didn't even attend the awards ceremony to receive my Certificate of Merit.

This self-hatred was one of the primary reasons I attempted suicide on so many occasions: I thought I was good for nothing, not even at being a mother. This feeling was compounded by emails that I found written by a family member to my daughter. For years this person had been 'explaining' to her what a messed-up mother she had. My daughter had been sworn to secrecy. When I discovered these emails, I felt exposed, betrayed, raw, naked, rejected and hurt. My justification, when I attempted suicide on that occasion, was that everyone would be better off without me.

Thank God, He had another plan for my life. He exposed the deadly lie for what it was - an attempt by the devil to perpetuate the harm that had been done to me. The damage caused by these vicious emails, in both my life and my daughter's, is on the mend now. In hindsight, I don't believe I would have tried to take my life if my love for myself had not been so fractured.

Learning to love *me* took time. I needed first to recognise that I did not actually love myself at all. I needed to believe that God not only loves me, but wants me to love me. I needed to pause in front of that mirror, 'open' before God, and say simply: "God, I don't love me, help!"

He did, of course.

Some of that help came from reading the Word. We are created in God's image: "Let us make man in our image, in our likeness."[1] The Latin translation is 'imago Dei' which means 'image, shadow or likeness of God.' It is as though God did a photocopy of Himself and we were the result - it is a mind-blowing thought! But if the reality of that truth actually sunk in, would we think that our bodies are ugly? Would we look at God and say that He is ugly, stupid or worthless? Then, how can we think that about ourselves? In Psalms David writes: "I will praise you because I am fearfully and wonderfully made."[2] How can we criticise something that God has created 'fearfully and wonderfully?' Should we get to a point where we dislike it so much that we want to destroy it?

Imagine that you are in Heaven. You are floating around as a spirit in the workshop of God. He is hard at work creating your body. Even

---

[1] Genesis 1:26
[2] Psalm 139:14

though He has created billions of bodies before, yours is completely unique: from the little lines on your fingertips through the intricacy of your DNA to the complexity of your character. As you watch you see that He is being very careful about every detail - He makes your body exactly the way that He thinks is best. You do not know the reasons why He is doing what He is doing, but He has such a look of loving care on His face as He works, that you know it must be for the best. You know that He can see the whole of your life spread out before Him and He can see how you fit into the grand tapestry of time. He can see how every detail that makes up the essence of 'you', will be perfected for His grand and loving purpose. Finally, He is finished and He presents you with your body and its matching personality.

Can you imagine, at that point, telling Him that He has done a terrible job?

If you can, then you have either been influenced by the barrage of media telling you how your body is meant to look, or you have taken cognisance of the negative things that others have been telling you.

One of the most powerful books I have read recently is Nick Vujicic's: "Life Without Limits." He was born with no legs or arms. Do you know what he would say when he was in that workshop and God handed him his body without any limbs? In his book he writes: "...God's love is so real that He created you to prove it." He thinks his body *proves* the love of God! He goes on to say: "...for every disability you have, you are blessed with more than enough abilities to overcome your challenges."

This book not only made me shamefully aware of how pathetic it was to complain about my physical body, but it also showed me where my feelings of worthlessness came from. He writes: "It's a lie to think you're not good enough. It's a lie to think you're not worth anything." I agree - it was a lie that nearly killed me, more than once.

God is a better judge about whether you are worth loving than you are. He has judged you worth loving so much so that He sent Jesus to die for you. Jesus would have died on the cross if you were the only person on the planet. Do you know better than God? By not loving yourself, you are saying that God is wrong, that you are not worthwhile. Not loving yourself to the point of wanting to kill yourself, means making a final declaration that you know better than God and that you disagree with His truth.

If you still feel that it is impossible for you to love yourself, then you are most likely blaming yourself for something. You feel that by forgiving yourself you will be condoning whatever it is that you have done. Holding onto this blame has, at its root, pride. If God has forgiven you then who are you not to forgive yourself?

Whilst God has been telling us the importance of loving ourselves down through the ages, the world of psychology has only recently discovered its benefits. It has been labelled 'self-compassion.' Psychologists have created an interesting exercise that might help with learning to love yourself: The idea is that you trick yourself into treating yourself better. Pretend that a loved one is in your shoes. Now ask yourself what you would say to them. How would you advise them, given your situation? The idea behind it is that you would not criticise and condemn them the way you do yourself. Unwittingly, it supports the Bible: "love your neighbour as yourself."[1] It turns the verse around slightly to read: "love yourself like your neighbour would love you." In so doing you become aware of how unfair you are being on yourself.

Once we have learnt to love ourselves, we can begin to learn how to love others in a way that will benefit them. When you walk in love you will become more confident because you will know that you are doing the right thing. When you walk in love people will want to be with you.

Imagine that we are walking down the road together and I say to you: "Hey would you like some chocolate?" You say: "Thanks! I'd love some!" Then nothing ... no chocolate appears. So you might ask: "Nita ... um ... the chocolate?" I then, rather infuriatingly, explain to you that I don't have any. That is how it is when it comes to loving others before we learn to love ourselves - we cannot give away what

---

[1] Matthew 22:36

we do not have. Only once you have learnt to love yourself, you will be ready to love others.

But that can seem an impossible task when you have been badly hurt. People have hurt me with the things that they have said and the things they have done. I don't know why people hurt people. I was wrongly taught not to ask 'why' early on:

In my late teens I visited my sister who was running my step-father's farm with her husband. One night, after a party, I was sent to sleep in one of the manager's houses because the main house was full of guests. I was just about to go to bed, when the manager walked into my room, and without a word to me, began to hit me. My surprise out-weighed the pain. I hardly knew him! What could I have possibly done? I blurted out: "Why?" He answered by hitting me once more. When I asked: "Why?" a second time, he said: "If you ask me 'why' one more time, I will hit you again." I couldn't help myself, my response was automatic: "Why?" I said frantically. Again, I felt the sting of his hand across my face. This exchange continued in a surreal dance – I asked 'why' and he hit me.

My 'why's' took on a broader significance. I was asking 'why' about all the traumas I had faced. Eventually he stopped hitting me for as little reason as he had started. He left me to crawl through the night, in the fog, to the main house.

I have since come to realise the benefits, not only of asking why, but seeking justice. In those days, the cruelty of the politically corrupt system of policing under the Apartheid regime meant approaching the police was a last resort so the manager's crime was never reported. Instead, he was reprimanded and dismissed. I never got an answer to my question: "Why?"

But I can guess why: "Hurt people hurt people." People often hurt others because they have been hurt. This is not a rule (for example, I was seriously abused and haven't abused my children), but there is certainly truth in the idea. Realising that people are hurting you largely because they are operating out of some pain inside them, helps one to be compassionate.

What I find really hard to understand though, is Christians who hurt Christians. I have been on the receiving end of interfering busybodies, gossips, slanderers and, sometimes worse, the well-meaning Christian meddler.

One would think that because we have the love of God in us and because we are constantly being taught to love (and in many cases we are teaching on love) we would act in love and not hurt each other. Paul recognised this problem and writes: "If I speak in the tongues of men or of angels, but do not have love, I am only a resounding gong or a clanging cymbal. If I have the gift of prophecy and can fathom all mysteries and all knowledge, and if I have a faith that can move mountains, but do not have love, I am nothing. If I give all I possess to the poor and give over my body to hardship that I may boast, but do not have love, I gain nothing."[1]

Clanging gong people are found in pews as well as behind the pulpit. They are filled with self-righteousness disguised as holiness, knowledge disguised as wisdom and ambition disguised as love. We see people in the church who, professing the servant heart, offer themselves as mentors and counsellors. We trust them with our secrets and shame, only to realise that they are serving no one except themselves.

Over the years, while running home-groups, my husband and I have from time to time been alarmed at the extent of this phenomenon; of hurting Christians who hurt Christians. Many wounded people have landed at our door, despondent, angry with the church and ready to leave because of the perceived lack of love they encounter from pastors and congregations alike.

But a lack of love is not the only reason why the hurt from a Christian seems to sting so badly. It is also because of our expectations. We are doubly disappointed when Christians hurt us because we tend to place them on pedestals where they are expected to behave better than ourselves and others. We especially expect our pastors to have some kind of supernatural, instant, deep understanding about us and to have the solution to all our woes.

---

[1] 1 Corinthians 13

We ask them for help with a preconceived idea about how we think that help should be given. We set a standard for them to which we ourselves are unable to adhere. We expect their wisdom and response to be akin to that of God, failing to see that they are just as fallible as we are. Often, we rely on them, instead of relying on the Lord.

We need to become more gracious about receiving help from others. If someone gives their opinion without you asking for it, listen quietly, evaluate what they have to say with the help of the Holy Spirit and receive or reject it. But we should avoid lashing back at them if we disagree. If we ask for help, we need to accept that the help we will be given will not always be that which we require. If we disagree with the advice given, we can love them for trying and move on.

It is not only the well-meaning advice that hurts. Sometimes we are hurt by another's jealousy, revenge, anger or pride. In an attempt to escape these attacks, we often end up 'throwing the baby out with the bathwater' by cancelling out whole groups of people because of the actions of one. For example, a woman abused by a man, might end up hating all men.

This is against what we have been taught. Jesus commanded us to love others. He says that this is the greatest commandment after loving God. "Love your neighbour as yourself."[1] This is for their sake as well as ours. I have found that one of the best ways to cheer myself up is to help others. Nick Vujicic writes: "Yet I also believe that when you do unto others, blessings come to you as well. So if you don't have a friend, be a friend. If you are having a bad day, make someone else's day. If your feelings are hurt, heal those of another." We do not and should not wait until we are healed emotionally before we reach out to others. God comforts us so that we can go and comfort others. He "comforts us in all our troubles, so that we can comfort those in any trouble with the comfort we ourselves have received from God".[2]

---

[1] Matthew 12:31
[2] 2 Corinthians 1:4

I hear you saying: "If you understood what I had been through you wouldn't ask me to do that." Maybe someone has said very cruel things about you or your work has gone unappreciated for years or you have been robbed and cheated or your opinions have been slated or your reputation wrecked. But the Bible makes no exception. God doesn't say: "When you are over this hurt, then go and love others." Whatever has happened to us, no matter how hurtful, we are instructed to love anyway. Of course it is easier to love those who are kind to us, but it takes an 'extra something' to love those who hurt us, especially when they are not apologetic. This extra something comes from God. It is He who gives us the love to love those we consider unlovable.

But we need to decide to do it. We need to shift the focus from ourselves to others. The devil wants you to focus on getting what you want and he wants you to be miserable when you don't. One thing that I have found that sometimes helps is trying to imagine yourself in their situation. Look at it from their point of view. Harper Lee writes in "To Kill A Mockingbird: "You never really understand a person until you consider things from his point of view — until you climb into his skin and walk around in it."

Gossips destroy relationships and reputations. When a person is down and having troubles the harmful tongue of a gossip can tip them over the edge. Christians often disguise their gossip with false reasoning: "I am just telling you this for the purpose of prayer," or "I am only telling you this because I am so worried about her."

The Old Testament Hebrew word translated as "gossip" means "one who reveals secrets, one who goes about as a talebearer or scandal-monger." A gossip is a person who has privileged information about people and proceeds to reveal that information to those who have no business knowing it. Gossip is distinguished from sharing information in two ways: The intention of the gossip is to build themselves up by making themselves appear as knowledgeable while making others look bad. It is also distinguished by the type of information that is shared: faults, failings and potentially embarrassing personal details. Even if the intention is not to harm, it is still gossip.

Paul speaks about how God pours out His wrath on those who rejected His laws, including gossips.[1] God instructs us how to deal with gossips and anyone who hurts us – this is the **Right Response to Hurt**:

- "Go and show him his fault" [2] - Have a private conversation with the person. Stop talking to everyone else about the problem in an effort to justify your actions. Do not go to your friends, your pastor or even your family first, but rather to the person who has hurt you. If you go to others it would make you the gossip! If at all possible keep this matter between the two of you.
- "If he will not listen, take one or two others along" – Make sure that you choose people who will act in love and who do not have a grudge against the person themselves.
- "If he refuses to listen to them, tell it to the church" – this is a last resort and only used if the problem directly affects the church.
- Forgive the person - Ask God to help you.
- Love them – This may take the form of a prayer for their blessing, if seeing them is impossible for some reason.
- Be brave and go back into the community and church as soon as possible and face everyone.
- Move on with your life - Drop the issue by not speaking or thinking about it anymore. Leave it in God's Hands. He sees every tear that you have cried and He is your Protector and your Defender so leave Him to do His good work.

The damage that has been done may take a while to heal in your heart and in the lives of others. But over time the drama will be forgotten and people will move on. No one is ever as interested in your life as you think they are.

Our good work is to love people – all people, but we don't have to let everyone we meet become close friends. We are to choose those wisely. Surrounding yourself with a good set of godly friends will

---

[1] Romans 1:29-30
[2] Matthew 18:15-20

help you when times get tough; people who can remind you what the word of God says, people who love you and people who also believe that God will keep his promises.

We need to shy away from those who tempt us into getting tied up in the things that are bad for us or those who constantly drag us down with negativity. In the book of Proverbs we are warned not to hang out with angry people because bad tempers are contagious.[1] Other people's misery can be passed on to you. This sounds like a minefield, but if we ask God to help us choose the right friends, He will guide us about who to take into our confidence.

God knows what love is because "God is love."[2] We often turn this around: "Love is God," by idolising the idea of love, and we set out on a lifetime quest for that false, surface, mushy feeling we think is love. I call this counterfeit of love the 'love drug' because it is highly addictive.   On our endless quest to fill the hole that should be occupied by genuine love, we sacrifice our morals and the feelings and rights of others. We try to fill the gap with our love for material things, or our love of success, by idolising the body image or a bastardised 'Hollywood love'. This drug has been manufactured by the devil to keep us just satisfied enough so that we do not look for the real thing. At its core is selfishness – we want what we want now, for us, to meet our own ends. Real love, the love God has for us, is clean, perfect, innocent, sacred, good, honest, virtuous, dependable and ethical. Its virtues cannot be described because it is as deep as God is endless. The fake counterpart barely skims the surface.

This invisible God reveals His love for us through his Word, His Son, the Holy Spirit in us, His Creation, others to us and us to others and in our daily lives.   He "is over all and through all and in all."[3] The more time we spend with our God of Love the more we will be able to love ourselves and others.

---

[1] Proverbs 22:24-25
[2] 1 John 8
[3] Ephesians 4:6

His love is everlasting - it "stands firm forever."[1] You may feel that He doesn't love you when you look at your circumstances, but that is because you are seeing them through your limited vision. The truth is that he loves you deeply and "that in all things God works for the good of those who love him who have been called according to his purpose."[2] Your circumstances, or your view of them, do not change the fact that God is working, in love, in your life right now.

You may ask: "How can God love me?" You may not be able to believe that He could possibly love you – what you have done and who you have become weigh so heavily on your heart. But God knows that you feel this way, so much so that He labours this point in the Bible in an effort to reassure you: "...neither death not life, neither angels nor demons, neither the present nor the future, not any powers, neither height not depth, nor anything else in all creation, will be able to separate us from the love of God that is in Christ Jesus our Lord."[3] It is His Love that will heal you in those deep, hard to reach places. I know because He has healed me.

Perhaps you, like me, have been conned into chasing that false 'love drug' and have been left disillusioned, throwing out the whole concept of love as impossible to attain and simply not worth the effort. What we really need is to throw out our dependence on the false copy and soak ourselves in the real medicine of God's kind of Love.

God is clear about how He wants us to love Him: "Love the Lord your God with all your heart and with all your soul and with all your mind and with all your strength."[4] I became deflated when I first read this, thinking that it was an impossible task, until I heard that God not only teaches us how to love Him, He gives us the love in the first place! We just need to ask.

---

[1] Psalm 89:2
[2] Romans 8:28
[3] Romans 8:38
[4] Mark 12:30

Here is a promise God makes to us: "Delight yourself in the Lord and he will give you the desires of your heart."[1] Delight for me brings to mind images of a child opening their Christmas presents. That innocent, uncluttered 'wow' moment is how God wants us to feel when we think about Him. But we won't feel like this if we are not trusting Him and obeying Him. Doubt and guilt will stifle delight. Delight in Him with a clear conscience and with trust that He has you firmly in His loving arms.

Loving God, others and ourselves is an action, like the act of getting dressed in the morning: "And over all these virtues put on love, which binds them all together in perfect unity."[2] We 'put on love' just like we put on clothes. The clothes themselves were bought and paid for by Him. He even bought the body we put them on. If we want to know how to 'do' this love, we only need read the washing label on our love-clothes. We love Him by getting to know Him and by obeying His Word. We get dressed covering our whole bodies with His love and holding them close to us all day. As we look at ourselves in the mirror, we see how these clothes have improved our appearance in every way. We head out, thanking God for His Love, determined to spread the news about the most fantastic Tailor in town!

Help me to love me.
Show me how to love You.
Help me to love others and see their needs.
Give me friends who are godly.
Help me to have no 'issue' with anyone today.
Help me to focus on what is important to you – love.
Teach me how to delight in you.
Remind me to 'put on love' every day.

---

[1] Psalm 37:4
[2] Colossians 3:14

Why Don't I Feel like God is All I Need?

My Dear Child

I am the Lord God Almighty who created the heavens and the earth. I am the beginning and the end and everything is in my Hands. Even though you may not understand my power and majesty, I want you to respect me.

I am also your Heavenly Father. I long for you to know me as your Abba Father, and for you to lay your head against my chest and experience my Love.

I have shown myself to you in my Creation, in my Word and in so many areas of your life. When are you going to get to know me? When are you going to realise that I am all you need?

Forever

Your Heavenly Father

Some people think it is disrespectful to call God: "Daddy." They argue that it is being over familiar and does not show the honour and respect due to the powerful Creator of the Universe. You, like me, may find using this term of endearment difficult. God was a scary figure to me for many years, as were most men, so calling Him 'Daddy' made Him somehow more approachable.

The first time I really began to focus on the concept of God being 'my Dad' was when I read a book called: "The Father Heart of God" by Floyd McClung. I started to realize that I was filtering the concept of 'God being my father' through my experiences of my own earthly father who had been far from perfect. In fact there was rumour that he had molested a family member and that same rumour suggested that I too had been sexually abused by him as a child. I haven't, to date, remembered any actual abuse, except for when I have been very drunk. Then I 'remember' horrific scenes of abuse that seem to be taking place during some kind of ritualistic ceremony. But my memory of these events remains clouded. I have been to professionals to help me recall these incidences, without success. I have been told numerous times that all other 'evidence' points to the fact that I was abused, but I am left frustratingly unsure as to what exactly happened. But even if I wasn't abused, the mere suggestion of it, and the uncertainty of not knowing for sure, has caused great pain in my life.

There was no way for me to approach him about any of this because all these 'rumours' only started filtering out of the family closets after he died. This lack of closure has added to my feelings of powerlessness and hopelessness over the years, but oddly, I felt guilty. If I was accusing him of this horrendous act, and he was innocent, then I was guilty of not honouring him. I had loved him and didn't want to sully his name with false accusations.

So began a long quest to find the truth. I went to psychologists and councillors and quizzed family members and I have racked my brain to try and remember: Has he ever said anything in particular that could indicate abuse? Have I seen him in the nude? These types of questions were traumatic ones to ask, and left me feeling disgusted. I remember him having an embarrassingly short night gown. I remember him telling me that he would 'know' when I lost my virginity. I remember him boasting that he had a 'chance' with my teenage friends. I also remember him telling me that the Bible condoned sex between a father and his daughters, and that it was only modern man that had made it a taboo. When I was trying to drown my memories in the bottom of a bottle I did remember something else: His gold pocket watch swinging back and forth in front of my eyes...

His favourite party trick was to hypnotise people. He also boasted about drugs he could get that would make people do things faster and others drugs that would make them sleep.

When I quizzed family members about this, I got alarming responses: While visiting me at my father's house, my grandmother had found me comatose on the couch. She could not wake me. She was convinced that I was drugged or hypnotised. Was I? I will probably never know. Another family member, in response to my investigation, said: "Oh that! Everyone knew! He used to boast about it!" I was so shocked by his comment that I clammed up and the chance to question him further passed. I have not seen him since and it is not the sort of thing one can write in an email. But maybe this is an excuse, maybe deep down inside, I don't really want to know.

So the concept of God being my Father confused me. In fact, I was scared of God and He was something to hide from. I saw him as a stern, old, bearded guy who sat on a throne in Heaven and scanned the earth, ready to hand out punishments for any wrong-doing. I could sort of relate to Jesus by thinking of him, sitting on a rock with children playing at his feet, telling strange stories. So when I learnt that one of God's names is 'Abba Father' I had to think about it long and hard for it to sink in. It is an Aramaic word best translated 'Daddy' and is the term that a child would lovingly use to speak to their father. Of all His names, this is the most significant one that explains how He relates to His people.

While we are all 'children of God', not all of us are entitled to call Him, "Abba Father." This is a privilege reserved only for a born-again Christian.[1] When we are born again we become adopted into His family and reign as "co-heirs with Christ." As such we can approach God with "confidence, so that we may receive mercy and find grace to help us in our time of need."[2]

He considers believers to be His children: "But when the time had fully come, God sent his Son, born of a woman, born under law, to redeem those under law, that we might receive the full rights of sons. Because you are sons, God sent the Spirit of his Son into our hearts, the Spirit who calls out, "Abba, Father." So you are no longer a slave, but a son; and since you are a son, God has made you also an heir."[3]

I have also seen others visualize God as a distant, stern taskmaster who disapprovingly glowers down from a faraway heaven, ready to punish at the slightest sign of sin in us. But as I began to study the

---

[1] John 1:12,13
[2] Hebrews 4:16
[3] Galatians 4:4-7

concept of God being 'Abba Father' I learnt just how far from the truth that was: He is quick to forgive and slow to anger. He loves us more than any earthly father could imagine loving their child. He is our refuge and our strength – our Strong Tower. He is the Rock beneath us and the Shield in front of us. In short, God is Love.[1]

The more we get to know this Love, the more we will become enveloped by it and the more the world that rages around us will 'grow strangely dim'. When we take that leap of faith, off the high wall of fear that we created in a pathetic effort to protect us, we will feel His loving wind gently holding us up and cuddling us in its warmth.

But getting to know God is more than knowledge gained through study: it is tapping into the power that is ours as His heirs. It is about being able to *be* in His presence. Just as the wind gives power to the windmill and the battery gives power to the torch, the Lord is our power source. We can ask Him to put His battery in us (through the Holy Spirit) and then be turned on! His power will surge though us and give us the strength to do whatever we need to do and face whatever hardships we have to face. When we feel as though there is nothing we can do to change our situation, we can cry out: "Daddy, please help!" Charles Trumbull said: "Prayer releases the energies of God". Perhaps we would all like the power of God to be released in our lives. But how do we get that to happen?

I believe it is because we don't really *believe* He is there and intimately involved in our lives. I was blessed to have an amazing revelation that truly made this fact a reality in my life:

This story began a few months ago, while my husband and I were watching a program about Pope Francis. When the camera panned across the magnificent ceiling of the Sistine Chapel depicting Michelangelo's stunning painting of the 'Creation of Adam', I recognised it immediately. As I contemplated that famous gap between the finger of God and the finger of Adam, I noticed something: God is stretching out from heaven while Adam is

---

[1] 1 John 4:8

nonchalantly lounging back. I remarked to Richard how true to life that is – God makes so much more of an effort than we do.

The next evening Richard went to Home Group, alone as always, because my pain often prohibits me from going out in the evenings. While they were praying for me, a dear friend of mine said she saw a vision, similar to the Michelangelo picture of God reaching to man, and told Richard that she felt someone should reach out to me with the same action. Thinking that this was unlikely to be a co-incidence, we sheepishly tried what she had suggested that evening - Richard prayed and pointed at me with his finger. Even though no great lightning bolts flashed out of the sky, something was beginning to happen...

In the morning I got a text from the same friend saying that she had a song in her head that she believed was for me: Godfrey Birtill's "Just One Touch". After having my morning quiet-time with God, I lay on my bed and played the song on YouTube.

Very gently, like a soft wind, the Holy Spirit flooded my entire body. Words really fail me when I try to explain the rest of this story. I just lay there, covered with intense goose bumps as this breathless, light, contented feeling came over me. While it compares to no other, it is not new to me. I have felt it a few times over the course of my life. Years previously I had seen a massive out-pouring of the Holy Spirit when it fell on the town where I was living in South Africa. The feeling I was experiencing that morning was stronger and more powerful than anything I had known before.

I didn't become aware of the words of the song until he began to sing the words "bless Ireland", when suddenly the feeling became more intense. It felt as though it was pouring in through the left side of my neck. Surprised, I asked God why, and was reminded that I had half my thyroid removed the year previously. Since the operation my hormones had been out of balance causing all sorts of problems in my body. So I began to wonder and hope that perhaps I was being healed.

Suddenly as I lay there with my eyes closed, I saw the cosmos. Even though I saw it in my mind it was not in the same place where I reason or where I have dreams. It was more like a movie being screened just behind my eyelids, only the picture was clearer and I knew I was not the author of it. As I was moving between the stars, I heard a deep, crackling, rumbling noise.

What appeared to be the 'back' of the universe began to rip apart, much like paper would tear; only the substance seemed as though it was alive. A Spirit came out of this rupture and I knew it was God - like a man but not like a man. Everything is like Him but He is not like anything in the world. I felt His Sheer Power as He moved with purpose and direction straight towards me and touched me.

I felt everything good all at once.

Love overwhelmed me.

I had heard that He loved me many times, and I had seen the power behind this fact when I led people to receive Jesus as their Lord by telling them He loved *them*. But a fault in my thinking became suddenly clear. I had been saying to myself: "Yea, sure he loves me. He loves everyone." I had missed an essential point, one that pales in the telling: that He loves me individually and personally.

I began to cry. Streams of tears poured down my face and soaked my pillow. I felt deeply loved, more loved than one can explain or imagine. Me - Nita Tarr - totally and absolutely loved, just as I am, by the Creator of the Universe.

Then tears of joy became tears of sadness as I realised that this experience would pass. I didn't want it to stop.

God made something profound known to me, as I lay there on my bed that morning, not in words or in the picture on my eyelids, but more like all types of communication at the same time. He 'showed' me that He was enough for me. I knew that He is all I need. I understood at that moment, a verse in the Bible that I had heard so many times: "The Lord is my portion; therefore I will wait for Him."[1]

---

[1] Lamentations 3:24

Once this experience had passed I decided to print out the words of the song: "Just One Touch." Amazed, I read the first verse: "...pride stops us stretching out our withered hand, yet God has stretched out to heal us." It reminded me about the comment I had made to Richard about Michelangelo's painting two nights earlier.

I became particularly interested when I read the lyrics: "heal us," and began to wonder if God was trying to tell me something. At this stage I had been in severe pain for about three years. My symptoms included severe pelvic pain, a throbbing, hot leg from an operation that didn't work, a myriad of symptoms from unbalanced hormones, back pain and sporadic blinding headaches, so I wondered if I was being healed. I didn't feel any relief at the time, but I hoped that maybe healing was on its way.

When I went back to tell my story to my friend from Home Group, she was amazed and mentioned that she had never realised the words of the lyrics were about the painting. I was astonished because I had presumed that was why she had suggested the song to me!

This experience changed me. I now *knew* that I was individually and personally loved by the Creator of the Universe. But this knowledge didn't seem to change my circumstances. In the weeks that followed, I felt under siege. When I questioned God about why I hadn't been healed, why our finances were still in shambles and why some of my relationships remained broken, He gently reminded me about the whole point of the revelation: *He is enough.* I shouldn't need my life to be going wonderfully well; the realisation that He was right there with me, loving me, was all that I needed. This all-powerful, all-loving God is right there beside me. I don't need my relationships to be restored or healing to come or our finances to be sorted out - I have Him! He is our All-You-Need God.

As the weeks passed I learnt to put that reality into action, and I discovered that truly believing He is there and loves you, and that He wants to be intimately involved in your life, is the key to tapping into the Source of Power. Once you are tapped into the Source, power flows in your life.

But the story doesn't end there. Believing that there was a strong possibility that I was in the process of being healed, I decided to go off all thyroid medication the day after this experience. I wanted to be able to tell if my hormones levelled out.

I first had a thyroid blood test done then I waited for about a month before I had another blood test done. But while I waited I was content. I believed: "My flesh and my heart may fail, but God is the strength of my heart and my portion forever,"[1] and understood for the first time that His Grace "is sufficient for you, for my power is made perfect in weakness."[2] I waited ... knowing that He was with me.

There was no need to 'conjure up faith' for healing or for anything else I needed in my life. I could rest in the knowledge that the Almighty Creator of the Universe so loved me that He sent His Beloved Son to die on the cross for me so that I could be with Him forever. I was *convinced* that I could not do any of it without Him.

Have you reached a place where you know you cannot do it alone? Do you want to be plugged into *the* Power Source? Then truly believe that He is right there with you now. He loves you and is in control and working everything out. Nothing is too difficult for Him. You might not have the experience that I had, but that does not make it any less of a reality in your life. He is touching you right now, wherever you are and whatever you have done or not done - He loves you anyway. Is there anything else you could possibly want? So, take courage and be filled with hope and peace - God is with you.

After taking no medication for my thyroid for about six weeks I had more blood tests. When I asked the doctor for the results, she said: "The results were interesting Nita!" All my thyroid levels were normal!

Spurgeon, known as 'the prince of preachers' said: "You are my portion, O Lord. It is better to have our good God than all the goods in the world! It is better to have God for our All than to have all and

---

[1] Psalm 73:26
[2] 2 Corinthians 12:9

be without Him. He who possesses God; lives at the wellhead and drinks from the ever-flowing Fountain. He who owns the choicest worldly goods, apart from Him, only drinks of the foul leavings which remain in the corners of earth's broken cisterns. What is the whole universe compared with Him who made it? What are the base pleasures of sin compared with the fullness of joy which always dwells at God's right Hand?"

There seem to be so many things that we think we need: health, money, security, love and acceptance. So how can we honestly say: "God you are *all* I need?" It doesn't sound logical, let alone possible. But if we don't get what we want and yet have a firm understanding that God is with us, while being deeply in love with Him, those things will fade in importance. Believing in this All-You-Need God is the key to being content and at peace in all circumstances.

He came to live in us when we gave our lives to Him and He wants us to get a better understanding of who He is as we continue to walk with Him. As we get this clearer picture, we begin to realise that He is indeed all we need. A song from my childhood says it so well: "...and the things of the world will grow strangely dim in the light of His glorious face."

Perhaps you are asking: "Why don't I feel like God is all I need?" Understand that this is a process. We know this only dimly in the beginning and then, as we apply this fact to each circumstance we are going through, it becomes a reality. For example, when you stop reading this book today you may go and open your post. It might contain a bill that you cannot pay. What you think you need is money to pay the bill - right? That sounds logical. But if you picture God standing right there next to you with your bill, then how would your thoughts change? Would you still be as concerned about it? If this All-You-Need God was a reality in your life, wouldn't you discuss the bill with Him? Wouldn't you hand Him the letter, and without worrying about it, snuggle up peacefully with Him, knowing that He will help you deal with it somehow at the perfect time?

If you are struggling to believe in this All-You-Need God, then ask Him to help you. God says: "You do not have because you do not ask."[1] This is exactly the kind of prayer that the Lord delights in answering. It is like someone telling you that they would like to spend more time with you to get to know you more. Wouldn't you love that? So does God. He instantly answers the prayer to get to know Him more intimately, and He will honour any efforts of yours to try to seek Him. Other prayers, like paying for the bill, might take a little longer or even get answered in some way that you hadn't even thought about. While you wait for an answer to those prayers, don't give up getting to know Him. Don't stop looking at His Face just because you are waiting for something from His Hand.

Imagine a child going to their Father and asking for a new toy. Being all-wise He can see that if He granted the child's request, it could cause the child (or someone else) pain. She is too young to understand the reasons, so He does not offer any. Instead He takes the child onto his knee and comforts her and says: "No, not yet." At that point the child can either choose to have a hissy fit and storm into her room, slamming the door behind her, or she can decide to cuddle up to his warm chest, knowing that her Father loves her and will do the very best for her.

She lies on her bed, with the pillow over her head, feeling sorry for herself and mulling over the apparent injustice: "He has the money in his wallet! He could easily just get me what I want!" This thinking flicks a dangerous button inside her brain: The Rejection Button. Once switched on, default avenues of thought explode: "He is not listening to me. He doesn't care for me. He has abandoned me!"

This button is most often pushed because of peoples' past experiences. For example, they have been rejected in some way by their earthly father and therefore think that their heavenly Father will reject them in the same way. But if you have become a child of God, He promises that He will "never leave you nor forsake you." It is a promise, and God keeps His promises. So he has not and will not reject you. It might look different to you, but He is working in your life for your good even if you cannot see it. He has you in the palm of His hand and He is personally involved in all aspects of your life.

---

[1] James 4:2

175

The Rejection Button can be taken off the keyboard of your brain by creating a different pathway for your thoughts to travel down. Recognise who it was that rejected you and realise that it is not God doing the rejecting. Try to pinpoint the exact time you flicked that switch for the first time. This may be the result of some deep rejection you suffered in your early life. Rejection can be a deep wound that sometimes needs healing by talking to a therapist. But we know that God will never reject his children, so if we ever find ourselves thinking those kinds of thoughts we can remind ourselves what His Word says: "For the Lord will not reject His people."[1]

But perhaps the child is not lying on their bed mulling over the unfairness of her situation. Maybe she thinks her request has been denied because she is being punished for some wrong-doing. This may be so. Very often, with unwavering justice, God does not grant our requests until we have recognized, admitted and turned from sin. The Father is not punishing the child by not giving her what she desires, but rather taking the opportunity to teach the child a lesson.

When the child first gets that nagging, gentle urge deep down inside that some aspect of her life needs to be changed, she simply needs to go and tell her dad that she recognises that she has done something wrong and say sorry. One may ask: "If God can see it all anyway, why do I need to tell him what I am doing wrong?" God wants us to recognise that what we did was wrong *for our sake* because that is how we grow. Only that which is recognised can be worked on and changed.

He is not an uptight parent who only wants to hear good things from us. When we come to Him and show him our pain, He doesn't say: "Stop being such a cry baby! If you carry on crying like that I will really give you something to cry about!" We are coming to our Abba Father, our Dad in Heaven, who understands more than any human could any ever understand. He sees our feelings of rejection, frustration, confusion, loneliness and heartbreak. He loves more than any earthly father could love. So we can come to him when we are a mess and know that He will treat us with mercy and kindness.

---

[1] Psalm 94:14

Once we have told God about what we did wrong, then we can be assured that Jesus died on the cross for this exact moment – to forgive us. We can then tell God how thankful we are that He no longer sees us as dirtied by our sin, but that He sees us as spotless as He sees Jesus. He says that when you say sorry for what you have done, your sin is removed from you "as far as the east is from the west". Very often, attitude can stand in the way of our requests being granted.

But there is another reason: You also need to make sure that you have done everything to mend relationships around you. God wants us to live in unity: "Anyone who claims to be in the light but hates his brother is still in the darkness."[1] This does not mean that if you don't like someone you are not a Christian. We don't have to like everyone and approve of their actions but we are also not meant to treat people as enemies or competitors. We can choose to love them even though we don't like their actions. The Bible has specific instructions about this to husbands: "Husbands...be considerate as you live with your wives, and treat them with respect...so that nothing will hinder your prayers."[2] There is a clear link to our prayers being answered - we need to mend relationships around us: "as far as it depends on you, live at peace with everyone."[3] You might discover that the other person is too bitter or hurt to respond to your attempts to restore the relationship. In this case, look to your own healing by forgiving and making sure you have dropped the issue in your heart. If you have honestly tried to make amends, then God won't let a broken relationship stand in the way of answering your prayers.

Phillips Brooks, an American clergyman and author wrote: "Prayer is not conquering God's reluctance, but taking hold of God's willingness." Our requests may not be answered when or how we would like them to be answered, but God hears you and He is acting on your behalf and for your good because He loves you.

---

[1] 1 John 2:9
[2] 1 Peter 3:7
[3] Romans 12:18

While asking our earthly or heavenly Father for things is a large part of our relationship with him, it should not be the main focus. Imagine how disappointed you would feel if your child only asked for things all the time and never bothered to get to know you. It would cause you to feel more like a vending machine than a human. But how do we get to know God's character?

To have a revelation that will lead to a real grasp of this All-You-Need God we need to look at who God says He is in the Bible. I will only be focusing on some of God's attributes, but the ramifications and depths of each point are so broad, that I suggest you meditate on each one. When you do this, you will notice that He becomes brilliantly real to you.

Our Abba Father is...

- Holy and cannot accept or even look upon sin.
- Love - He doesn't *have* love, He *is* love.
- Merciful – He does not punish us as our sins deserve.
- All-knowing – He sees and knows all things.
- All powerful and has no limits.
- Present in all places at all times.
- Unchanging.
- Righteous and just - He is fair and impartial.
- Self-sufficient – He does not need anything outside of Himself.
- Wise – He does everything with infinite wisdom and He only acts for our good.
- Faithful – He keeps His promises.
- Graceful - He grants merit where it is undeserved.
- Our Comforter - He is filled with compassion.
- The Source of all blessing, fullness and fruitfulness.

His attributes are breath-taking and may cause us to fall in reverential worship at His feet, especially when we realise that this awe-inspiring, amazing God is intimately involved in our lives and working things out for our good.

As your awe for this All-You-Need God grows, your fears will abate. When calamity strikes you will need a God who, while diminishing your reliance on self, will enlarge your faith and astonish you with His mighty saving miracles. The longer you spend getting got know Him, the greater He will become. In his book, 'Prince Caspian', C. S. Lewis allegorises this exquisitely: Lucy sees Aslan the lion for the first time in a long while. She is surprised by his size: "Aslan, you're bigger." The great lion replies: "That is because you are older, little one." Slightly confused she answers: "Not because you are?" Aslan explains: "I am not. But every year you grow, you find me bigger."

We all need a deeper revelation of this amazing God so that we, like David, can say: "Praise the Lord, O my soul, and forget not all his benefits – Who forgives all your sins and heals all your diseases, who redeems your life from the pit and crowns you with love and compassion, who satisfies your desires with good things so that your youth is renewed like the eagle's."[1] This God is, and should be, enough for us.

Lord I don't understand how You can be all I need in life. Help me to be deeply convinced of your Presence. I need so many things but I want You to be everything. Show me how you are 'my portion' and all I need. I want to get to know You more. I want to be able to really see you as my Father, Creator, Comforter and Friend.

---

[1] Psalm 103:2-5

Who is My Real Enemy?

My Soldier

There is a whole world, the spirit realm, which is not visible to the naked eye. But this is not a world that you need fear.

I am all-powerful and have overcome the powers of evil. They will, however, plague you from time to time. While I do not want you to become obsessed by them, I also don't want you to ignore them.

So, put on your full armour, and with the authority of the name of my Son, Jesus Christ, resist these forces and they will flee.

Your Conqueror

Two wars wage: Over the battlefield in our soul (which includes our minds) and a larger one that covers the earth. This is what happened to John in the War on Earth:

Nobody told John he had signed up for war. He had heard someone speak about the King, and what he stood for, and he knew it was the only way he could be saved. So he had pledged his allegiance. But now the celebrations following his commitment have died down and he becomes aware of the distant sound of metal against metal. Curious, he goes to investigate.

Frightened, but strangely drawn, he belly crawls his way towards the sound. As he draws closer he sees there is a massive battle underway, both on the ground and in the air, for as far as the eye can see. Demons, with contorted and grotesque faces and bodies, fight with magnificent angels, whose wings reach from above their heads to the ground. Once airborne, these creatures clash with such force that it feels to John that the air is shaking. Below them people, some wielding swords, are trying to help the angels. To one side he notices a platoon of demons marching to join in the war. They hold banners high above their heads - Pride, Jealousy, Disunity, Self-Righteousness – he can only read a few. Some demons, sitting to the side, seem to have the sole job of shouting words of discouragement. John notices that some of the people lose hope as this barrage of criticism continues unabated, and they leave the battle. But others, in the thick of it, keep looking towards something at the right of the field. Adjusting his eyes, John sees something magnificent: sitting astride his powerful horse is his King.

A deep love overwhelms him and he instantly knows what he should do. Rushing, with a loud animal-like shout, he ploughs straight into the writhing group. It feels like he has been hit by a brick wall. No matter how much he swings his fists, kicks or shouts, he gets nowhere.

One demon, who had been watching him from a distance, flies past his head laughing. He swings around trying to punch the ugly face with the hardest right hook he can muster, but, as he does, he sees that the demon is called Doubt. He misses and is knocked sprawling; face down in the mud. Once down, he is trampled by man and demon who continue to fight above him. Covering his face, John cries out for help.

Suddenly he feels the strong arms of someone picking him up and placing him, bruised and bleeding, near a group of tents. As he turns around to identify his Saviour he sees his King riding off.

Just then a Tall Man comes towards him with a wry look on his face. "New recruit, eh?" he says almost laughing beneath his breath as though at some private joke. When John nods, he continues: "Only a Newbie would go into that without armour on. Come on let's get you kitted out."

As John follows him to one of the tents, the Tall Man explains that when John was conscripted into God's army, he became an enemy of the devil, who they call The Accuser. "I see you have already felt his attacks?" When John explains about being pushed over by Doubt, the tall man replies: "Ah yea, his favourite target is the new ones."

To John's embarrassment, the Tall Man begins to take John's clothes off once they are inside the tent. John is just about to object, when he looks down and sees something shiny under his clothes that he had never noticed before.

"This is your breastplate" the Tall Man explains. While John is running his hands over the ornate, cool silver covering his chest, the Tall Man continues: "This will protect your heart. You know – where your emotions are, like how you feel about yourself and your trust in others. This breastplate was put there when you were conscripted and is called the Breastplate of Righteousness. It is a constant reminder to you and to the forces of evil that because the Son died to take away your sins, the King now completely approves of you."

John can't help thinking about the shame he had felt when he was face to face with the King. The Tall Man takes off the scruffy hat on John's head and reveals a solid looking helmet. "You need this if Doubt ever attacks you again. It will remind you that you were saved."

Then, kneeling down he takes off the broken boots from John's feet and there, wrapped around like a second skin, are the best boots he has ever seen. "These will help you with conscription. When the demons try to persuade you that telling others about the King is a waste of time and that the job is too big, these boots will give you courage to spread his proclamation of peace."

Standing up, the Tall Man points to John's belt, which appears to be holding all his clothing in place: "This is the belt of Truth. The Accuser will try to come against you with lies – even lies that sound like the truth. Knowing that you have this belt will set you free from them."

Walking to a large wardrobe in the corner of the tent, the Tall Man takes out an incredibly large and uniquely crafted shield and sword. Handing them to John he explains: "When the demons try to hurl temptations, trials and the fiery darts of insults at you, use this shield to defend yourself. It is the Shield of Faith and it will help you to see beyond what is happening to you, towards the victory that is ours." John is thrilled to get the sword and listens intently as the Tall Man explains: "This is the only part of your armour that is used to attack rather than defend. This is the Sword of the Spirit and with it you will be able to beat the enemy back. When you wield it you are wielding the Word of God."

John is not listening as the Tall Man continues to talk. His mind is racing ahead. He is excited about going back onto the battlefield to try out his new armour. The Tall Man, realising John is no longer listening, allows him to leave.

On re-entering the battle John begins to make out the names of some of the demons: Rejection, Bitterness and Shame. He notices a demon called Hopelessness grip onto a person who has just been battered by other plaguing demons. John sees that the person is a Christian and that his Helmet is awry on his head and his Belt is so lose that it is nearly falling off. As John is fighting to get close so that he can help, he sees that Hopelessness is not alone. Depression has been hovering over the man's head. John is suddenly hit by a dart of Insecurity, but he raises his Shield to fend off any further attacks and holds his Sword ready. Sheltering behind his Shield, John half turns to see how the Christian is getting on.

To his horror he sees that the Christian is in the mud, lying in a foetal position. He is no longer able to see the King. Hopelessness and Depression are laughing as they hover over him. "I love his part," Depression says ominously, "If we just stand here, he will take his own life. We don't even have to do anything. It's genius!" They roar again with laughter.

John sees a glimmer of fear cross their faces when they see him standing on the other side of the man, fully armoured and determined to do battle. As he raises his Sword, ancient wisdom and truth begin to pour out of his mouth. Just as he is about to deliver the final blow, he notices that the two demons are looking over his shoulder. John glances back quickly, and there, resplendent on his horse, is the King. Filled with overwhelming joy, John looks back at the two demons. But he only catches a glimpse of their bent, twisted backs disappearing into the thick of battle.

Kneeling, John wraps his arm around the cowering Christian. They both look up at the King and thank him together as He reaches down and takes the Christian up onto His horse. As he leaves, John realises that the Christian will probably be taken back to the tent to be cared for. Exhilarated by his encounter, he becomes even more determined to fight on.

Suddenly, it is as though the stuffing has been punched out of him. He is so badly winded that he falls to his knees. He looks up to see his attacker, and to his surprise he sees a Christian! Getting to his feet, John realises the problem: the Christian is so blinded by Self-Righteousness, Deception and Gossip, that he cannot see clearly. "This Christian thinks he is fighting for the King!" John thinks to himself in horror.

The blows keep coming. John, who is stunned and not wanting to hurt him, lowers both Sword and Shield. Fiery darts are now piercing his heart. Shocked and hurt, John falls to the ground. As he looks up to plead with the Christian to stop hurting him, he notices two more demons have entered the fray – Pride and Ambition. They are a powerful, dreadful pair.

The arrows sting and the blows seem to pierce the parts of John that hurt the most. Down, and almost wanting to give up, he feels those strong hands lifting him out of the mud. He is on the horse of the King.

Back in the tent, recovering, John begins to wonder what went wrong. He realises he should have kept his Sword and Shield up. But there was something else that was missing. His reverie is interrupted by a young soldier walking into the tent. "The King has told me to give you this note," the soldier says and then leaves.

Taking the note, John reads: "In my Name they will drive out demons." Expecting a long treatise that could explain his complicated situation, John is surprised at how short the note is. A light begins to dawn on him as he starts to realise what was missing – he hadn't been using the authority of the Name of the King.

He thinks about the note and the battle over the next few days as he rests. He is never alone. Christians busy themselves around his bed, feeding him, tending to his wounds, reading to him from the Big

Book and singing songs that sooth and comfort. They teach him about love and tell him that without love on the battlefield, he would be ineffective. During those few days of rest, John makes many friends who, he knows, will remain close to him for life.

Refreshed, fully armoured and wielding a banner that reads: 'Love,' John re-enters the battle. The first thing he notices is a group of people huddled with their backs towards him, so that he cannot see their faces. As he walks closer he realises that they are Christians. A huge demon has his wings wrapped over the group and his name is Fear. As John edges closer he can hear them telling each other fearful stories and he notices that their Swords are down and their Armour is in tatters.

This time John uses the name of the King as he wields his Sword. As soon as he does, a beautiful chorus of angels swoop in and begin to fight with Fear, who cowers back. Delighted at this victory, John reaches down and helps the dazed Christians to their feet. After encouraging them to take up their Shields and Swords again, they head out together to fight for their King who is standing by.

The afternoon goes by in a whirlwind of battle. But even while it rages around him, John is content. Every time he feels even the slightest fear, he looks up to his King, who is always close by.

As the sun is about to set, a Striking Woman catches John's eye and to his amazement she is coming straight towards him, smiling. When they begin talking it is as though she has been a friend forever. She says everything that John wants to hear and is very complimentary. He hangs onto every word. She is such a welcome relief from the battle that John decides to sit down with her to continue talking in more depth. They talk right through the night about how things could be different and how this battle shouldn't have occurred in the first place. John begins to see the futility of his cause.

At sunrise, John is tired but so engrossed with the Striking Woman, that he has not noticed a band of demons who have sidled up behind them. John is transfixed and, as she continues to talk, he begins to see that she is wise. She tells him about a world far beyond the battlefield, where the King is not ruler of all.

Suddenly the King appears, as if out of nowhere, and gently gives John an order. Not wanting to appear ignorant and unmanly in front of the Striking Woman, John tells the King that he will follow orders later....maybe.

All at once the demons, who John now sees are Deception and Lies, pounce. As he staggers to his feet, he hears the Striking Woman laugh – a hysterical, nasty laugh. He turns to look at her, but she has vanished, taking her alluring charms and beguiling lies with her.

John begins to fear - a gripping, raw fear in the pit of his stomach. He wants to run and hide in a small dark place far away from all this bloodshed but he feels paralysed. As he looks at the battle he longs for the Striking Woman and her words offering quietness away from all this pain. "It's not fair," John says falling to the ground, "this is too hard and I didn't ask for any of it. This is not my fault. Why should I have to go through this?" He begins to wail at the thought of the injustice of it all.

He sits there for so long that cramp sets into his legs and he feels physically ill. Just then he realises that there is someone wailing a lot louder than he is and he recognises it as the cry of a child. Immediately he stops his own plaintive cries and gets up to try to find where it is coming from. As the mist parts he sees a horrible sight: sitting waist deep in the mud is an Infant. Around her a band of jeering demons are flying in a circle. Each one takes a turn at prodding her little, thin body that is weak from starvation and crying.

Forgetting his woes, John adjusts his Armour. Shield raised and sword held out in front of him, he advances against the bony, black demons. As he does, he notices they are Starvation and Abuse. Seeing him, they squeal and back off a short distance, just enough for John to scoop the Infant into his arms. He immediately reaches into his pocket and takes out the last of his bread. The ravenous Infant eats, nestled behind his Shield, as he turns back to the gyrating demons. They are clearly bothered by the sight of the child eating and begin to back off. Disgusted, he runs his sword through Abuse, who staggers away howling. Starvation follows suit, gnashing its teeth.

John looks down at the muddy Infant and speaks gentle words of comfort and love to her. She responds by clinging to him with her little hands. His heart melts. Saving the child has left him feeling strangely fulfilled and good about himself. Something warm stirs within him and he looks around for the King.

He is standing next to John and smiling down at him. He takes the Infant into His arms. Falling to his knees John says: "Lord, I am so sorry I doubted you!" The King kneels besides him and encircles him with a hug. "I love you John," He says. Tears of gratitude flow to John's eyes and he asks: "Lord what can I do for you?" Cupping John's face in His Hands the King replies: "I want your unconditional surrender John." Startled by his reply John queries: "How Lord, how do I surrender?"

"Cast your burdens on me." The King replied. Then taking the Infant from John he adds: "Come John, let's walk together and I will show you how." John stands up and shaking the dirt of the battle off himself, he walks hand in hand with the King, secure and loved.

Inspiration for this allegory comes from one of my favourite verses: "Finally, be strong in the Lord and in his mighty power. Put on the full armour of God so that you can take your stand against the devil's schemes. For our struggle is not against flesh and blood, but against the rulers, against the authorities, against the powers of this dark world and against the spiritual forces of evil in the heavenly realms. Therefore put on the full armour of God."[1]

We are 'flesh and blood'. The devil and his demons are the 'powers of this dark world'. This is not a fantasy, it is real and it has been raging since Satan fell from Heaven and it is still going on around us all the time. The war is between truth and lies; life and death.

We have no reason to fear. Even though Satan has some power, he is no equal to God Almighty, because he is a created being, made by

---

[1] Ephesians 6:10-13

187

God to be an angel before he rebelled.[1] The Bible also reassures us: "You, dear children, are from God and have overcome them, because the one who is in you (that is God) is greater than the one who is in the world."[2] Evil will be defeated every time in any match because God is all-powerful. He never struggles against the devil. Satan was a vanquished foe from the beginning of time. Through the work of Christ on the cross, we have victory over sin, death and the works of the evil one. The Bible states that Jesus came so that "he might destroy him who holds the power of death – that is, the devil – and free those who, all their lives, were held in slavery by their fear of death."[3]

For now, Satan wages war against Christians. He "prowls around like a roaring lion looking for someone to devour."[4] But at the final judgement he will be "thrown into the lake of burning sulphur," where he will be "tormented day and night for ever and ever."[5] Now he works desperately, on borrowed time, knowing that it is short because his final judgement is inevitable. Our Prince of Peace shall return and Satan will be tossed into his dreadful dwelling for all time.

In the meantime we are performing 'mop-up operations' by standing against the devil and his demons. Demons are spirit beings with evil personalities. Their objective is to deceive, condemn, tempt, defile, oppose, resist, control, steal, afflict, kill and destroy. We are their target. As soon as we became children of God we became their enemy. Jesus said to Peter: "...I will build my church and the gates of Hell will not overcome it."[6] We, the church, are in enemy territory, but God assures us that the powers of darkness will not prevail.

Believing in this unseen world can be difficult for some, but it was easy for me, because I once saw an angel. When I was eight years old, while living with my mum and sister in Camps Bay, Cape Town, I

---

[1] Isaiah 14:12-15, Ezekiel 28?13-17
[2] 1 John 4:4
[3] Hebrew 2:14
[4] 1 Peter 5:8
[5] Revelations 20:10
[6] Matthew 16:18

was sitting on the edge of the bed when a glowing light caused me to look outside. My bedroom, which I shared with my mum, had long windows that reached to the floor and overlooked a balcony. Beyond, the vast Atlantic Ocean twinkling in the moonlight became eclipsed by the being that stood there. A soft, but penetrating light emanated from this towering figure. Huge wings reached from above its head to the ground. The only thing I can remember about its face is that it had a square jaw. But what stood out the most was its sword; it was huge, shoulder height to the ground. I sat there, totally calm and secure for a short while, and then lay down and fell asleep. It was years before I told anyone about my visitation – I didn't want their doubt to spoil my experience.

Interest and focus on the demonic can become extreme. In the 1970's, the church was swept by a wave of renewed interest in all things supernatural. After reading a book on the subject I began to imagine demons in all sorts of things. For example: in a piece of antique furniture or a statue of an owl. If something went wrong during my day, I would ascribe it to demonic interference. This unhealthy focus on things demonic can lead to fear and warped thinking. Either ignoring demons or becoming obsessed with them can be dangerous; we need a balanced, Bible-based perspective.

While not all Christians who kill themselves are driven to it by the demonic, I believe demons have a hand in many suicides. We can see a few examples of this in the Bible: After the devil had used Judas for his purpose, he then used the power of guilt to drive him towards self-destruction.[1] The demon possessed boy mentioned in Matthew threw himself into the fire and then into water, showing his suicidal tendencies.[2] The man with a demon called Legion at Gerasene constantly tried to cut himself with stones.[3] While there is no way of knowing the extent of demonic involvement in suicide, we can be fairly certain that it does exist. The devil wants us to be ineffectual, and failing that, he wants us dead.

---

[1] Matthew 27:5-10
[2] Matthew 17:15
[3] Mark 5:9

I have known two Christians who have taken their own lives. Both had given their lives to the Lord shortly before they died. I knew them well and there is no doubt in my mind demonic forces were at play. Even though they agreed that they needed deliverance, they kept putting it off. I think they were probably scared – understandably so. But unfortunately they died in the interim. I strongly believe they were driven to suicide by demons.

Many churches today, while strong in other teaching, are amiss in not training believers to be soldiers, active in spiritual warfare. Do we know how to "pull down strongholds"[1] or "resist the devil"[2] or "wrestle with principalities and powers... rulers of this dark world?"[3]

We need boot camp. We need practical knowledge. We need to learn how to "fight the good fight."[4] Satan has a plan to destroy each one of us, our families and our communities. We are not to closet ourselves away, hoping that we will not be noticed. We are not to have a defeatist attitude - because we are not on the defensive, we are on the attack. We are meant to be taking ground for God in our lives. We are also not to be reactive by only dealing with these forces when they attack, we are to be constantly moving forward, spreading the light that God has placed within us into the world. We have not been called to sit back and watch Him and His Angels fight. We have been called into His army to gain territory in our lives and in the world for Christ. Our weapons are truth, peace and justice. We advance on our knees and destroy with love.

Demons can invade and possess a human body. In so doing they can control that person more effectively than if they were on the outside. The Bible calls the person with the indwelling spirit "possessed."[5] This word suggests total ownership and as such there is much debate surrounding it. The personality of the demon takes dominance over the personality of the individual. A Christian, who is 'possessed' by the Holy Spirit, rarely has this type of complete

---

[1] 2 Corinthians 10:4
[2] James 4:7
[3] Ephesians 6:12
[4] 1 Timothy 1:18
[5] Mark 9:17, Luke 4:33, Mark 1:23

subjugation. I believe that a Christian can become possessed to a certain degree, though only temporarily and not to the same extent as a non-believer. Demons also influence our thinking and actions - some call this demonic oppression.

Indwelling or interfering demons should always be considered to be trespassers. Our bodies are the temples of the Holy Spirit and as such, demons are on hallowed ground when they encroach on our territory. These trespassers will continue living unlawfully until they are confronted and challenged on the basis of legal rights. The devil has no rights over us whatsoever and it is up to us to tell him so. Demons consider the body which they are possessing to be their 'house.'[1] They are liars and deceivers and need to be driven out. Just as Jesus drove the money changers out of the temple we too, with the same authority given to us by Him, can tell demons to leave.

You may be asking: "How do I know if I have a demon?" This varies widely from person to person, however there are a few 'symptoms' that can present themselves. While these are not a sure sign of the demonic (and some of these can have other causes), this may help us to decide if we need to seek help. While any one of these points does not mean that you have demonic problems, it can be an indication that a problem exists. Final discernment should come from God via the prompting of the Holy Spirit.

Possible symptoms of demonic activity:

- A Lack of Control in any area in your life - You feel that something you are doing is beyond your capacity to stop e.g. addictions, swearing incessantly, thoughts that seem to be going in a loop, emotions that soar or sink down or urges that don't seem to go away.
- Living continually in the past or in the future, e.g. if your thoughts are ruled by "what ifs" and "if onlys" and you find it difficult to 'be in the moment.'
- Mood Swings - You are on an emotional roller-coaster and flare up at a moment's notice or you plummet to the depths of depression at the smallest difficulty.

---

[1] Matthew 12:43

- A sudden interest in the occult - If you are drawn towards things that are darkly mystical e.g. psychics, fortune-tellers, Ouija boards, horoscopes, movies and music with satanic themes.
- A sudden change in personality, e.g. a person who was once placid may become aggressive.
- A sudden change in intelligence – You find you can work things out easier and have a deeper knowledge of things. This change normally goes hand in hand with feelings of grandiosity. An extreme example of this would be Hitler, who mesmerised millions with his oratory.
- A persistent feeling of heaviness or fear that will not lift – This may be depression but it could be caused by a demon. King Saul had a "tormenting spirit."[1] This can manifest in nightmares, irrational fears, phobias and headaches.
- Difficulty in maintaining your Christian walk - Praying, studying the Bible, praising and obeying God become a relentless uphill battle.
- Continual Defeat in certain areas of your life e.g. on-going financial, health and relational problems.

It must be stressed that these symptoms can have their root cause in other areas, for example, financial problems could be caused simply by your over-spending or, a sudden change in personality, can signify a medical condition. Medical help should also be sought in the case of some of these symptoms. However, if they persist, demonic involvement should be considered. We need to be guided by the Holy Spirit when it comes to the discernment of evil spirits.

The 'good news' about learning that you have a demonic problem is that once the demon is cast out, the problem dissipates.

It you are concerned that you have a demonic problem but do not want to ask for prayer from a leader in the Church, you can deliver yourself of demons. As a believer you have the same authority as anyone who has a 'deliverance ministry.' The authority comes through the Name of Jesus. You will also need the Power of God, which is available to us and greater than the power of the enemy:

---

[1] 1 Samuel 16:14

"But you will receive power when the Holy Spirit comes on you."[1] Jesus gave this power through the Holy Spirit to his disciples: "...he gave them power and authority to drive out all demons and to cure diseases..."[2] Before going against the forces of evil you need to be sure that you have both the authority of the Name of Jesus as well as the power of God through the indwelling Holy Spirit. You have authority as soon as you have committed your life to Christ, and the power of the Holy Spirit is received once you ask for it.

However, it is advisable to seek help from someone who is experienced. Demons that have been plaguing a person for a long time are sometimes difficult to discern – familiarity blinds us to them. A person, newly delivered of a long standing demon can often say: "Oh, I thought that was just me!"

I have had demonic problems. In a previous chapter I mentioned my deliverance from a spirit of fear. But there have been others: I was set free from a generational demon (one that was passed down from my father's involvement in the Free Masons) and, once delivered, I was freed from many problems, for example, lying. I was also delivered from a spirit of addiction. Once it was cast out, I found it much easier to give up the habits that had previously enslaved me. I was also delivered from a sexual demon (probably as a result of rape and molestation) that freed me to enjoy an intimate relationship with my husband. When the spirit of guilt left, I began to grasp the wonders of what Christ did on the cross for me. There were other demons that have tried to hover around me over the years, but with the help of a gift of discernment I am able to recognise when they are around.

Earlier on in my life, I normally asked leaders in my church to pray for deliverance for me, but over the years my husband and I have developed a 'deliverance ministry' and we now pray for each other. Thinking back though, I wouldn't have liked to have delivered myself when I first noticed that I had a problem. Some of the demons spoke through me to the leader who was praying for me: "There is no point in trying to cast this demon out because this is my fault!" That was a

---

[1] Acts 1:8
[2] Luke 9:1

demon influencing my thoughts, and the elder needed to be astute enough to know not to consider what it was saying. Also, I needed the care and comfort of others after the deliverance because I felt dizzy and drained. Self-deliverance is not always possible or recommended so if you are new to this, it is advisable to get help from a person who has this particular ministry. After you have experienced deliverance in the hands of an experienced believer, you will be better equipped to 'keep your house clean.'

Getting help from others is often neither possible nor practical so you may want to consider self-deliverance. Outlined below are my suggestions for the steps and prayers that will guide you to freedom from demonic bondage and interference:

- **Accept God** as Lord of your life - If you have not given your life to Christ, the simple prayer below can act as a guide. Once you say and believe the words you are praying in this prayer, you will begin your relationship with God. If you believe that you are a Christian, there is no harm in praying this prayer again:

I am sorry Lord for the things I have done wrong in my life. Please forgive me. I believe that Your Son, Jesus Christ, died on the cross so that I could be forgiven and set free. I accept Jesus as my personal Saviour now. Thank you for saving me. Thank you for this free gift that I now receive. I welcome you into my life to be with me forever. I gladly receive your Holy Spirit into my life now. Thank you, Lord Jesus, that I am saved. Amen.

If you have demonic activity in your life, you may find this prayer extremely difficult to say. It may be more beneficial to you if you ask a leader in the church or a person who has a deliverance ministry to help you.

- **Surrender to God** - The process of surrendering to God is the process of tearing down thought patterns (strongholds) that keep you from yielding to Him. You can be freed from any habits that have gripped your thoughts, mind or body by surrendering yourself to God.

Lord, I surrender my whole life to you, the past, present and future. I surrender myself to you and all that I am. I give up my choices, my will, my memory and my understanding about how I think things should be. I give it all to you. You are my King and I want to follow You wholeheartedly. I refuse to give the devil another day.

- Tell God that you want nothing to do with the devil.

Lord I want to have no part in anything that the devil is trying to do. I only want to follow You.

- **Acknowledge your position** in the Kingdom - You are a child of God, made in His image. The Bible specifically tells us that we have greater authority than the authority of demons. Demons are forced to yield to the authority given to you in the Name of Jesus. During His final speech before ascending to heaven Jesus said: "And these signs will accompany those who believe: In my name they will drive out demons."[1]

Lord, I am Your Child and an heir to your kingdom. Thank you that I have Your Power and Authority in the Name of Jesus.

- **Recognise your armour.** You may not fully comprehend the importance of your armour, but that does not matter, you became clothed in it when you received Christ as your King.

Lord, thank you for this armour. I put on the helmet of salvation, the breastplate of righteousness, the shoes that are shod with your Word, the belt of truth and I take up the shield of faith and the sword of the Spirit.

- **Command the demons to leave** – If you have specifically discerned the names of the demons you can address them by name. The most common demons that I have come across are: Pride, Rebellion and Unforgiveness. It is sometimes necessary to tell them to go a few times. If you are suicidal you may have a demon called Suicide.

Now, evil spirits that are in or controlling me, I am speaking to you. I command you, in the name of Jesus Christ to leave. You have no place

---

[1] Mark 16:17

in me. I am a child of God. I cast you out by the Authority of God and the power of the Holy Spirit.

A suicidal person may have a demon of death speaking into their minds. While you are praying you may have overwhelming feelings of hopelessness and thoughts of death – press on and tell the demon to leave. It has to leave at the Name of Jesus. Ask God to send His angels to guard you. Do not be afraid, this demon cannot harm you. It can only try to get you to harm yourself.

Demon of death I tell you, in the Name of Jesus Christ, to leave. I am a child of God and I do not want you in my life anymore. God has promised me a life abundant and death will come when it is God's Will. Stop speaking into my mind now. It is a waste of time. I want to live.

Or you may pray:

My life is in God's Hands. Through Jesus Christ I now belong to Him. My life is His to give and to take away. Nothing can separate me from the Love of God. I pray, as Paul did in the Bible: "For I am convinced that neither death nor life, neither angels nor demons, nor anything else in all creation, will be able to separate us (me) from the love of God that is in Christ Jesus our Lord."[1]

If you feel no release at this point, then read out scriptures, especially ones that relate to the demon, for example, if you believe that you have a demon of unforgiveness, then you may say:

God said we are to be 'forgiving (towards) each other, just as Christ God forgave us.[2] *So I forgive as I am told to do! Now, demon of unforgiveness, leave in the Name of Christ my Saviour.*

Some illnesses can have their root in the demonic, for example, major trauma can bring on sickness. When a traumatic event occurs in a person's life, they can become plagued by a demon of fear. This demon can affect us physically by attacking our immune system and our body. The person may lose hope as fear gains more territory in

---

[1] Romans 8:38
[2] Ephesians 4:32

their thoughts. Praying against this demon of fear (or even a spirit of trauma) may relieve physical symptoms:

In the Name of Jesus Christ I command you, demon of fear, to leave. The Word says: "God did not give us a spirit of timidity (fear), but a spirit of power, of love and of self-discipline."[1] So leave in Jesus' Name.

There may be manifestations of the demons as they leave and this can show in many different ways: a pressure on the throat or other parts of the body, prior to the demon leaving; a hot or cold feeling; a cough, a sigh, a grunt or even vomiting. Sometimes the 'feeling' that you get is related to the demon, for example, the demon of fear may manifest by you feeling particularly scared just before it leaves. However there is nothing to fear, God is with you. There is often a perceptible feeling of release as the demon leaves. Whatever the feeling, the actions that were associated with the demon will become easier to resist.

- **Be filled with the Holy Spirit**.[2] It is clear from the Bible that an evil spirit can return if the 'house' is left empty. The house must be filled. Pray that the Holy Spirit comes and fills you and every nook and cranny of your home:

Come Holy Spirit I welcome you afresh in my life. Please fill every area of my mind, body and home.

- **Thank God and praise Him**.

Thank you, Lord, for setting me free. You are awesome and I love You.

After you have been delivered, you need to hold onto your deliverance by:

- Acknowledging that you wear the full armour of God.
- Guarding your thoughts - most demons that enter come in by attacking your thoughts. Refuse to fill your mind with violent, sexual or demonic images in movies, video games or books.

---

[1] 2 Timothy 1:7
[2] Matthew 12:43-45

- Speaking positively not negatively - Negative speaking often characterises demonic problems. We need to be careful that we are not agreeing with demons with the things we say.
- Saturating yourself in the Word - Jesus withstood the temptation of the devil by quoting scripture. We too can resist the devil by thinking or even saying passages from the Bible.
- Crucifying the flesh - Don't give in to worldly temptations, but rather practice obedience and discipline.
- Praying continually - Get into the habit of praying about all things.
- Surrounding yourself with loving Christians – Don't isolate yourself: "Let us not give up meeting together."[1]

It is not necessary to go around thinking about demons all the time in order to keep them at bay. In fact we are advised to think about all things that are true, lovely, of good report and honest.[2] However, if we feel an evil presence is attempting to disrupt our minds or interfere in our lives, we should be quick to exercise the authority we have in Christ by telling them to leave.

This is *not some mental trick that you need to perform*; this is you relying on God to achieve what would be impossible for you to achieve on your own. Remember that it is not your battle: "Do not be discouraged, the battle is not yours…"[3] We need to remember who is in charge of the battle. At the head of our army and presiding over every battle in your life…is God…all powerful and supreme. Then we too, with Paul, will confidently say: "In all these things we are more than conquerors through Him who loved us."[4]

---

[1] Matthew 10:25
[2] Philippians 4:8
[3] 2 Chronicles 20:15
[4] Romans 8:37

Why has nothing changed?

Believer

I know that you have heard many stories about how others have accepted me as their Lord and Saviour and how their lives have been miraculously changed and it has left you feeling confused because the things you want to change have not.

Know that a great deal has changed in your life – you have me guiding you every day towards a better future and you have the assurance of being with me for eternity.

Some things take time to change, for example, becoming more like me. This is a process, so if you come to me, I will show you how.

Your Friend

Jesus

You may be totally convinced that God is intimately involved in your life and yet feel as though nothing has changed. You may have heard that "you are a new creation; the old has gone, the new has come,"[1] but, in some ways, you continue to feel the same as you always did. Why has nothing changed?

We are three-part beings consisting of our body, soul and spirit:[2]

- **The body**, or as Paul called it our 'tent' where our spirit man lives,[3] does not go to eternity with us.
- **The soul** consists of our conscious and subconscious minds, our emotions, passions, desires, discernment and decision making facilities.

---

[1] 2 Corinthians 5:17
[2] 1 Thessalonians 5:23
[3] 2 Corinthian 5:1-5

- **Our spirit** is that which is eternal within us - God is Spirit[1] and our spirit is our link to God. When you were born again the real you became reborn as God breathed His Spirit into you. This Spirit is what makes you permanently tied to God. So even though your mind and body remain unchanged, your Spirit has been recreated. At that rebirth your spirit becomes permanently united to God for eternity.

Our souls look earthward, whereas our spirit's focus is heavenward. So when the Paul writes: "Therefore, if anyone is in Christ, he is a new creation; the old has gone, the new has come,"[2] he is explaining what actually happened when you said the prayer of salvation – you became a 'new creation.' You still have the same thoughts as you did before, for example, if you thought about pornography before you may still think about it, if you worried about your finances before you may still worry about them.

Our souls, where our thoughts and reasoning take place, are not born again. This sets up a constant conflict between soul and spirit. Even though our spirit is born again, we may often ignore the promptings of the Holy Spirit by insisting on doing things our own way: our souls are trying to govern our thoughts and actions.

Paul divides believers into two categories, those who allow their sinful natures to rule (in other words those ruled by their souls) and those who follow the Holy Spirit: "Those who live according to the sinful nature have their minds set on what that nature desires; but those who live in accordance with the Spirit have their minds set on what the Spirit desires."[3] He goes on to explain the dire consequences of the former: "The mind of sinful man is death, but the mind controlled by the Spirit is life and peace; the sinful mind is hostile to God...those controlled by the sinful nature cannot please God."[4]

When you were saved it is as though you were given a new house in the best possible location called The Kingdom. As you walk into the

---

[1] John 4:24
[2] 2 Corinthians 5:17
[3] Romans 8:5
[4] Romans 8:6-8

house you notice that all your Old Stuff came with you. As you look at it, familiar feelings begin to stir: the table where so many hurtful family arguments took place, the picture given to you by that person who told lies about you, the single earing that reminds you about the time you were robbed...the memories about past hurts and wrongs begin to flood back, threatening to ruin the excitement you felt at getting the gift of this new house.

As you look at your Old Stuff you notice something that you haven't noticed before – most of it is broken, worn out, dirty and smelly. You wonder how you ever lived with these things in your life before. Then you begin to panic about how you are ever going to sort out the mess, and the task seems impossible.

Suddenly you get a good idea and decide to sweep the jumble under the carpet and squash the clutter into the cupboards. The bulging doors barely shut and there is now a big bump in the carpet that keeps tripping you up. The mess, you decide, doesn't look right in your beautiful new house. So you begin to do a thorough spring clean. You make a few piles: things to be aired, things to be fixed, things to be cleaned and things to be thrown away.

Half way through this spring clean you look around and, to your horror, notice that everything is much messier than it was when you began! Things are waiting in the passages to be put into other rooms, rubbish bags are tossed everywhere, cleaning up apparatus and liquids are strewn across the floor. It looks as though a whirlwind has blown through your house and you feel too tired to do anything about it. Disillusioned, you begin to think that perhaps it was a bad idea to have started in the first place. You were hoping it would all get better and it is in fact, looking worse.

Despondently you collapse on the couch and survey the mess, grumbling quietly to yourself: "Nothing has changed. Why did I bother trying in the first place?" The more you grumble the higher the pile seems to get. By the end of the day, as darkness is about to fall, the mess looks insurmountable.

A pang of horror grips you as you realise that well-wishers will be arriving at any moment. There is no way that you can sort out this pandemonium before they get there, so you frantically jump up and draw the curtains while reassuring yourself: "No one will know I'm at home, maybe if I keep as quiet as a mouse they will leave. I will see them at church anyway, so there is no need for them to see me now. Yes, that will be ok, because I will be dressed nicely and I can smile and sing 'hallelujah' and no one will know what my house really looks likes inside."

This is how I felt for many years after I became a Christian. I felt, and was told, that I glowed on the outside and that 'Jesus shone' in my face, but I knew what was going on inside of my mind. I still held grudges against people, I still had bad habits and addictions, I battled with a temper that would flare up and I was resentful and sometimes unkind to those around me. But as soon as I went to church I 'put on a happy face' along with my make-up and smart clothes to hide what was really happening beneath the surface. My soul (mind, emotions and will) needed to come into line with my spirit. I needed to become more 'spiritually minded' by learning and choosing to think as the spirit man inside me thought, and not be governed by my flesh (or 'soul man').

It is sometimes difficult to tell a believer apart from a non-believer because many believers, once saved, continue to think, talk, act and speak like non-believers. Nothing seems to have changed. Paul refers to them as still being conformed to the world: "Do not conform any longer to the pattern of this world, but be transformed by the renewing of your mind."[1]

The act of being transformed implies a complete renovation or metamorphosis of your mind. It could be likened to the same change that occurs to a caterpillar when it becomes a butterfly. It didn't simply put on a pair of wings and immediately fly off; it had to be completely changed in every way. It was transformed over time and we too are called to be 'metamorphosed' by the renewing of our minds.

If you have reached a point where you are thinking about suicide then you need to look at the state of your mind. Your spirit, aligned

---

[1] Romans 12:2

with God, wants to move forward but your soul is holding you back using invasive tactics; negative thoughts like: "there is no point", excuses like: "nothing I do will make any difference", cover-ups like: "none of this is my fault. If others changed, things would be better" and with a lack of discipline: "It's just the way I am. I can't help it!" This is a battle; a smaller and more insidious one to the war spoken about in the previous chapter: this is the Battle for Soul City:

Not so long ago, the people of Soul City were ignorant of the Overlords that held them captive. At its centre, a Gaping Hole threatened to engulf the teetering buildings clinging round its sides. There was no rest as the citizens laboured unceasingly, trying to fill the Gaping Hole. But the more they worked the more they realised they needed to work because it seemed the hole could not be filled. A loud-speaker blared out constant reminders to them about their past, their failures and how they needed to work harder to fill the Gaping Hole.

Towering above the long lines of bowed figures scurrying to fill the Hole, massive billboards promised relief at the end of the day. Each time the task before them became intolerably boring or back-breakingly hard, they would glance up at these flashing signs and crave for what awaited them.

At night the city would vibrate. Every fantasy could be fulfilled. Vats of enticing cocktails kept the citizens coming back for more. They would lie under the bulbous barrels and drink, but they were left thirstier than ever before. They ate from tables dripping with delicacies, but they never felt full. When their stomachs could take no more, they injected themselves with chemicals that made the moment euphoric. Many could never take the needles out because when they did, Soul City looked unbearably dark.

Million were transfixed by the Overlord's interactive monitors on which carefully designed war games were screened. Points were awarded for those who killed the most people. As they played they became numb to suffering and indifferent to death. Many left, their frayed egos having been bolstered, wanting to kill. Conscription booths, ready to oblige, were conveniently waiting to sign them up.

Massive Pits had been dug in the middle of stadiums. Citizens filled the stands betting on numbers, dogs, horses and anything they could find to try and beat the odds. The house, run by the Overlords, always won. But this didn't deter them as they continued throwing money into the Pit. When the last of their money had gone, they fought with others for theirs.

In the early hours of the morning, feeling empty and alone, they would look around for someone, anyone, to try to soothe their aches and scratch their itches. But no matter how wrapped up in another they became, they were left feeling empty.

Such was the life they had become accustomed to when The Prince arrived. There was great rejoicing when he ousted the Overlords from their penthouse strongholds and when he filled the Gaping Hole. He took the power from the bulbous vats, interactive screens and stadiums, but then something strange began to happen in the city.

People, called Soul Men, could still be seen trying to fill the Gaping Hole. They continued to strive as though their lives depended on it. A particularly miserable bunch of Soul Men, who missed the loudspeaker, picketed in the streets for its return. When their objections were ignored they took it upon themselves to shout about their own failures to anyone who would listen. Some still talked with fondness about the Overlords while others spoke in private, thinking that they would be ostracised if they spoke out loud about their yearnings for what had been. Some could be seen hanging around the vats, screens and stadiums and dabbling in what they had to offer even though the allure was now gone for them and the hold had been broken. They became easy targets to scavengers who lurked in the dark alleys.

When these Soul Men met the Prince, instead of thanking him for saving them, they hung their heads in shame. They were used to tyrannical rule and could not believe that this smiling, loving man, offering so much for free, could be genuine. He understood everything and tried to encourage them to change by showing them that the Gaping Hole had been filled and that the power was broken over the things they used to crave.

This allegory, the Battle for Soul City, illustrates how someone who has made the initial decision to have Jesus in their life struggles to get rid of old habits and complexes from the past. These emotional conflicts sabotage our thoughts and we end up asking: "Why has nothing changed?" For change to occur, our entire mind needs to come under the authority of our new Lord, Jesus Christ.

This battle is won by bringing our minds under control. The Roman poet Horace wrote: "Rule your mind or it will rule you." The devil wants to rule our minds because he knows that if he can rule our thinking he will have control over our lives. We are used to letting our minds wander wherever they please, but if we want to gain victory over difficult areas, we need to bring our minds under control.

The first practical step, after agreeing that you need to take back control, is to practice keeping your mind thinking about what you want to think about.

Our minds can wreak havoc in our lives by running rampant with thoughts that go unchecked. Some of these thoughts are **Poisonous Thoughts**, like:

- "No one loves me, not even God. But I don't blame them because I have done so many things wrong."
- "I fail at everything I do."
- "People are always so horrible to me."
- "There is no way I will ever recover from this."
- "There is no point in trying; I will always be this way."
- "Everything is going wrong."

These Poisonous Thoughts seep into our lives like toxins, causing decay and death. The Bible explains that we are to "take captive every thought to make it obedient to Christ."[1] We need to 'run' our thoughts past God as we think them.

---

[1] 2 Corinthians 10:5

When I first heard the concept of 'taking your thoughts captive' or 'you can control what you think,' I dismissed it as impossible. Not only was I totally convinced that I could not control all my thoughts, but I became angry with anyone who suggested I could! My thoughts 'just happened' and there was nothing I could do about them. They crept up on me without me even being aware that they were there and suddenly, there I was, thinking something.

When I decided to try to think about what I was thinking about I was surprised. There were so many thoughts that I was having that were dangerous and negative. For example: insecurities and fears went unchecked. I realized that my brain really was controlling every part of my life – the way I spoke, acted and reacted - and it was affecting my health.

In an effort to renew my mind, I began to try to become aware of my thoughts and to control what I was thinking. This was very, very difficult. First, I acknowledged the thought by stopping and asking myself what I was thinking at any given time, and as I did so, I started to realise just how damaging my thoughts had become.

About a year ago I was driving down the avenue that leads to our home, I was feeling a little low until I noticed an exquisite tree that had just come into bloom. It was so beautiful that I stopped the car and stared at it in wonder. Beautiful voluptuous yellow flowers hung down from its willow-like branches so that there was barely a leaf in sight. I was looking forward to looking at it every day for a while... I needed cheering up.

After a few days, I passed it again and saw that it had been cut down and all the branches and flowers were tossed onto the driveway. I was sad and thought: "Every time I find something I like in life it is taken away from me". Then I paused and thought about my thought, as I had been training myself to do. I asked myself if it was true, and realized that there had been significant moments in my life where I had something that made me happy, only for it to be taken away from me. This thought was so deeply entrenched in my brain that I had begun to think that it was the pattern of life: All good things get taken away. I questioned my thinking and as I began to dig deep into my memory I found all sorts of things that had been taken from me –

my cat was taken away when my mother got remarried, my first sports car was stolen before I had a chance to drive it, my modelling portfolio and all negatives had been stolen, I had not received my rightful inheritance... the list went on and on. Then I hit bedrock when I realized one of the biggest losses I suffered as a child: I felt as though I had lost my mother when she had remarried. This fear of loss had been set deeply in my soul and it was dictating my thoughts. My automatic response had become: "Ah, don't get too close to something (or someone) because it will be taken away from you." I tried not to enjoy things or even love things because I feared they would be lost. I became scared to love and fearful of enjoying life. The 'toxic thought' had spread its poison.

To reverse this way of thinking, I began to reason with myself: I thought about all the people and things that had not been taken from me and that I still had. I also thought about all the things that had been restored – the little inheritance I had received had increased a hundred times its original value, I had many cats, my current car is the best I have ever owned and my mother and I are best friends. Then, during my next quiet time, God confirmed this thought by showing me in His Word that He restores.[1] It wasn't long before that way of thinking was completely gone. The re-programing of my brain in that area was complete – the garbage had been flushed out.

Steps to Renewing Your Mind:

- Decide to think about your thinking.
- Consider your thoughts throughout the day - Think about what you are thinking about whether you are driving, having a conversation with someone or sitting in a class or office.
- Think before you speak - Find out what is causing you to say what you say.
- Think after you speak – Get into the habit of analysing your conversations, asking yourself why you responded the way you did. Be careful not to be obsessive about this and don't condemn yourself for what you said.
- Ask God to help you - Pray that the Holy Spirit makes you immediately aware when a damaging thought comes into

---

[1] Joel 2:25

your mind: "Help me Holy Spirit to recognize these thoughts and help me throw these wrong thoughts away."

- Don't meditate on negative thoughts – we should consider things that have been said that are negative, but mulling over them will only cement them in our minds. If you find yourself thinking about things that people have said that offend you and make you feel rejected, then stop yourself from thinking this in mid-thought and instead quote a scripture in your head that directly opposes that thought.
- Think healthy thoughts – Get your mind thinking about things that will add to the quality of your life.

Being in constant pain brings a barrage of negative thoughts into my head. I sometimes think I will be in this pain forever. This thought keeps me awake at night, and that is when all poisonous thoughts seem to be the hardest to control: "What if this is it? What if my son grows up with a mother who is too sick to play?" As these thoughts ruminate with no sign of relief, I am left physically exhausted, emotionally drained and spiritually spent. I have found the only way out is to:

- Oppose the thought - Directly opposing that thought is the only way to find peace in amongst the pain. It may not sound logical, but it works. For example, I remind myself that God heals. In those dark moments in the middle of the night, I literally hurl this Scripture at the wrong thought: "I am the Lord who heals you."[1] It is short and easy to remember and to the point. God heals. There is hope. Even though the pain may continue, my thought pattern changes, and with it my sense of well-being. My brain is being re-programmed.
- Find Scriptures that oppose your negative thought ahead of time so that you are prepared.
- Decide that no matter how hard it is, you will train yourself to think the way God wants you to.
- Exercise self-control – Don't make excuses like: "I can't control myself!" Recognise that what you are really saying is: "I don't want to control myself." Then ask God to help you make the changes you need to make.

---

[1] Exodus 15:26

We go to great lengths to ensure that we don't eat anything poisonous, why then do we seem to be so careless in guarding our minds against poisonous thoughts? In the same way that we choose to eat foods that are good for our bodies, we need to purposely think thoughts that will enrich our minds.

Here are **Ten Healthy Thoughts**, written in quick, easy-to-remember sentences so that they can be dwelt on easily throughout the day:

- **"I can control my thoughts"** – Decide once and for all that you will do whatever it takes to 'take your thoughts captive' by thinking about your thinking and controlling the contents of your thoughts.
- **"I will never give up"** – Realise that this hardship is only for a time and that you can make it through.
- **"I can do this because God helps me"** [1] - Look at difficulties as challenges that you can overcome and learn from with God's help.
- **"I forgive quickly"** – Practice forgiving no matter how difficult it feels.
- **"I refuse to worry or fear because God is with me"** – There is no need to be anxious because you can trust God and He is in control.
- **"I love people"** – If someone irritates or hurts you, decide to love them anyway.
- **"I will enjoy every day"** [2] – Focus on beautiful things in your day, no matter how small.
- **"God is enough for me"** – When you find yourself wanting more, remind yourself that God is sufficient.
- **"God provides all I need"** [3] – Be assured that God is your provider and believe He will supply all your needs.
- **"God loves me"** [4] - No matter how many times you 'fail' in your eyes, remember His love for you does not change.

---

[1] Philippians 4:13
[2] Psalm 118:24
[3] Philippians 4:19
[4] 1 John 4:16

Remind yourself how much He loves you and tell Him how much you love Him!

The best way to train your mind to think Healthy Thoughts is to set yourself small goals. At first, try thinking healthily for half a day, then a full day, then two days and so on. Eventually this way of thinking will become habitual and your mind will be more balanced, happier and in line with God's will.

Help me to be more like Jesus.
Help me Lord to think about my thinking.
Make me aware, Holy Spirit, of negative thought patterns.
Help me to have self-control.
Help me to think before I speak.
Thank you that I can do anything I need to do because You are with me.
Help me to guard against negative thoughts like wanting to give up.

I Can't Help It

My Dearest Friend

You are weary of this perpetual uphill battle that you feel you are losing. I know you feel as though you don't want to keep trying anymore and you want to give up. You are tired of making promises that you break, tired of seeing disappointment in the eyes of those you love and tired of making an effort and failing. You think that there is no point in trying anymore because it just doesn't make any difference.

Listen carefully, my child: No matter what you are battling to overcome today – you are not an exception to my Word. It applies to you in whatever circumstance you are facing. I have promised that everyone can have freedom and live life to the full.

No matter what you are going through, you can be healed, delivered and saved,[1] because I came so that you could have life to the full.

Just keep remembering that you, and your situation, are not exceptions to any of the promises and regulations in my Word. If I say it is so, then it is.

Your Friend

Jesus

The Holy Spirit, like a GPS, helps us on the Road to Recovery.

I want to go to the place offered on the holiday brochure – the one away from this rut that has become my life. The glossy pictures promise peace away from this groove that has trapped me for so long. This won't be the first time I have tried to go on the Road to Recovery but each time my efforts have been frustrated and I have been forced to turn back.

---

[1] Joel 2:32

As I page through the well-worn brochure I see, yet again, that the directions for getting there are simple: "Remain on the road. It is straight and narrow." But as I look out of my sitting-room window, I see a tangle of so many roads leading out from my home that the confusion threatens to hold me back ... yet again.

My family, perched on the edge of their seats looking expectantly at me, try to egg me on: "We can't take this anymore. You need to do this for us," they say in unison, leaving me feeling as though they have ganged up on me. Fighting back rebellion that threatens to derail my good intentions, I nod and try to reassure them: "This time is different. This time I will do it." I can tell by their expressions that they remain unconvinced.

"How am I going to find my way there?" I wonder to myself as I look out the window again. A fog is creeping in over my upturned dustbin vomiting its contents over my unkempt lawn and over my house that has become so dilapidated that rain travels well-worn paths to buckets placed strategically throughout. It makes me feel as though I am suffocating – I have to escape. I have to find relief from this wreckage that I call my life. As I search for answers, an idea comes to me: "I could rely on my GPS, surely it will get me to that place where I can be better." Encouraged, I grab my car keys and head for the door.

As I set off, there is a nagging feeling that I have forgotten something, and I begin to panic about what I have left behind. As I begin to make a U-turn, I reason further that I need to take my family with me: "After all, I cannot do this on my own. It will be too much of a shock to my system if I just leave everyone and everything I have ever known. It won't even be fair on them!"

Disgruntled, my family pile in the car while I try to make a quick decision about what I will actually need for the journey and what I can do without. Then, with the car riding low under the extra weight, I set off once again. But as soon as I do, I realise my mistake: Everyone has different ideas about how to get there, and they are making their opinions known... loudly. My 'other-half' drones on and on that I should stop and ask for directions and moans constantly that I am either driving too fast or too slow or too close behind the other cars. Granny is whining non-stop about needing the bathroom and the kids are chanting: "Are we there yet?" Their cacophony makes it hard to concentrate on the road. So I turn back and drop them off. I can and will do this trip on my own.

Before I leave home I set the course on my GPS. I find Road to Recovery categorised under 'Historical Sites' – it has obviously been around for a while. Without the continual chatter from everyone else, I can easily focus on the voice of the GPS. As I follow its guidance, it leads me out of the mishmash of roads that is my neighbourhood and I feel hopeful anticipation. Perhaps this time will be different to all the other times I have tried.

Reaching the Road to Recovery, I see that the brochure didn't lie: the road is as straight as an angel's flight. Reassured that I am on the right path by the silence of my GPS, I continue.

After a boring, uneventful few hours, a huge neon sign flashes an advertisement for a pit stop up ahead. My tummy is grumbling and my mouth is dry. The water I had brought with me doesn't sound as tempting as that which I know will be on offer if I simply take a detour off the Road to Recovery.

As I turn to take the exit, the GPS, in its calm and measured way, warns me that I am going in the wrong direction: "Turn right at the next round-about." I ignore it. I am focused on looking for the next sign that will lead me to what I now crave.

The road twists and turns so many times that I no longer know where I am. The GPS is now blaring out directions so much so that I turn up the radio to drown out her incessant voice. The pit stop, glowing under its red neon light, is crouched around the following corner.

It is as seedy and tacky as it is expensive. I mumble, "rip off" under my breath, and look up to give the scantily dressed waitress my order. Her face is made of wood. She has strings attached to her arms and legs and as she walks back to the kitchen with my order, they trail behind her along the ground. All the other diners have clocks where their faces should have been. Maniacal music skittishly prances from the jukebox in the corner. It is difficult to eat because the walls seem to be closing in on me. The food makes me feel ill and the drink intoxicates - the whole experience leaves me feeling dizzy, dirty and damned.

As I walk back to my car I realise that I have doubled back and have virtually landed in the same place I was when I began my journey. Slightly despondent, but also more determined after my 'dirty experience', I reset my GPS and continue once more. This time I am determined to get back onto the Road to Recovery and stay on it until I reach my destination.

I feel better as soon as I turn back onto the highway. Deeply in thought about the detour I had just made, a sign flashes past me. As I drive along I begin to wonder what it might have said. When an exit comes up, I begin to panic that maybe I am meant to have taken it. The GPS is silent. Confused and slightly panicked, I take the next exit. I am barely conscious of doing it – I simply take the turn. The road is desolate and going in the opposite direction to the one I am meant to be on. I begin to feel lost and immediately turn the radio down. The measured voice of the GPS, calmly giving instructions, can now be heard. This time I follow, as an old Turkish saying comes to mind: "No matter how far you have gone down a wrong road, turn back."

Once on the Road to Recovery again, I feel like nothing can prevent me from reaching my goal. I begin to sing merrily to myself and smile at the passengers in the other cars. Feeling particularly carefree, I ignore the warnings that my mother always gave me, and stop to pick up a Hitchhiker. As soon as he gets into my car, a wave of pungent body odour hits me. But I am used to bad smells from those I used to hang around with and get chatting to pass the time. He is vague about where he is from but he says he knows a much shorter route to where I am going. He is so convincing that I follow his instructions, take the next exit, make a left turn at the crossroad and go under the bridge. I have no clue where I am, but presume my well-dressed travelling companion does. After a very long time I realise we are back at the same diner that I left hours previously – back almost to where I had begun my journey. Devastated, but now in need of rest, I walk into the heaving diner, past the people clocks, past a cat dancing on its hind legs, past two bar stools in a boxing match and place my order with the wooden waitress. I scoff down my food, trying to ignore the chaos waging around me. This time I feel so sick after eating that I can barely walk out. Retching and guarding against fainting, I make it to the door. The Hitchhiker is close on my heels: "If you eat something else you will feel better." He says. "Just one more..." I say "No," and tell him that I no longer want him to accompany me on my journey. He immediately slinks off to speak to a person, one with a normal looking face, who has just arrived.

Sick to my stomach and confused by my own brain, I drive back onto the Road to Recovery. I am deeply saddened by all the time I know I have wasted and I now become even more determined to stick on the road until I reach my goal. I begin to play word games in my mind: "The Road to Recovery is paved with good intentions." My intentions are good – nothing is going to stop me this time. The road is straight, and I know that if I just listen carefully to my GPS, I will reach my destination and rest, recuperation and recovery will be mine.

Whatever you are battling, this Road to Recovery is one that you will need to take: People will try to tell you how to do it and for what reason; you may want to return to that which feels more familiar; you may make friends with people who have a bad influence on you and the demonic may influence your thinking. By listening to the Voice of the Holy Spirit, we can guard against taking detours and stay on the road. The Spirit will tell you when you have taken a wrong turn or when you need to do a U-turn. CS Lewis writes: "Progress means getting nearer to the place you want to be. And if you have taken a wrong turning, then to go forward does not get you any nearer. If you are on the wrong road, progress means doing an about-turn and walking back to the right road; and in that case the man who turns back soonest is the most progressive man."

But sometimes the 'noise' from our past is so loud that we are no longer able to hear the Holy Spirit's promptings.

I could not be called a 'progressive man' at all. I took so many wrong turns when I was trying to give up drinking that I lost count. In an attempt to drown out my painful memories, I sometimes drowned out this Voice. I record one of these detours in my diary:

"Lindy (my sister) and her family come to stay with us over Easter. Without giving it any serious thought I started drinking and then went out on the town. I couldn't get up for Easter morning and the usual guilt and self-loathing followed. Needless to say my family were concerned and mum said she was 'mortally wounded'. I asked Richard to get the AA Handbook from the Internet. I don't want to deal with this; all I want is for my problem to go away completely. I want to live life victoriously through Jesus Christ."

I read the AA Handbook and went to their meetings a few times, but I found praying to 'a higher power' unacceptable and could not relate to the other alcoholics spiritually. I also thought that if I confess: 'I am an alcoholic' for the rest of my life it was as though I was admitting that I would always be that way. I wanted to say: 'I am healed of being an alcoholic,' and then carry on drinking moderately. These were, of course, all just excuses in a long line of other excuses. They were excuses that led to detours. Years later, when I had truly run out of them, I went back to AA and got equipped with some valuable tools and insights that helped me on my Road to Recovery. But that came much later - I stayed weaving on and off that Straight Road for a while longer.

In those days I was convinced that I couldn't stick to anything. I wrote: "So often I watch people get deeply inspired and then totally committed to a 'cause' or 'direction' – nothing seems to deter them on their victorious march. I want that in my life, instead of this un-victorious wafting I seem to be prone to. I knew that the only right direction was the one Jesus wants for me and that all true inspiration comes from Him. I have sometimes felt that I had grasped this, only to see the most intense intentions and projects crumble by the wayside. There have been so many projects that I have started with great gusto, only to fizzle out before coming to fruition – acting in movies, being a gospel singer, teaching underprivileged children, inventing a board game, counselling battered women, to name a few. Many times I wondered: "Why can't I stick to things and see them through? Trying to give up drinking was no exception – I just seemed incapable of doing it.

A few years after the last diary entry, I still seem to be struggling: "I must change or I'm going to die. I know I can be different. I see where I am and the gap is so wide that the only bridge is God – only some Power as great as He can span the chasm. I need You, God, in my life permanently, not intermittently." I relate to Paul who writes: "I do not understand what I do. For what I want to do I do not do, but what I hate I do."[1] Whether you are battling an addiction, a compulsive behaviour or a mental health problem you may, like Paul, feel as though you do not understand why you do the things you do and why you cannot stop doing them.

Before we embark on this journey down the Road to Recovery we need to ask three important questions: Do I need to take this journey? Is there any point in going on this journey? Do I want to go on this journey?

Do I need to take this journey?

We are often the last to know that we have an addiction or a mental health problem. Below are two checklists that may help indicate whether you need to take this journey or not. The most common **Signs of Addiction**:

- **Isolation** – You may find yourself withdrawing emotionally or literally. Addicts often excuse their behaviour as 'needing to relax' or that they need to 'relieve the tension' or because it helps them 'to forget.' They think they owe it to themselves to continue in their habit. They prefer to spend their time with people who have similar addictions, so when they are 'trying to kick the habit' they tend to avoid old acquaintances and end up being isolated.
- **Secrecy** - You may try to hide your addiction from others. This also leads to isolation.
- You may have **lost interest** in activities that you previously enjoyed.

---

[1] Romans 7:15

217

- **Mood swings** – these may include irritability, depression, fatigue, sweating and anxiety. These negative emotions can improve suddenly once you have been 'satisfied' by your habit.
- **Money troubles** – 'Feeding' your addiction can be costly, either because it is an expensive habit or because you have less time for work.
- **Dishonest behaviours** – you may be lying and even stealing to cover or support your addiction.
- **Denial** – You may deny that you have a problem and excuse your behaviour by saying things like: "I can't help it!"
- **Withdrawal** – withdrawal symptoms can vary from fairly minor feelings of agitation to major sickness and even death (as in the case of serious drug abuse). When withdrawing from major addictions it is always advisable to seek medical help.

The longer you stay on an addictive substance the greater the damage to your body and the more difficult it becomes to stop. Therefore it is important that, as soon as you suspect you have a problem, you take immediate action to deal with it.

If you are unsure about whether you are suffering from a mental illness, this list outlining the **Early Warning Signs** may be an indicator that you need to get help.

- Mistrustfulness or suspiciousness
- Changes in personal hygiene
- Emotions that do not fit the situation
- Vague or rambling speech
- Speech that does not make sense
- Unusual ideas or beliefs
- Suicidal thinking
- Extreme anger, hostility or violence

This list is not definitive and if you do not experience any of these symptoms it does not necessarily mean you do not have a problem. With some types of mental illness, such as bipolar disorder or schizophrenia, you may not realize the extent of your problem. Friends or family may think that: "something is not quite right."

Seeking medical help is advisable in these circumstances because early intervention can help reduce the severity of an illness and it may even be possible to prevent or delay the development of a major illness altogether.

Is there any point in going on this journey?

Are you thinking that your problem is too big to overcome? Perhaps you have tried so many different treatments and methods that you are ready to give up. Maybe you are even thinking of giving up on yourself because you have tried and failed so many times before. If you are think: "There is no point in trying anymore, I may as well just let this take over," then you have decided that you, or your situation, are the exception to the rule.

God offers *all of us* freedom and life abundant and therefore they must be possible to attain – no exceptions! Your problem is not new to God and it is definitely not so uncommon that God cannot deal with it. Here are some examples of **Exception Thoughts**:

- **"Everyone has tried to sort this out**. There is just no use trying anymore" - Maybe a professional has told you that your problem is unique or maybe you have been diagnosed with a disorder that you will 'just have to live with' or maybe you have even been called 'a freak' because of it. But although others can be ignorant, uneducated and cruel, God sees and He understands your struggle. Your situation is not unique to God and the Bible say that nothing is too difficult for Him.[1]
- **"I was just born this way"** - But if God made you that way then He will give you the power to overcome all obstacles, but you need to be absolutely sure that the way you are is it in alignment with His Word? For example, if He says you are not to be addicted to strong drink, you cannot pass your addiction off on having a genetic predisposition for it. If your behaviour goes against the teaching of the Word, then you need to change your behaviour. However, if you were born with a physical disability, He can give you the power to live a

---

[1] Jeremiah 32:27

happy and productive life while you hope and pray for healing.

- **"The way I am is normal"** - Perhaps you have been brainwashed by the media or 'scientific evidence' that condones a habit or lifestyle contrary to Scripture. But the promises of the Word are for those who trust and obey.
- **"God doesn't say anything about my problem** in the Bible" - Maybe you think that your problem is not mentioned in the Bible, for example, bulimia or self-harm. However, it does say: "Do you not know that your body is a temple of the Holy Spirit...You are not your own; you were bought at a price. Therefore honour God with your body."[1]

Jesus tells us why He came and why he was willing to die such an excruciating death on the cross: "The thief comes only to steal and kill and destroy; I have come that they may have life, and have it to the full."[2] Believe that your problem is not an exception for God and that you can live 'life to the full' and make the decision to take this journey.

Do I want to go on this journey?

Perhaps you feel that giving up your habit, lifestyle or addiction will not give you a fuller life. You may not even want to stop because of the pleasure it brings you. Maybe you even feel that you *need* it and that life would not be worth living without it? Maybe you feel trapped between your desire to be obedient to God and your desire for that which gives you pleasure. If so, then you have been trapped by a lie, which is: "I cannot be happy without this." Whether the 'thing' that is making you happy is a substance, an imaginary friend, a persistent habit or urge that brings relief or comfort, a 'wrong' relationship, a mental 'high' or a thirst or hunger – the lie remains the same: "You will not be happy unless you continue thinking/doing/having it." Remember, you are no exception – you can have an 'abundant life' and be happy, free from whatever it is that is holding you in its clutches.

---

[1] 1 Corinthians 6:19
[2] John 10:10

I wrote this entry in my diary: "Dearest Father God, I have really messed up my life. I never got control over my emotions or my life and selfishly sought death. Paradoxically though, I loved You and needed You and sought You. But neither quest, for death or You, was single-minded. I now choose Life, I now choose You. I now ask You to intervene if my flesh chooses death. Be my strength. For in You I can trust but I still have to prove myself to me. For I believe You love me still and yet I can only see my past failures. Pick me up Lord, and put me on higher ground. Take me to that place I can't seem to get to - that I can't see. That place closer to You and further from me. I chose Life Lord. I choose You again."

I had decided once more to embark on the Road to Recovery and what I discovered was incredible: He didn't just help me to stop drinking alcohol; He got me to a point where I didn't want it anymore. You too can become happy to be without that thing which is holding you captive. He will not only make you stronger to resist it but He will take away your desire for it. Happiness without that thing that is holding you captive is possible. God can heal, restore, rebuild and give us the strength, not only endure while we are on the road, but to enjoy the journey. Faith must result in action or it will die - our Christ-like characters need to grow or they will fade away.

Whether you are suffering from a persistent habit, an addiction or a mental health problem, the next step after believing that God can and will help you is to give yourself the **PEP Talk**. This consists of quick reminders to help you on the Road to Recovery. PEP stands for:

- Persevere
- Educate
- Pray

Persevere

We need to remind ourselves to persevere - especially when the going gets tough. Perseverance may be defined as steadfastly continuing on a course of action in spite of the obstacles, difficulties and discouragements that may be encountered. If you are battling mental illness, persevere with your treatment, persevere in praying for a miracle and in searching for what God wants you to do.

The Bible instructs us to: "Make every effort to add to your faith goodness and to goodness, knowledge; and to knowledge, self-control; and to self-control, perseverance; and to perseverance, godliness; and to godliness, brotherly kindness; and to brotherly kindness, love. For if you possess these qualities in increasing measure, they will keep you from being ineffective and unproductive in your knowledge of our Lord Jesus Christ."[1] While God empowers and enables us to overcome, there is a responsibility on us to practice these qualities listed above – one of them being perseverance. We are called upon to persevere during trials, sickness, persecution and affliction in the face of temptation.

There are two misconceptions about temptation - one is that only 'bad' people are tempted. It is simply not true – even Jesus was tempted in the desert by Satan,[2] and all Christians are tempted many times during their lives. No one is exempt. There is no 'level' that you can achieve in your Christian life where you will be free from temptation. Of course the things that tempt you today will not necessarily be the same as those that tempt you in the future. You can get to a point where that which used to be tempting to you, no longer bothers you at all. It can become easier to say 'no' to temptation; this can either be instant or take time. But, no matter how impossible it feels to you, God has promised he will not allow us to be tempted to the point of not being able to handle it: "And God is faithful; he will not let you be tempted beyond what you can bear. But when you are tempted, he will also provide a way out so that you can stand up under it."[3] Remember there are no exceptions – all temptations can be resisted.

Another misconception about temptation is that it is a sin. Thinking about something sinful is not a sin but letting it settle down and take root in your thinking is. Martin Luther once said: "You cannot keep

---

[1] 2 Peter 5-8
[2] Luke 4:1
[3] 1 Corinthians 10:13

birds from flying over your head, but you can keep them from building a nest in your hair."

For years I asked God to take away the temptation of alcohol and I got angry with Him when He didn't do it. I even excused my drinking by saying to myself: "Well, if He cannot be bothered to heal me of my drinking problem (and it would be so easy for Him to do), then why should I bother trying!" What I was failing to understand was that while He may not take the temptation away, He will teach us how to resist and give us the strength we need to overcome. I then began praying for the right thing: self-control when faced with the temptation to drink.

The Bible says we are meant to endure when we are tempted: "Blessed is the man who perseveres under trial,"[1] and the King James Bible says: "...that endureth temptation," going on to promise what will happen if we do: "for once he has been approved, he will receive the crown of life which the Lord has promised to those who love Him." This 'crown of life' speaks of authority given to those who see it through to the end. When you are obedient in small things, you will be given authority over bigger things on earth and in heaven. If we resist the temptation to give in to sin, we will be blessed in various ways, including:

- Blessed by not doing the wrong thing anymore – which always leaves you worse off e.g. you don't gamble and lose all your money or you don't drink and get a hangover.
- Blessed by our characters being strengthened – we become better people in so many ways. For example we become more disciplined or more tolerant of others.
- Blessed with a deeper relationship with God.
- Blessed by a special reward in Heaven.

It would be impossible for me to cover the specific aspects of all cures to all addictions and mental health problems in this book, so I cannot stress enough how important it is for you to get support for this journey. I learnt invaluable lessons from going to AA. For example, I found it very disheartening to think: "I will never drink

---

[1] James 1:12

again." The prospect of a life without alcohol just looked too huge to comprehend. So, I learnt to give myself smaller goals: "One day at a time." And I sent myself more manageable and 'do-able' goals. "I will not drink today." If you cannot find a therapist, psychologist, counsellor or support group for your particular problem in your community, then try to find support online. The advantage of online support is that you can remain anonymous – even though all real-life support groups should offer this privacy.

Educate Yourself

Once you have decided to travel the Road to Recovery, your next step is to educate yourself about your problem. Find out as much as you can by seeking the advice of professionals and doing your own research about your mental illness, habit or particular addiction. God says: "my people are destroyed from lack of knowledge."[1]

In this chapter we have considered only those addictions that have been known to lead to suicide. Cigarette addiction has not been covered, even though it may lead directly to death. It may also lead to a point where you may want to kill yourself because you have been diagnosed with a terminal cigarette-related illness.

Your suicidal thoughts may well be linked to your addiction or mental health problem. Statistics vary around the world, but according to studies, over 50% of all suicides are associated with alcohol and drug dependence. Substance abuse is the second most common risk factor for suicide after major depression and bipolar disorder. However mental health problems and substance abuse cannot be dealt with separately, they are often intricately intertwined in relation to suicide. It is estimated that 90% of all people who take their lives were suffering from mental illness or substance abuse problems at the time of their death.

Alcohol and drug abuse often lead to suicide for a number of reasons:

---

[1] Hosea 4:6

- They increase psychological distress and feelings of hopelessness, loneliness and depression.
- They enhance and facilitate aggressive behaviour, including self-aggression.
- They change an individual's expectations of their lives.
- They inhibit effective coping strategies.
- They often lead to social decline e.g. marriage break-up.
- They can lead to depression and loss of self-esteem.
- They produce increased impulsiveness and a weakening of normal restraints against dangerous behaviour.
- They promise to ease the distress associated with the act of suicide.

Many of the points in the above list could refer to other addictions, like gambling (between 12 and 24% of pathological gamblers attempt suicide), pornography, self-harm, sex addiction or even an addiction to shopping.

So it is a crucial step on the Road to Recovery to get a diagnosis and to learn as much as you can about your addiction or mental health problems. One of my problems, with not being able to give up alcohol, was that I didn't agree with the diagnosis. When I looked at other alcoholics, I came to the conclusion that I wasn't one.

Recent studies by the National Institute on Alcohol Abuse and Alcoholism (NIAAA) have dispelled the myth of the 'typical alcoholic' and identified five subtypes:

- **Young Adult** Alcoholics - Most are in their mid-20s and had early onset of regular drinking and early onset alcohol problems. More than half come from families with alcoholism, and about half have a psychiatric diagnosis of antisocial personality disorder.
- **Young Antisocial** Alcoholics who often have mental health problems - More than 75% smoke cigarettes and marijuana, and many also have cocaine and opiate addictions.
- **Functional** Alcoholics - Typically middle-aged, well-educated, with stable jobs and families. About one-third have a multigenerational family history of alcoholism. One-

quarter had major depressive illness at some time in their lives.

- **Intermediate Familial** Alcoholics - Middle-aged with about half from families with multigenerational alcoholism. Almost half have had clinical depression, and 20% have had bipolar disorder. Most smoke cigarettes, and nearly one in five report cocaine and marijuana use.
- **Chronic Severe** Alcoholics - Mostly middle-aged individuals who had early onset of drinking and alcohol problems. High rates of antisocial personality disorder and criminality.

Once I was able to see that I didn't have to fit the standard view of being an alcoholic in order to have a problem, I could deal with it. I now find it easy not to drink, and I can drink moderately, however I choose not to. My husband enjoys a couple of glasses of wine with his dinner on occasion and it does not bother me at all. I have fun when I go out and don't feel like I need it to help me to enjoy myself. When hardships come, the bottom of a bottle is not my first port-of-call as it once was.

While you are educating yourself about the symptoms of your problem, the treatments available and receiving advice from others who have overcome, remember to pray.

Pray

The Bible offers two more ways to overcome temptation: "Watch and pray so that you will not fall into temptation. The Spirit is willing, but the body is weak."[1]

'Watching' means that one remains vigilantly on guard. I have found that planning in advance how I will respond, helps me to resist temptation. It is not always easy to respond in the correct manner when you are caught unawares, so try to plan strategies ahead of time. Ask God to help you to recognise the situations or people that can cause you to give in to the temptation. Be determined to get good at spotting the things in your life that cause you to 'fall' and run from them.

---

[1] Matthew 26:41

But, at the point when you are about to reach for that bottle, give in to that habit, surrender to that addiction or fall into that damaging thought pattern, that is the exact moment that you need to cry out to God. At these crucial, life-changing times "Help!" is sometimes all we can muster – and it is enough – God will hear. Martin Luther said: "The fewer the words, the better the prayer."

Please give me a sound, balanced mind.
Lord show me the truth about this problem – show me if this is something that is contrary to Your Word.
I am sorry Lord, for all the times I have given in to temptation.
Please heal me miraculously.
Help me to endure this treatment.
Help me to recognise when temptation comes.
Help me to persevere when faced with temptation.
Help me to be self-controlled.
Help me to avoid the people and situations that cause me to fall into sin.
Protect me from the evil schemes of the devil.

I Cannot Go On Like This Anymore

My Dear Child

Inevitably, you will be let down by things of this world, so you would be wise to place your hope in Me alone. When you do, I will show you how to remain hopeful, no matter what is going on around you.

You will become brave and strong, strengthened by My power. Endurance and patience will be yours as you rest, content in my will for you. You share in the inheritance of all believers in the kingdom of light, having been rescued from the dominion of darkness, so live your life in hopeful expectancy.

My hope will see you through all the storms of life.

Your

Redeemer

I barely saw my handsome Uncle John when he walked up the path to our house, I only had eyes for what he was holding – a giant, stuffed pink bunny. Laughing at my uncontainable excitement as I jumped up and down, he explained that the bunny had called to him from the shelf in the shop: "Do you know any pretty little girl who will love me?" I was thrilled to be his mommy and I called him Bugsy.

We went everywhere together. He was hugged, thrown, dragged, pulled, snuggled and loved until he was very threadbare. I chatted to him about everything, and he listened intently. At first, Bugsy had a rather charming, dishevelled look, like a gentleman in a romantic novel, but later, when his stuffing began to fall out he looked as though he needed an operation. As he sat forlorn on my bed, I imagined him saying: "Nita, please help me, I am falling apart!"

One sombre day, my Mum became a physician and I a nurse as, taking out needle and thread, she attempted to sew poor Bugsy together again. While nursing him back to health I noticed that the stitches were coming apart and the stuffing was forcing its way through the holes. As I looked at his broken body, I realised he would never be up for rough and tumble anymore. He had become delicate.

Suddenly I had a bright idea and, taking a little blue jumper from one of my dolls, I put it over poor Bugsy's patched up body. He had a new lease on life. Even though he had bits broken and patched up on the inside, he had a new outer layer that kept him together. Bugsy was ready for a few more years of rough and tumble!

I have become a bit like that giant bunny and it feels like my body is 'falling apart'. It has been four years since I first began to experience pain that felt like shards of glass scratching me on the inside, with hot lightning bolts shooting down my legs. Headaches were frequent and lasted for days and I was always bone-weary. Doctors are still not certain about what is causing my pain but they have made several diagnoses, including interstitial cystitis and pelvic dysfunction. I have tried well over twenty types of painkillers, to no avail. Very often the side effects of the medication out-weigh the modest relief I sometimes receive. I have run the gauntlet of medical professionals, who have prodded and probed and found all sorts of other little things wrong, but nothing offers any real relief from the relentless pain.

For years I looked for help and also spent hours on the Internet trying to find a possible diagnosis and cure. While 'Googling your pain' can be very helpful, and I think we should take an active and informed part in our medical health, it can also be alarming. It can cause great anxiety as one wades through a quagmire of possible explanations for one's pain, thinking that they may apply to your specific condition. While it is good to do your own research, especially on the side effects of medication, when you have any concerns, it is best to take them to your doctor.

But, until I found relief I felt, along with Bugsy and the psalmist, that I was 'falling apart': "Everything's falling apart on me God; put me together again with Your Word."[1] I sometimes felt that my stuffing was falling out faster than I could put it back together again as I battled to get answers for my problem while the pain persisted unabated. The psalmist's plea became mine as I cried out to God for help. Faithful as always, He answered by covering me with a little blue jumper – called Hope. Such a small and seemingly insignificant word, once understood, gave me what I needed to continue.

When you are without hope, you believe there is no chance of anything good happening in your life and you think nothing will change. This kind of thinking is extremely destructive and will lead you on a downward spiral. An emotion common to suicidal people is an overwhelming feeling of hopelessness.

So what is hope? I used to think it was a vague thought that maybe something good would happen, like: "I really hope that will happen." But that is not what the Bible means when it talks about hope. Hope is a real, conscious thought. The dictionary says it is "to desire with expectation of attainment" or "to expect with confidence". It is a favourable and confident expectation, synonymous with trust. It is the voice of purpose - where dreams begin. It speaks to you and reassures you that 'this too will pass.' Hope reminds me of the times I used to go sailing:

The sky is pregnant with rain and scowling over the little yacht. It once felt big, secure and robust, able to sail the world, but it now feels tiny, a speck on the bulging, dark ocean. You read the weather warning and check your co-ordinates and realize you are in the path of a force ten storm. Forty-eight knot gale force winds are expected with thirty foot waves. You see it coming but are powerless to stop it.

So it is with us: inescapable storms of life come.

You furl the sails. It is hard work bringing them down on your own. You begin to wish that you had someone to help you, but you were too busy preparing for the trip to ask anyone on board, besides you know that no-one can do anything as well as you can. Now you stand

---

[1] Psalm 119:107 The Message

drenched, on the rolling deck, trying to pull down whipping sails in the icy wind. You know you have to try to do everything you can to prepare for the storm.

You frantically look around for anything to ease the blow that is sure to come. You try to slow your boat by releasing the sea anchor, hoping that this little parachute will give you some control. You secure everything that could blow away or whip around and cause damage and then, thinking there is very little else to do, you baton down the hatches and go below.

The storm rages on for hours as you try to comfort yourself with something to eat and drink, but nothing eases the fear that is taking hold of your heart. You feel very alone. No-one else is going through this. You *are* alone.

Looking out of the porthole, you can barely see anything except the white of the foam-topped waves. The noise becomes deafening, like some vicious sea monster circling; ready to devour. Panic grips as your mind begins to race - cataloguing all the horrors to come. You feel entombed and claustrophobic and want to get out, but the storm is so fierce now that you doubt you will be able to open the hatch.

Then, almost imperceptibly, you think about God. He is all-powerful, surely He can help. You pray. Nothing happens. The boat lunges forward over the top of a wave, sending all your books and crockery crashing to the cabin floor. "Fat lot of good that prayer did!" you moan. The boat suddenly banks, sending you flying across onto the bunk on the port side. Terrified, thinking that it is a vengeful act of God, you cry out an apology to the Almighty.

When you slowly open your eyes, scared of what you might see, you think you see something shining through the porthole. You rub your eyes again to try and focus. It is a light! You realize that if it wasn't for that last jolt that sent you flying to the other side of the cabin, you may never have seen it.

This is how it is with many things in our lives: That which we think is there to cause harm, is often the beginning of something that will save.

But you are not sure it will save. Perhaps it is just a low star, or another storm tossed boat or your imagination. Suddenly a massive wave hits the boat broadside and you are slammed against the wall of the cabin. You open your eyes and realize your face is pressed up against the porthole and you have no choice but to look out. Past the angry waves, past the foam flying off their crests, over the dark depths you see the light of a lighthouse!

"The Lord your God is with you, He is mighty to save."[1]

You pull yourself up and get yourself into a position where you can focus on it exclusively, as you do, the light seems to grow larger and the waves smaller.

"Turn your eyes upon Jesus
Look full in His wonderful face
And the things of the world
Will grow strangely dim
In the light of His Glory and Grace."[2]

It seems as though you sit staring at the light, propped up on your aching arms, for what seems like an age – but the light does not seem to be getting any closer. Panic sets in: "Maybe I'm going to sail right past. Ah, it's probably for someone else and not for me," you think with resignation.

"He gives strength to the weary
And increases the power of the weak
...but those who hope in the Lord
Will renew their strength."[3]

As you focus once again on the light, you see that while it remains unmoving, you are still being tossed like a ragdoll. It is as though it has been there from generation to generation, solid and immovable. It was there long before you were born and will be there long after

---

[1] Zephaniah 3:17
[2] Composer - Helen Lemmel,1922
[3] Isaiah 40:29

you die. Its unchanging, faithful service gives you assurance as you contemplate how it has guided, saved and led so many others to safety for so long. It is a stronghold in times of trouble, a refuge for the weary and a beacon of hope for the hopeless. It rewards those who follow with shelter from the storm.

A strange thing begins to occur, as you focus and become more determined to follow the light, it is as though it is getting closer. You feel energized. Suddenly there is a deafening screech followed by a loud crash. The gut-wrenching truth becomes apparent as you realise that your mast has broken and you are in more trouble than ever before. A glance towards the light tells you that it is not getting closer fast enough. "If I don't get there now, it will be too late!" you decide. The howl of the wind seems to get louder.

"So do not throw away your confidence; it will be richly rewarded. You need to persevere so that when you have done the will of God, you will receive what he has promised...But we are not those who shrink back and are destroyed, but of those who believe and are saved."[1]

The noise of the storm becomes more real than the memory of the light, and the comforting thoughts you had about its promise of hope, now seem as far away as the light itself.

"But when he asks, he must believe and not doubt, because he who doubts is like a wave of the sea, blown and tossed by the wind. That man should not think he will receive anything from the Lord; he is a double-minded man, unstable in all he does" [2]

Hours have gone by since seeing the light, so you begin to feel dead inside, beyond hopelessness and ready for death. "I am so tired that I probably imagined it," you say out loud to the empty cabin. "It was never there. I just wanted to believe it was there so that I would feel better."

---

[1] Hebrews 10:35-39
[2] James 1:7

"For in this hope we were saved. But hope that is seen is no hope at all. Who hopes for what he already has? But if we hope for what we do not yet have, we wait for it patiently."[1]

Sitting on the bunk, alone and lost, you take stock of your situation. No matter which way you look at it, you cannot see anything else you can do or any way out of it. Your only hope lies in following that light and getting to the safety of the harbour. Once again the thought of it gives you a glimmer of hope: "It is there. I can be saved. I could be all snug in a bed with a cup of hot chocolate soon." Thoughts of people and things you love begin to caress your mind. They are there, waiting for you to return: "This will pass. Thank you, God." You pray, a glimmer of hope beginning to stir.

"Be joyful in hope."[2]

"Rejoice in the Lord always. I will say it again: Rejoice! The Lord is near. Do not be anxious about anything, but in everything, by prayer and petition, with thanksgiving, present your requests to God. And the peace of God, which transcends all understanding, will guard your hearts and your minds in Christ Jesus."[3]

Suddenly you notice a light shining across the cabin table! You look out and with elation you see that you have drawn closer to the lighthouse. Now, even though the storm continues to rage relentlessly outside, something has changed. You feel a kind of joy that makes no sense at all. "Woohoo," you shout excitedly, "thank you Mr Lighthouse person!" you shout, feeling silly and happy.

"May the God of hope fill you with all joy and peace as you trust in him, so that you may overflow with hope by the power of the Holy Spirit."[4]

The boat has changed course and the wind now seems to be carrying it against the tide towards the light. It is as though the wind is on your side. "I know, I can help this go a lot quicker," you think

---

[1] Romans 8:24
[2] Romans 12:12
[3] Philippians 4:4-6
[4] Romans 15:13

excitedly. A plan begins to form in your mind and, braving the fifty knot winds, you open the hatch. Water pours into the cabin and the rain lashes down but, thankful of your wet-weather gear that is keeping you as dry as a bone, you stagger to the tiller. You can barely grip the wet, slippery wheel between your hands. Once you do, it seems as though it has a mind of its own and it pulls against every effort you make to turn it. The yacht seems to be going in the wrong direction, so you try to come about. Realising that nothing you do is going to help, you return to the cabin exhausted by your own efforts.

"Trust in the Lord with all your heart
And lean not on your own understanding;
In all your ways acknowledge him.
And he will make your paths straight."[1]

Knowing that you have done everything you can, a thought occurs to you: "There is nothing more I can do about this." Surrendering to whatever the future may hold, you secure the hatch and lie down to rest. "Rest is fuel for the soul," you think as you drink deep of its power.

"Rest in the Lord and wait patiently for him" [2]

As the light from the lighthouse fills the cabin, you go out onto deck and start the engines. The battered little boat revs into action. Keeping your eyes firmly on the light, you negotiate your way safely into the harbour. As you jump off the boat to tie the ropes around the bollards, you are overwhelmingly grateful to be on solid ground.

"Your path led through the sea,
Your way through the mighty waters,
Though your footprints were not seen."[3]

Perhaps the storms of life have hit you hard and maybe you feel that the magnitude of your problem is so great that you cannot see your

---

[1] Proverbs 3:5
[2] Psalm 37:3 KJV
[3] Psalm 77:16

way out. Hopelessness has set in and you are screaming inside: "I cannot go on like this anymore."

You may feel:

- That nothing good will ever happen to you - you, think that these feelings are justified given what doctors or others have told you or what you 'know' about yourself.
- Alienated – you have thoughts that you don't fit in and that you are different to everyone else.
- Abandoned – you feel that you have been deserted by God or others during your darkest hour of need.
- Powerless to do anything that may bring about lasting change. Nothing can take you out of this mess, restore that relationship, heal that broken heart, help you to give up that habit or take away that pain.
- Incapable – you don't feel up to making the changes necessary.
- Overpowered – people you know (or your circumstances) have left you feeling crushed, bullied and 'trodden on.'
- Trapped – by your own actions and thoughts or the behaviour of others.
- Exposed and threatened and unable to do anything about it.

Whether the weight of your worries and burdens have been laid on you by your own actions or the behaviours of others, you may have decided that there is no way out. You can't after all, argue against the facts.

Hope is the little blue jumper covering these facts. We worship a God who is greater than the facts because He can do anything. He is all-knowing, all-seeing, all-powerful and wise beyond our imaginations. He promises to save you from the storm and you can be certain that He keeps His promises.

So, how do we put on this hope jumper? How can we attain this hope that leads to joy that is solid and lasting; the kind of joy that will see us through when the going gets tough and the pain feels unbearable? Then, having found it, how do we keep it no matter what? How do we change from thinking: "I really hope this will happen" to being a 'prisoner of hope'?

God promises that if we become 'prisoners of hope He will restore double what we have forfeited: "Return to your fortress, O prisoners of hope; even now I announce that I will restore twice as much to you."[1] In other words, where we were once trapped by negativity, now we can be locked up like a prisoner within the bounds of hope. It is as though we become helpless against hope as all that we do, think or say becomes subjected to an all-encompassing hope that things will change and that God has a plan. This hope should and can surround us, inhabit our thoughts and govern our lives.

But you cannot have hope without trusting God. After all, you are not relying on yourself to get you out of this mess. You are not relying on the doctors or other people or the government. It is God who you are trusting. We have hope when we trust despite the evidence. When everything looks like it is against us and there is no hope, we believe that things can improve. When you cry out to Him to help, He will rescue, restore, heal and deliver. Knowing that our God is a God of hope, and that everything He says is filled with hope, we can become 'prisoners of hope.' Once we do, miracles happen.

Maybe you have run to church, during these dark hours, and knelt in the pews hoping that the fire of God would reign down on you and wipe away all hardship. "How," you think as you kneel there, "can I get the fire of God in my life?"

This is an acronym, **The Pews Fuse**, listing the first steps to help regain and maintain hope:

- Pour Out Your Heart
- Expectantly Believe
- Wait Patiently
- Seek God

---

[1] Zechariah 9:12

Pour Out Your Heart

David tells us how we can speak to God: "Trust in Him at all times...and pour out your heart to him."[1] This suggests that we splurge our thoughts, hardships and desires to God. It sometimes takes us getting to our lowest point, our darkest moment, before we cry out to God in this manner. C. S. Lewis writes: "God whispers in our pleasures, speaks in our conscience, but shouts in our pain. It is His megaphone to rouse a deaf world."[2]

The Creator of the Universe is giving you an invitation today: "Come to me, all you who are weary and burdened, and I will give you rest. Take my yoke upon you and learn from me, for I am gentle and humble in heart, and you will find rest for your souls. For my yoke is easy and my burden is light." Our gentle Lord is waiting for you to come to Him and tell Him all that is on your mind.

Expectantly Believe

Once you have poured out your heart to Him, you may need to wait a while before you see any results or get any answers. This wait can be more tolerable if you live your life with expectancy. According to the free dictionary online despair is "a complete absence of hope," but I think it is also the absence of expectation. Hope can be defined as the confident expectation of good – we believe that something good is going to happen to us, to our family or our country. Those who despair have no expectations of good occurring.

We can choose to wallow in despair or we can make a decision to be a hero to ourselves – to rise up and believe against all odds that things will change for the better.

For many years I found it hard to expect that anything good would happen to me. This is probably understandable given the years of pain, abuse and trauma that I had suffered. Slowly, imperceptibly, I sunk into a destructive pattern of negative thought that had

---

[1] Psalm 62:6
[2] Matthew 11:28-30

detrimental consequences. I felt, with every suicide attempt, that all expectancy of hope in the future drained away from me. It sometimes felt as if something else was robbing me of hope. I wasn't wrong.

The devil will send one trouble after another into our lives until we begin to believe that nothing good will ever happen. We sometimes stand in agreement with him when we, like some harbinger of gloom, tell all who will listen about our woeful prediction of future tribulation. He wants you to believe that nothing good will happen to you because he is well aware that this will lead to hopelessness and perhaps even suicide. He steals hope by planting doubt and negativity in our hearts and as long as he can keep us talking about how awful our futures look, he knows it is only a matter of time before we will want to give up. When you start down the path of trying to find hope, you will discover that the devil will connive to deter you. He will try to give you every reason to think that your situation is hopeless. That is when you need to say: "I refuse to lose hope!"

Even though your troubles remain, you become expectant of change. That expectation for the better is hope. When I was a child, one of my favourite things was getting a lucky packet - a large, brightly coloured bag, filled with sweets and a surprise gift. I loved the anticipation of not knowing what toy I was going to get. I enjoyed waiting for the surprise so much more than actually getting it, that I used to play a game with myself: I had to wait until I got home before I could open the packet! The expectation was greater for me than the fulfilment. I was so convinced that something wonderful was in that packet that I was willing to wait for it. It would change our lives if we could have this Lucky Packet Attitude.

A large aspect of hope lies with our attitudes - hope is having a positive attitude. According to an old Amish proverb: "A negative attitude is like a flat tire. You won't get very far without changing it." The problem is that we want everything now, and when we don't get an immediate answer to our prayers, we lose hope that it will ever be ours. A Lucky Packet Attitude implies being content to sit in the back seat of the car, happy that we will soon see the favours that are ours as we journey with a loving God.

I have found that when I wake up in the morning and pray: "I expect great things to happen to me today," my day becomes an adventure. I have no explanation for it, but great things do happen.

Wait Patiently

Continue praying about everything, while you patiently believe that He is working in your life. Hope comes through patient belief. Jesus teaches us how to pray: "Give us today our daily bread."[1] In this prayer we are acknowledging that all things come from Him because He is our provider. We sometimes mistakenly think that we provide for our needs ourselves. Rather, we should recognise that all we have, comes from God and that He is well able and willing to take care of our daily needs. As we continue to pray, we are to wait patiently for God to answer.

Seek God

How can we really trust a God we haven't seen? It is natural for believers to wrestle with hope as we question why our lives have turned out the way they did and why God has allowed certain things to happen to us. But faith comes from reading the word[2] and where there is faith there is hope. When we truly believe that God is who He says He is, then our hope increases. This can best be achieved by hearing what God says about himself in His Word. We read that He sees us, deals with us individually in love, works things out for us in our lives and has a wonderful purpose for us. "For I know the plans I have for you," declares the Lord, "plans to prosper you and not to harm you, plans to give you hope and a future. Then you will call upon me and come and pray to me, and I will listen to you. You will seek me and find me when you seek me with all your heart. I will be found by you," declares the Lord."[3] Don't let your vision of the future be based on what you can see, but rather by what you can imagine – nothing is out of your reach.

---

[1] Hebrews 6:11
[2] Romans 10:17
[3] Jeremiah 29:11

Nothing can break this promise of God. According to His plan, you have a "hope and a future." We don't know what tomorrow holds, but we know Him who holds tomorrow. So when you cry out to Him in your despair you can be confident that He will answer.

Once you have been sitting in the PEWS - pouring out your heart to God, expectantly believing in an answer, while waiting patiently and seeking Him, you may begin to become aware of your purpose.

People who are overwhelmed by hopelessness have lost the sense of purpose for their lives and they feel as though their dreams have died. The Bible states: "Where there is no vision the people perish."[1]

Do you look back at your life and wonder where all those years went? Do you feel that you have wasted your life? Maybe you were passionate about something in your youth and it has since been buried under years of responsibility and irresponsibility. Maybe you think that opportunities have passed you by and that it is too late for you to achieve your dreams. Maybe you have never been particularly passionate about anything. Maybe you are still waiting to become passionate about something.

The purpose for your life, your 'vision' or dream, is like a movie directed by God. You are the star and the story of your future is depicted with alarming honesty and depth of insight. This is a handmade film. In it your capabilities are displayed, your talents used and your desires fulfilled. When times get tough you can re-play this movie in your head to give you courage, hope and perseverance for the future.

However, as soon as despair sets in, filming comes to a grinding halt. The film crew may scurry around doing their jobs but, without a star, filming cannot continue. Then if the star resigns, this unique movie will never be seen. No one will ever know what could have been, not even the star. So too with suicide: the purposes that God had in mind for your life die with you.

---

[1] Proverbs 29:18

But hope is the assurance that there is this special movie made about you; one that promises to give you a future beyond your wildest dreams. Knowing that He has a purpose for your life may give you a hope that will hold you steady in hard times. We need to tell God that we are available to fulfil whatever His vision is for our lives. If you cannot think of anything that you are interested in doing or passionate about then continue on with the Pews Fuse.

I was taking a nap, feeling pretty miserable about my life, when I got the idea for this book. It felt like the words: "Suicidal Christians," simply fell into my head. I believe it was a God-inspired idea because I wasn't even thinking about anything relating to this topic at the time. I had been praying for God to use me in any way that He wanted to for a long time. You too can have God-inspired ideas. He speaks to us in our difficulties and some of the time it is with ideas about ways out and sometimes it is to plant the dream that will see us through.

There are so many stories throughout history where people have triumphed against persecution, torture and all manner of hardship because they had a dream. Ask God to give you a dream so that you too, along with Martin Luther King, can shout: "I have a dream!"

It is not easy to keep a hold on hope when we feel we cannot take one more step forward because of pain or we feel sapped of energy or we feel there is no end to the daily grind of work or we are reeling from a barrage of hurtful insults or we have been diagnosed with a terminal illness. It is *then* that we need to believe: "He gives strength to the weary, and increases the power of the weak. Even youths grow tired and weary, and young men stumble and fall; but those who hope in the Lord will renew their strength. They will soar on wings like eagles; they will run and not grow weary, they will walk and not be faint."[1]

This narrative song that I wrote a few years ago, based on Isaiah, is an allegorical story about **The Eagle**:

Pillow-puff clouds in the heavens

---

[1] Isaiah 40:29-31

Gather over a darkening land.
The animals skelter for shelter
Because they don't understand.
Above them perches an eagle
Who steadies himself for flight
He knows he needs to confront
The dark to reach the light

Chorus
Soar eagle, soar
With the wind to hold and guide you
Climb eagle, climb
Above the storm.

He's not alone in his struggle
The wind fills out his wings
And he's carried aloft by the strong
Breath of the King of Kings.
Thunder roars at his efforts
Lightening attempts to blind
But he locks his wings and soars
To the heights he knows he'll find

His feathers grow cold with ice
But the wind guides him on
To the gentle warmth of a thermal
He can rely upon.
He's reaching the gates of heaven
Seeing further than before
With strength he faces the future
No matter what it has in store.

If you get close to despair you can have hope knowing that the Wind of God's Holy Spirit will lift you up and carry you farther than you could ever have imagined. In the coming weeks, if 'thunder roars at your efforts' or 'lightening attempts to blind' you can decide to have hope in God - a sure guide through any storm.

Lord, I cannot see my way through this storm, please help me.
Help me to become a 'prisoner of hope'.

Thank you for lifting me up when I could not go any further.
Thank you for being my strength when I am weak.
Thank you that you 'put me together' when I felt as though I was coming apart.
I expect great things to happen to me today.
I am available to fulfil whatever vision You have for my life.
Help me to pray as David did: "But as for me, I will always have hope."[1]

---

[1] Psalm 71:14

I Don't Know How to Pray

My Child

My greatest delight is being in a relationship with you. I long to speak to you and I want you to include me in every aspect of your life. I know how busy you are, but if you make a special time in your day, where we can talk deeply together, then time will miraculously become available for you to do everything else. Simply put me first.

Then speak to me throughout your day. Nothing is too insignificant to interest me and no problem is too large for me to fix. There is nothing you can tell me about yourself that I do not already know, so you cannot shock me. I will never leave you because of anything you have done. I am here to help in every way.

Tell me, my loved one, whatever is on your heart.

Always listening

God

Prayer is like a train. It is always there on the tracks, shunting along, stopping whenever it sees someone waiting to get on board.

When we hear about the Prayer Train, we hurry to the station, hoping it will take us to our destination. Once there, we are not sure how to catch it, having never done it before. There doesn't seem to be any ticket office and people are milling about looking vaguely lost. Someone has scrawled instructions on a piece of cardboard and hung it up on the wall: "Get on your knees, put your hands together and bow your head." Looking around you see that no-one else is doing it so, feeling embarrassed to try it in front of others; you slip into the bathroom to get more privacy. You try it for a while, but as you wait silently on your knees in the bathroom for the Prayer Train, it begins to dawn on you that you will not be able to see when it arrives. You also begin to doubt the validity of the instructions on the cardboard; they look like they were written centuries ago – maybe someone even made them up.

As you re-emerge on the platform, you notice a group of people who appear to be in a trance, all saying something out loud together. Tentatively, you touch one of them on the shoulder to get their attention. Bothered, a well-dressed lady turns around and, listening to your inquiry, she tells you that if you repeat the words: "Hail train!" twenty times, the train will come. Feeling confident that she must be right because so many are doing it, you begin to chant: "Hail train!" At first you are comforted by being in a group, but that soon wears off and leaves you with emptiness in your heart that matches the emptiness of the track. You make your apologies and begin to look around for anyone who might be able to help you catch this elusive Prayer Train.

You spot an enthusiastic looking man who seems to be moving from one person to the other giving advice. Encouraged, you cross to him and ask how you can catch the train. Delighted to be asked, he tells you, with no uncertainty, that you need to shout loudly at the train itself for it to come. He goes on to reassure you that if you truly believe that the train will come then it will. So you begin shouting at the tracks but when you try to believe that it is coming, even though you can clearly see that it is not, you feel a little silly. The Excited Man is right there by your side egging you on and when he sees that you are growing despondent, he tells you that you actually need to believe that the train is there. As you look down the tracks you try to believe that it is there, but the train doesn't arrive. "It can't be the train's fault, so it must be you!" he says. This sounds logical so you close your eyes and concentrate harder on 'believing', but when you open them, there is still no train. Confused, you sidle off, hoping the Excited Man won't notice you aren't there anymore because you don't want him to think that you are not one of the believing few.

Standing in a clearing and feeling lost and alone, you are just about to give up trying to find someone to help, when you suddenly become aware of your surroundings. The little station looks like something out of a children's novel: creepers cover old stone and brightly coloured flowers sit in window boxes. In front of the picturesque stone station, an ornate but comfy looking bench

246

beckons. Feeling exhausted, you decide to sit down and, as you do you beginning to relax, enjoying the sun on your face. That is when you notice something for the first time and you are amazed that you never noticed it before; a small Voice can be heard coming over the loud speaker – so quiet that it is nearly drowned out by the cacophony of people talking and chanting on the platform. As you listen closely you realise that the voice is giving what appears to be a history lesson about the station. You listen to the Voice telling the history of all the past trains that have come through and taken people to their destinations and you feel comforted. The Prayer Train will come.

Excited, you get up from the comfortable bench and go to the edge of the platform. Looking expectantly down the track, you see the train appear in the distance. As soon as it stops in front of you and the doors open, you embark gratefully.

No sooner have you sat down than it begins to occur to you that you have absolutely no idea where it is going. "What if I am going in the wrong direction?" you worry. So, as the train pulls into the next station, you hurry to get off.

You are left, alone, wondering where you are: "North is... um... ok... maybe there is GPS on my mobile. Ok, no signal. Maybe, if I stick my finger in the air and see which way the wind is coming from...? Ok. No wind. Right! Now what? How am I going to get where I want to be if I don't know where I am?" you wonder, becoming a little frantic.

Looking around this new station you see that there are many other people waving their mobiles around trying to get a signal while sticking their fingers up in the air. Everyone looks lost. You wonder if they all got off the train thinking it was going in the wrong direction. Your only option, you realise, is to get back on the train. You don't need to wait long before the next one arrives.

To your delight, as soon as you get to your cosy cabin, you notice that the Conductor has laid out a lavish feast for you. Even better – it is free of charge. There are delicacies that you have never tried before and the taste and aroma are indescribably delicious. Just as you are about to bite into one succulent looking pink puff ball, a thought occurs to you: "This cannot possibly be for me. I have never heard about trains serving this kind of food." You begin to panic with the next thought: "This cannot be free. Nothing is ever free. I bet I am going to get a huge bill that I cannot possibly pay!" Drooling but resolute, you push the food away from you, and try to pull yourself together by thinking: "Besides, I am meant to be concentrating on where I am going, not on having a party!"

As you sit there, tummy grumbling, you look over into the other cabins and envy those who are digging into their feasts. They are laughing and chatting and looking as though they are having a lot of fun. You draw the blind on your window and sit alone, mulling over the events of the day. "Something is just not right" you muse. "Maybe it is that Conductor who gives things away for free? I bet he doesn't even know where we are going." This last thought begins to grow in certainty in your mind.

As you mull over these things you see that there is a small, Morose Man perched on the edge of the seat opposite you. He seems to confirm your fears when he begins to tell you that there are rumours circulating that the Conductor is a shady fellow who carries a whip and who has been seen to use it on the homeless and even on children.

The Morose Mans' words are the last straw. Terrified and suspicious, you disembark at the next stop.

For what seems like an age, you sit on the cold platform taking stock of your situation: You are no longer home and you are not where you need to be; you don't want to be where you are and you don't want to do what you need to do by catching the train to get to where you want to be. You feel as though you are in limbo. But you know one thing for sure - you cannot stay where you are. There is nothing there for you. You reason that maybe you don't need to catch a train after all. Maybe you can walk to where you want to go. But you realise that this would be impossible because it is too far. Something has to change - but what? You have tried the train but it was not fast enough and you are not sure it is even going where you need or want it to go. No one seems to be able to help and you cannot put your trust in that Conductor, after all that everyone is saying about him!

248

As the darkness falls so too does the rain. Cold, hungry and frightened you cry out for help, but none comes. Slowly it dawns on you that you are in this predicament, not because of what has happened to you, but because of what you were thinking in your head. You realise you could be on the Prayer Train enjoying the lavish feast if you had not let your fears run away with you. You immediately feel sorry for listening to the Morose Man and being suspicious about the Conductor, who, after all, had only offered you a sumptuous feast. All at once, like a long lost friend, you see the lights of the Prayer Train in the distance hurrying towards you.

As you climb on board you decide that this time you will not only stay on the train until you reach your destination but, as you see the feast freshly laid out, you resolve to enjoy the ride.

The Bible tells us 216 times to pray whereas it never tells us to breathe. The difference is that breathing comes naturally whereas prayer is a decision. We can therefore deduce that God is emphasising the importance of prayer.

This Prayer Train allegory explains some of the difficulties we may face when learning how to pray: At first, we are unsure how to do it and then as we weigh up the many rules and methods on offer; we are riddled by doubt as to its effectiveness; we get impatient when our queries and requests are not answered as quickly or in the way that we would like, and we doubt the simplicity of the invitation from our Creator to allow it to encapsulate us wherever we go.

Prayer is a conversation, in thought or word, between you and your Father. It should not be guarded (after all He knows everything about you) and you should not feel scared to approach Him with whatever is on your mind. He wants an honest, open, sincere conversation with you. Prayer can be one of our most powerful tools and our deadliest weapon. When we are at our lowest, prayer restores our hope.

If suicide became my Default Button (as mentioned in the beginning of this book) prayer was the Delete Button. It was only when I learnt to *pray before* any attempts at suicide, that I became truly free of this devastating penchant. Instead of allowing hopelessness to push me over the edge, I stopped and prayed. I remember the exact prayer word for word because it was so short. As I sat on the toilet seat with the box of tablets in my hand, I yelled out: "God please help!"

Help came immediately. I went from having little control over my actions, to gaining a semblance of clarity about what I was doing. Even though my problems still looked insurmountable, I decided to stay alive simply because I knew God wanted me to stay alive. I believe God will always answer those crisis prayers immediately.

But sometimes, when we pray, it is as though God is not there and we may feel, along with Sylvia Plath: "I talk to God but the sky is empty." What do we do when our prayers are not being answered?

During the course of my illness, I have asked: "God, why don't you heal me? It is so easy for you, just a little flick of your finger and I could be healed." Some may feel that it was rude of me to ask God this question – but I was asking this question in the right way – let me explain:

In the book of Jeremiah God 'brought charges' against the Israelites for not asking whether He was in the situation with them: "They did not ask, 'Where is the Lord?'"[1] God wants us to ask this question because it reminds us what He has done in the past. However, we are to ask it in an attitude of enthusiastic remembrance of things He has done in the past and not in a complaining, whining manner. To illustrate this important difference: Imagine a child wanting their mother to take them to the shop to buy a chocolate bar. The enthusiastic-remembrance-method of asking would be: "But Mom! Last week you bought me chocolate, how about one this week?" The complaining-whining-method would be: "Mom you never take me to the shop to buy chocolate!" There is a subtle but significant difference – the one is recognising the Mother's provision, whereas the other is complaining about it.

So we can ask God why He has not granted our requests and we may even get an answer to that question while not getting what we are

---

[1] Jeremiah 2:6

asking for. But we should resist doubting God when it appears that our prayers are not being answered, because we do not have all the facts - only God does.

We are more likely to get our prayers answered if we learn to pray regularly. I sometimes get the feeling when people say: "I will pray for you," that they actually won't. We should only say that we will pray for someone if we are willing to follow through with the promise. I keep a notebook where I list all my prayers. As soon as I promise someone that I will pray for them, I write it in the list. I would never remember to do it if I didn't. This list has become a large one over the years and it has been a great faith-builder to tick off prayers as they get answered.

Praying should be a life style choice. Making a specific time in your day to have a good, long discussion with your Father will change your life. I can see a clear difference between when I used to pray occasionally and since I have begun to include Him in every aspect of my life. It would be impossible to mention all that has changed and all the benefits derived from this intimate communion. Suffice to say that while being enveloped by love I have seen the miraculous, gained wisdom beyond my capability, overcome mountains I thought too high and learnt how to enjoy my life.

We are told to pray "continually"[1] because it:

- Increases our faith
- Keeps us focused on Him and not on the difficulties we are facing
- Remind us that He is in control
- Keeps us obedient
- Keeps us humble
- Makes His Power and Wisdom available to us
- Makes us aware of opportunities
- Make us more available to hear His Voice

Prayer doesn't have to be a long conversation. It can be snippets of thoughts, little chit chats or simply a word, like: "Help!" We can also

---

[1] 1 Thessalonians 5:16

pray for specific things, like: "Lord, please help me find a parking." We are invited to pray boldly like the prayer of Jabez: "Oh that you would bless me and enlarge my territory! Let your hand be with me, and keep me from harm so that I will be free from pain."[1] He asked for God's blessing, for help with his work and for all 'borders' in his life to be expanded, for God to be with Him in all that He did and to be kept safe from harm and evil and "God granted his request."

Some people feel that they are 'wasting God's time' if they ask Him for what they consider to be 'little things'. But God exists outside of time, therefore being unlimited by it, he will not experience any shortage. Corrie ten Boom says it so well: "Any concern too small to be turned into a prayer is too small to be made into a burden." He desires to be in a deep relationship with us. Can you imagine someone being in an intimate relationship with you and all they speak about is 'important matters' (what a friend of mine calls 'admin')? It would become boring and tedious; communication that you would not enjoy. God wants you to delight in Him as He does you.[2] We need to include God in every aspect of our lives, for example, finding a good parking place (He is brilliant at it), baking a cake (He is the master Baker) or even getting dressed (we get very creative!)

Specific, longer times of prayer (sometimes called 'quiet times') can be set aside during your day at a time when you will be free from distraction. These times have become so valuable to me that I am sad if, for some reason or other, I don't manage to have them. But I have persevered because I noticed that my day goes better when I do.

As I lie snuggled up in bed, in the early hours of the morning, with my tea and Bible, I relish our time together and delight in every moment of being with Him. However, as with any long term relationship, things aren't always rosy. Sometimes I am bored and I feel I have heard it all before and none of it is relevant to me. Often it becomes hard going when nothing makes sense to me and I don't hear His Voice.

---

[1] 1 Chronicles 4:10
[2] Psalm 37:4

I have often been asked: "How do I hear God?"

Be still and listen: First, you need to 'chill out' in the knowledge that He is in control and supreme and loves you. "Be still, and know that I am God."[1] If you, or your life, are making too much noise, you may not be able to hear His 'still, small voice.'

- **Distinguish** - God often speaks to us in thoughts, so we need to learn to distinguish which is our voice and which is that of God. "God is a Spirit: and they that worship him must worship him in spirit and in truth." The Lord is speaking to our Spirits, not to our brain or ears. Sometimes it is difficult to distinguish actual words but rather He communicates by using a picture or an impression. One can find it hard to tell the difference between one's own thoughts and the words of God.
- **Practice** - Knowing the difference comes through practice. The more time we spend listening, the more we will know His voice. The more we read His Word, the more we will be able to tell the kinds of things He is likely to say from those He is not. God never contradicts himself, so you think you are hearing His voice, see if it lines up with His Word.
- **Trial and Error** - A number of times before, I felt an urge about something that I should or should not do and I have ignored it. For example: ignoring God's leading, I tell an intimate detail about my life to a friend and they turn on me. Another example: After praying for a parking, I might feel God is saying to go in a particular direction, I decide to do something different, only to see a parking place become available but now I am on the wrong side of the road.
- **Obedience** - Sometimes you learn to hear His voice by obeying Him. Some call it 'the voice of peace'. When you think that God is saying something to you consider it and see whether you feel at peace with about what is being said. You may not like what you are being asked to do, but behind that fear or reticence you will have a sense of peace that it is right. I have experienced this many times, but on one occasion it

---

[1] Psalm 46:10

253

saved us a lot of money: My husband wanted to buy shares in an aeroplane but I felt something was not right with the people who were offering this deal. The next time we saw the person was on the front page of a national newspaper having defrauded various people out of millions.

- **Read the Bible** - If we know His nature and the things He is most likely to say and do, we can become better at filtering out that which is not from Him.
- **Other People** - Sometimes God uses other people to speak to us about what He is saying. They might confirm something that He has already told you or they might tell you something that is new and that sits peacefully with you.
- **Takes Time** - But learning to distinguish God's voice takes time and having a regular prayer time will strengthen that bond.

Prayer should be our first reaction to everything. Abraham Lincoln obviously knew the importance of tapping into the wisdom of God: "I have been driven many times upon my knees by the overwhelming conviction that I had nowhere else to go. My own wisdom and that of all about me seemed insufficient for that day."

Having decided to pray more regularly, we may be left thinking: "I don't know how to pray." What better place to learn how to speak to our Father in Heaven than at the feet of His Son? When the disciples asked Jesus to teach them to pray, He showed them by example and began praying:

"Our Father in heaven,
Hallowed be your name.
Your kingdom come,
Your will be done, on earth, as it is in heaven.
Give us this day our daily bread,
And forgive us our debts,
As we also have forgiven our debtors.
And lead us not into temptation,
But deliver us from evil."[1]

---

[1] Matthew 6 9-13 English Standard Version

With this prayer, Jesus is giving us the ultimate nutritional requirements for our souls. It encompasses all that we will need to face the challenges in our day – we will be *'preprayered'* for anything! Many scholars agree that no matter how desperate your situation and even if you have reached the end of your tether, this prayer contains requests to cover every need. According to Augustine, "whatever else we say when we pray, if we pray as we should, we are only saying what is already contained in the Lord's Prayer."

This **Preprayered Prayer Pattern** consists of:

- Papa – "Our Father"
- Presence – "in Heaven"
- Praise – "hallowed be Your Name"
- Petition – "Your Kingdom come"
- Purpose – "Your will be done"
- Provision – "Give us this day our daily bread"
- Partnership – "Forgive us as we forgive"
- Protection – "Deliver us"

Papa

We need to approach God in this intimate way because it will change the tone of all our communication with Him. Instead of being a distant God, Jesus invites us to call Him, "Our Father." It is quite awesome that we, mere mortals, are invited to address the Almighty with such an intimate term 'Abba Father' which can roughly be translated as 'Papa'. If you have ever felt estranged from God and known that gaping loneliness, then truly grasping that God wants you to have an intimate relationship with Him will fill that hole. He hears equally the wailing of a little child, the prince or the pauper, the prisoner or the soldier. He is Father to the dying, the weak, the heartbroken, the strong, the cripple, the destitute, the orphan and the widow; all 'who are weary' and all who are downtrodden can sit on the lap of Papa and chat to Him.

Presence

We need to know that not only is His presence within us in the form of the Holy Spirit but He is our all-powerful King sitting on His throne in Heaven. The knowledge that we worship a God who reigns supreme above the thoughts and ways of men, and yet one who is present in our lives, should instil in us complete security. We are able to speak to Him at any time and know that He is right here with us. This is a gift beyond description - His presence is our best present.

Praise

The term 'to hallow' means to recognise as holy. In the book of Revelations John gets a vision of being in the throne room of God. God Almighty is on His throne, around him magnificent creatures worship Him night and day throughout eternity, without ceasing: "Holy, holy, holy is the Lord God Almighty, who was, and is, and is to come."[1] God not only made them, but He no doubt sanctioned the content of their song, so it is interesting that the words He most likes to hear and those He thinks are beneficial for us include recognition of His holiness. When we pray we should be overcome by awe and reverence and spontaneous adoration. Worship is the act where, with the help of the Holy Spirit, we intimately adore our Father in Heaven.

Worshipping God involves thanks-giving. Our prayer time with God should involve a time of spontaneous out-pouring of our thanks to God. I have found that when things get really tough and I begin to thank God, I become happier.

Petition

One definition of petition is 'a formal request.' In the Lord's Prayer, Jesus is inviting the children of God to ask Him for anything. Some people feel that it is rude to ask God for things, but He actually invites us to ask: "You may ask for anything in my name, and I will

---

[1] Revelation 4:8

do it."[1] Simply including Him in every aspect of your life makes all the difference. My children laugh at me because I always ask God for the closest parking. They used to think it was a trivial thing to concern God with, until they realized that I was getting the best parking in town! Now they pray for all the little things in their lives too and they have noticed how intimately involved God is in their lives. He delights in being in a relationship with us and wants to be involved in every aspect of our lives.

When Jesus was on earth he 'offered up prayers and petitions' to God. He did not say his prayers using gentle and beautifully spoken speech. The Bible says He prayed "with loud cries and tears to the one who could save him."[2] So pour out your heart to your Father in Heaven.

An important thing to remember is that this asking needs to be 'in His Name' - in other words in line with His Word and Character. If we are obedient to Him and sincerely following Him then our requests will naturally come alongside His will and His purpose for our lives. Not only do we need to pray for our needs, but we need to pray for the needs of others.

Some people take asking to an extreme, and their entire prayer life consists of using God as though He is a giant vending machine. Only asking God for things would lead to your relationship with God being unbalanced. Mother Teresa said: "Prayer is not asking. Prayer is putting oneself in the hands of God, at His disposition, and listening to His voice in the depth of our hearts." We should look to God's Face as well as His Hand.

Purpose

When Jesus prays: "Your will be done" it pre-echoes what He cries out later to God before His death: "Father, if you are willing, take this cup from me; yet not my will, but yours be done."[3] He knew the agony He was about to face, and He was not only telling His Father

---

[1] John 14:14
[2] Hebrew 5:7
[3] Luke 22:42

about His anguish but reaffirming His obedience to carry out His mission - no matter what. So too should we, when we look at our problems, tell God that whatever He wants for us is okay with us. Let us pray that God's perfect purpose will be achieved in this world as well as throughout eternity. We need to declare that 'His Will be done' (His Kingdom of righteousness, joy and peace) over ourselves, our loved ones, our church and our nations.

Provision

When we pray: "Give us this day our daily bread," we are acknowledging that God is our provider. God delights in meeting our needs. It is all His to give and He is generous beyond your wildest dreams. In fact, He promises to provide for you: "Therefore I tell you, do not worry about your life, what you will eat or drink; or about your body, what you will wear. Is not life more important than food, and the body more important than clothes? Look at the birds of the air; they do not sow or reap or store away in barns, and yet your heavenly Father feeds them. Are you not much more valuable than they? Who of you by worrying can add a single hour to his life?"[1] God sees and understands what you need and He is able to provide.

Partnership

We cannot be fully *preprayered* to face whatever may happen in our day, unless we forgive - because it restores our partnership with God. The Lord's Prayer emphasises two aspects of forgiveness: Ask for forgiveness and forgive others. Even though we were forgiven for all sin and will go to heaven, God instructs us to say sorry to Him when we pray. We simply acknowledge the things that we know we did wrong (but we cannot possibly know everything), assure Him that we want to change and ask Him for His help to achieve that and then thank Him for His forgiveness. Whenever you ask forgiveness of God, He replies: "Forgiven!" He never holds your failures over your head and He never condemns. Forgiveness is always ours when we ask for it.

---

[1] Matthew 6:25-27

There is a stern warning in the Bible that if we do not forgive others then God will not forgive us. The Lord's Prayer makes it clear that we are to do this on a regular basis. It restores our partnership with God and ensures that no root of bitterness takes hold of our hearts. So when you pray, think of someone who has wronged you and forgive them.

Protection

Jesus reminds us that to be *preprayered* we need God's continual protection against temptation and against the evil that is trying to derail us: "deliver us from evil." We need to remember to ask God to help keep us away from temptation as well as to resist it when it comes.

We also need to pray for protection against the 'powers and principalities' that are relentlessly trying to 'kill, steal and destroy' us and the work of God. Pray each day for a wall of God's protection to surround you, your loved ones, your efforts and your possessions.

In the Lord's Prayer, Jesus is helping us to be *preprayered* by listing all possible nutritional needs our souls may have. However, there is a necessary process that needs to occur before these nutrients can be absorbed. Just as carbohydrates, proteins and fats are prevented from being absorbed into the digestive system unless they have been broken down, so too are we unable to absorb the nutrients for our souls unless we are broken down by surrender:

- Surrender everything we are and everything we do to our Father who reigns supreme.
- Surrender our wisdom – We need to stop thinking that we know what we need and trust that God not only knows, but will work it all out for our good.
- Surrender to His Will – We need to be content with whatever He is doing in our lives and with whatever He chooses to do in the future.
- Surrender our feelings – We need to give up wanting to take revenge on others by asking for forgiveness.

- Surrender our pride - We need to stop wanting things done our way and become obedient to His Will.
- Surrender to His protection - We need to recognise that He is all-powerful, that He has won the battle and that "greater is He that is in us than He that is in the world."[1]

Sometimes, even with these instructions, we are at a loss about what to pray because our problems seem so complex and interwoven. God has sent the Holy Spirit for times like these: "We do not know what we ought to pray for, but the Spirit himself intercedes for us with groans that words cannot express."[2] He knows what to pray when we don't. At these times we can just bask in the presence of God and say: "Lord, I don't know what to pray, but I know that you know."

But what do we do when we think our prayers are not being answered? Everything today seems instant – coffee, cash machines, entertainment and information - whatever we want seems to be on demand. But prayer is not like that. God sometimes expects you to wait and pray until He decides when to answer: "Be joyful in hope, patient in affliction, faithful in prayer."[3]

So, continuing to pray when our prayers are not being answered requires perseverance. We are called upon to pray for our needs, then to wait patiently with faith while continuing to be persistent in prayer, until we receive an answer. We see this in the parable of the persistent widow. A widow comes before a judge with her matter, but when he refuses to consider her request she persists until he answers: "because this widow keeps bothering me, I will see she gets justice, so that she won't eventually wear me out with her coming!"[4] She can be thought of as a nag, but God is not trying to get us to force Him to cooperate with us, He is encouraging us to pray persistently until He answers. God is not playing some weird cosmic game with us by keeping us waiting. It is always for our own good:

---

[1] 1 John 4:4
[2] Romans 8:26
[3] Romans 12:12
[4] Luke 18:5

"Perseverance must finish its work so that you may be mature and complete, not lacking anything."[1]

So when your prayers are not being answered, the solution is: Keep praying!

Thank you that I can call you Abba Father.
You are Holy.
I am secure because you are in control.
May Your Kingdom of righteousness, joy and peace reign in my life, those of my loved ones, my church and in my country.
Thank you for all that you have given, please continue to provide all my needs and for the needs of others.
Please forgive my sins and help me to forgive.
Keep me safe from myself and from the devil.
I surrender to you today.

---

[1] James 1:4

Is Suicide A Sin?

My Own

I have been here since before time began and you can see My Hand working throughout history.

These are not subjects that you need fear discussing, but when you do, remember that I am Love. While everything else constantly changes, I never change - I am the same yesterday, today and forever. I will always be Love and I will always act in Love. You may not be able to see the reasons why I do what I do, but you will be able to get closer to the truth in all things, if you understand that I am Love.

I will never take my Guiding Hand off the affairs of men. In all these things I am Lord.

The Alpha and Omega

In this chapter I will be putting the Bible and what it says about suicide in context with the history of suicide in the church and in the Western world in general. After this overview, I hope that you will be in a better position to decide whether suicide is a sin and furthermore, whether it is (as so many think) the 'unforgivable sin.'

History is littered with junkyards piled high with big boxes. Inside each box we can find the taboos of each particular society – abortion, birth defects, rape, child abuse, homosexuality – to name a few. At some stage, all these forbidden subjects were locked in a box, tossed on the heap and the key was thrown away. We thought we were hiding them away, but they all just piled up until they became ugly blots on the landscape. Over the years we have learnt that the only way to truly begin to deal with a taboo is to find the key, open the box and attempt to be discerning about the contents. As long as these issues remain locked away, they cannot have the benefit of discussion by doctors, philosophers, law makers, citizens, victims and others. While airing them doesn't mean that they are being condoned or that they will vanish, it is the first step in the process of finding a solution. As long as things are under lock and key they cannot be openly considered. Once open, we can decide if what was inside the box was worthwhile, no good, a benefit to us or no benefit at all. Suicide has long been one such taboo.

The World Health Organisation issued a statement: "Worldwide, the prevention of suicide has not been adequately addressed due to a lack of awareness of suicide as a major problem and the taboo in many societies to discuss openly about it. In fact, only a few countries have included prevention of suicide among their priorities." They recognise that as a result of suicide being a taboo, efforts at prevention are hampered. There are still communities today who refuse to bury a person who has died by their own hand in hallowed ground and the families left behind often suffer enormous shame and ostracism. These attitudes make it very difficult for loved ones and professionals to offer the help that is so obviously needed.

Having an understanding of past attitudes to suicide can help us unlock present ones. As we read what others have thought on this subject, perhaps we can begin to make a more informed decision about what we think.

This taboo has not always been there. Over the years there have been many people who think that we have the right to die at our own hand. The ancient Egyptians regarded it as acceptable if you were faced with great emotional or physical suffering although a recently discovered poem suggests it was discouraged. This poem was commissioned by the King to encourage his subjects to find a solution to their despair and not to take their own lives. It reads: "Death is by my side today, like a well-trodden way ... like the longing of a man to see home ... I am laden with misery." It concludes: "...cling to life."

Suicide was fairly common in the Greco-Roman world as they believed it was acceptable under certain circumstances. As far as we know Socrates was the first person to openly debate the morality of suicide. He believed that humans belonged to the gods and therefore did not have the right to take something that did not belong to them – namely life. Ironically, he died having being forced to drink hemlock.   Epicurus, another Greek philosopher, encouraged his followers to die by suicide when their lives no longer afforded happiness.

The Romans took it a step further, believing it was the honourable thing to do if your honour was irretrievably lost and you faced public humiliation.   It was also considered acceptable in the case of the elderly.   No judgment was attached to such a death.   Two hundred years before Christ, suicide became the preferred method of execution amongst the Roman upper class.   Those who wished to kill themselves applied to the senate, and if their reasons were considered sound, they were given hemlock free of charge. Soldiers, slaves and those who had committed capital crimes were refused however, for economic reasons.   If you bought a slave, who subsequently killed themselves within six months of purchase, you could claim a full refund from the previous owner.   Those who committed non-violent crimes were allowed to return home after their trial, as long as they killed themselves within one day. Nero later took this mandatory suicide to the extreme by placing daggers on the dinner tables of his enemies.   Whereas suicides for these reasons were acceptable, suicides for petty reasons were considered cowardly.   An example of this would be Mark Anthony, who killed himself because he mistakenly thought that Cleopatra had taken her life.

The Bible mentions seven suicides and one attempted suicide. Two of the suicides are wicked men (Saul and Judas) ending their lives in humiliation, four of them (Saul's armour-bearer, Abimelech, Ahithopel and Zimri) are acts of despair or pride and only one of them is depicted as a hero (Samson). A closer look at these stories may give us a clearer picture of what the Bible says about suicide:

Abimelech's suicide[1], the first one mentioned in the Bible, was particularly humiliating. Having slaughtered his seventy brothers in a vain attempt to gain power and then burning a thousand people alive in a tower, he was trying to lay siege to another tower when a woman dropped a heavy millstone on his head, cracking his skull. As

---

[1] Judges 9:54

he lay dying he asked his armour-bearer to kill him to avoid the shame of being killed by a woman.

The story of Saul's death is in similar circumstances. We see Saul running from a fierce battle with the Philistines in hot pursuit. Wounded, defeated and no doubt aware of the Philistines reputation for torture having heard the story of Samson, Saul asks his armour-bearer to kill him. When he refuses, Saul falls on his own sword. In verse 13 we read "...because he was unfaithful to the Lord... ...the Lord put him to death..."[1]

However, this is not the end of the story. We later read about an Amalekite who reports to King David about Saul's death.[2] He explains that he came upon Saul who was begging him to end his life because he was already 'in the throes of death'. It seems that Saul had not been able to kill himself. The Amalekite obliges. Either the Amalekite was lying to the King to get a reward for killing his enemy, or the account is true and he merely helped Saul end his life. In the earlier account it said he fell on his sword but it does not say that he died. The Amalekite may have arrived after his failed attempt. Scholars have many differing views about how Saul died, but all would agree that it was under painful and humiliating circumstances.

This story gets even more convoluted.[3] The day before this event a medium had apparently conjured up Samuel from the dead. This apparition had told Saul: "Because you did not obey the Lord ... (He) will hand over both Israel and you to the Philistines." So we can see that Saul's death was a divine judgement for the sin Saul had committed. But the apparition's following prediction is interesting: "...and tomorrow you and your sons will be with me." This could lead one to believe that God was assuring Saul that he would go to heaven because we can presume that Samuel was in heaven. The Hebrew translation, 'with me' is directly translated 'along'. One cannot even translate it as "you will come along with me" because it reads more like "and tomorrow you and your sons...along." It is

---

[1] 1 Samuel 31:3-6
[2] 2 Samuel 1
[3] 1 Samuel 28:16-20

more likely that the ghost of Samuel is saying that Saul will be in the same state as he is – that he will travel 'along' the same path.

It does not look like God had a merciful and forgiving attitude to Saul – quite the contrary. Earlier the apparition says: "Why do you consult me, now that the Lord has turned away from you and become your enemy?" One can be sure that an enemy of God is unlikely to go to heaven. Also, upon hearing his fate, 'Saul fell full-length on the ground, filled with fear because of Samuel's words." This is not the action or emotion of a man who has been told that he will be going to heaven. So we cannot deduce from this that Saul went to be with God after his suicide. God gave Saul time to repent, but when he chose to continue sinning, he died as God had warned he would.

This story is of particular interest to anyone who needs clarity on the issue of assisted suicide. Assisted suicide is where the person asks for help to die, and performs the last act that leads to their death. Saul requests assisted suicide on two different occasions – firstly from the armour-bearer and then from the Amalekite (unless the Amalekite was lying). The first denies his request and the second obliges. Rightly, the armour-bearer did not want to kill God's anointed. We need to bear in mind, when asking ourselves whether assisted suicide is in God's will, that we are anointed.[1] Therefore, having received the anointing of the Holy Spirit from Jesus, it is clearly wrong for us to help someone to kill themselves. This text gives no sanction for assisted suicide.

A pitiful, copy-cat suicide taking place on the edge of this battlefield was that of Saul's armour-bearer. The Bible says that he was 'terrified'[2], probably because he too knew the reputation of the Philistines for torture. So, after refusing Saul's request, he too fell on his sword, dying alongside his master.

The next suicide we read about it that of Zimri who reigned for only seven days, having murdered the entire family of King Elah.[3] When

---

[1] 1 John 2:20
[2] 1 Chronicles 10:4
[3] 1 Kings 16

he realized he was surrounded, he fled to the palace and set it on fire burning it and himself to the ground.

The next two suicides mentioned in the Bible are similar: Both Ahithophel and Judas betray their masters and then commit suicide.

During the reign of King David, Ahithophel was an advisor to Absalom, David's son, who was plotting to overthrow the King David.[1] When his plan failed, he hanged himself. Whether he was angry at his advice not being followed or shamed by being disrespected is unclear but Ahithophel, in essence, killed himself because of problems at work.

The only suicide we read about in the New Testament is that of Judas.[2] He was a man who knew Jesus well and who was part of the inner circle of his best beloved friends. I believe that when he told the chief priests and the elders where Jesus was, he had no idea that it would result in Jesus' crucifixion. But when the reality of what he had done sunk in, and he saw that Jesus was condemned to die, 'he was seized with remorse and returned the thirty silver coins to the chief priest and the elders. "I have sinned," he said, "for I have betrayed innocent blood". Perhaps he was trying to reverse what he'd done or maybe he was hoping his act would spark some remorse in them so they might free Jesus. However, even though they were priests, they showed little sympathy for his guilty conscience. Realising there was nothing he could do to reverse what he had done and utterly broken "he went away and hanged himself."

It is impossible to know exactly why Judas hanged himself. The most likely reason is that he saw death as an escape from the enormous guilt he felt. Death would not have relieved him from this guilt, instead, what he desperately needed, was the absolution of his guilt that could only come from the exact One whom he had betrayed.

The death of Judas has raised many questions, but the only question we need to ask for the purposes of this book is: If Judas was damned to hell, was it because of his action of betraying Jesus or because he

---

[1] 2 Samuel 17
[2] Matthew 27:5

committed suicide? This is a hotly debated topic. It is true that Jesus described him as "one doomed to destruction so that scripture would be fulfilled."[1] Some speculate that this comment is referring to Judas being 'doomed' to such despair that he kills himself and others say it is refers to him being doomed to hell as a result of either his act of betrayal or his act of suicide. There is another explanation: In other translations Jesus says 'son of perdition' which is only used elsewhere in the Bible to refer to Satan. Jesus might not have been talking about Judas at all, he may be referring to Satan indwelling Judas.

At the last supper, while Jesus was feeding a piece of bread to him, Satan entered Judas.[2] Jesus knew what Judas and Peter would do, and yet he still chose to break bread with them and love them. Jesus probably saw Satan enter him but He did not stop the preordained plan of God. Just because Judas was 'possessed' does not absolve him of the responsibility of his actions.

Judas never heeded Jesus' warnings and he rejected the mercy and forgiveness that He offered before his betrayal. Never in the Bible does he call Jesus 'Lord' or 'Master', as the other disciples did, he only ever refers to Jesus as 'Teacher'. Perhaps he was damned for the same reason all are – if we do not acknowledge Jesus as our Lord and Saviour. We cannot know the definitive answers to these questions. The realm of eternal judgement is God's territory and not ours. However, we do know that our God does not make an offer for forgiveness only once, and if rejected, forsake the individual for ever. We are told repeatedly about God's endless love and mercy.

When Jesus was on the cross He said: "Father, forgive them for they know not what they do."[3] I believe that He was asking His Father to forgive, not only those who had tortured and hung him, but also those who had played a part in getting him to the cross – Judas included. Perhaps Judas, having been a close friend of His, was foremost in his mind when He asked His Father to forgive.

---

[1] John 17:12
[2] John 13:27
[3] Luke 23:34

A thought that confirms this view is that Jesus' called Judas a "son of perdition" *before* he had committed suicide, not after. So it may not be referring to his eternal punishment as a result of his suicide at all, but rather his punishment to come as a result of his betrayal.

There is no doubt in my mind that Judas committed a heinous act. However, he repented and did what he could to undo it. Surely if mercy was offered to Christ's murderers, then the same mercy might have been offered to Judas? There is no way for us to know for certain because eternal judgement is the realm of God. But we can also not surmise that Jesus, by supernaturally knowing ahead of time that Judas would kill himself, was damning Judas to hell.

There is another Biblical suicide that is particularly interesting because, on the surface, it could appear that it not only had God's assistance, but also His blessing.

The Philistines paraded Samson before them during a party with his eyes gorged out. While they jeered and shouted at him, he prayed: "...strengthen me just once more, and let me with one blow get revenge on the Philistines for my two eyes."[1] It is clear from Scripture that he wanted to die because he said: "Let me die with the Philistines!" God miraculously granted this request. Samson pushed on the pillars that held up the temple bringing it crashing down, killing himself and all there. The Bible says: "He killed many more when he died than while he lived." It goes on to note that he had an honourable burial in the tomb of his father. It is interesting that the New Testament does not mention his failures or his alarming death, instead he is praised by Paul, along with a few other faithful few, who "through faith, conquered kingdoms, administered justice, and gained what was promised."[2]

This strange story raises a number of questions: Did God see his suffering and grant him the power to end it? Without supernatural strength he would never have been able to bring the building down and therefore God gave him the means by which he ended his life. Is

---

[1] Judges 16:28
[2] Hebrews 11:32

this another Biblical picture of assisted suicide, where God is the 'assistant'?

Although Samson knew that his action would bring about his own death, he is not acting primarily to end his own life. His pain and need for revenge are secondary to the plan that God had. Samson was merely an instrument of God. Thomas Aquinas's rule of double effect may be at play here. This is a rule that helps to assess how permissible an act is. It deals with the question about whether it is acceptable to do something that will bring about good results (namely the death of the Philistines) while using unethical methods (namely his suicide). Samson's death can be seen as a secondary effect to the more far reaching primary effect seen in the deaths of so many wicked Philistines. As a result of his final act, an entire ruling dynasty was wiped out - which probably saved many Israelite lives in the long run, and changed the course of history forever.

Forgetting the lofty purposes of God, we could argue that Samson asked God to help him die and God granted his request. This could lead us to think that if we asked God to help us die, then it would be acceptable for us to take our lives. But we need to remember that this was achieved through a supernatural act of God. In order for that to happen to someone today it would be like a person who wanted to die, walking past a building and asking God to let it fall on his head. That is very different to jumping off the same building and on the way down asking God to kill you.

Therefore we can say that Samson's death was closer to being a divine act than a suicide. In his last moments he was able to do more for his people than he had done in his entire life previously. It was, arguably, a heroic deed and not an argument for assisted suicide.

The only attempted suicide we read about in the Bible is in Acts.[1] Paul prevents the attempted suicide of a jailer who was under the mistaken belief that all his prisoners, including Paul, had escaped during an earthquake. Thinking his career and even his life would be in jeopardy, he resolved to fall on his sword. Paul stopped him and, that night, he and his whole family got baptized.

---

[1] Acts 16:28

I have taken the references to actual suicides in the Bible, however there is another consideration: Jesus said: "Anyone who hates his brother is a murderer, and you know that no murderer has eternal life in him."[1] Does that mean that if you think in your heart about killing yourself, then it is as if you had? If this were the case then David, Job and others in the Bible can be considered to have committed suicide because they all mentioned not wanting to live anymore. Therefore even those who have considered suicide need to consider the question about whether suicide is a sin or not.

Suicidal Christians have been a fact since the early days of Christianity. After Christ's many believers chose suicide over the gruesome religious persecution they were facing, for example, being eaten by lions. There were some Christian writers, during those early days of the church, who suggested that suicide should be a goal for those who were particularly pious. As a result, the numbers of mass suicides and martyred deaths rose so alarmingly that Jewish elders forbid the bodies of suicides to be buried in hallowed ground. This seems to be one of the main roots of the stigma of suicide that we know today.

Early Christians began to condemn suicide because Judas had killed himself – it became a sinful act by association. During the 4th Century St. Augustine publicly condemned suicide as a sin, thus concreting the first official position of the church on the matter. He stated that suicide contravened the sixth commandment: "Thou shalt not kill" and therefore Christians had no right to take their lives.

In the years that followed there was a flurry of edicts and proclamations that outlawed suicide. Then in 348 AD the Council of Carthage condemned those who had died by their own hand and in 363 AD the Council of Braga denied proper burial rites for all known suicides. This resulted in all martyrs, who had died by their own hand, being struck off the list of martyrs in 305 AD. In an attempt to try and prevent people from committing suicide, the church had birthed a stigma steeped in fear and shame that remains to this day.

---

[1] 1 John 3:15

During the 13th century Thomas Aquinas wrote Summa Theologica which was a collection of theological writings pertinent to the Church. In it, he strongly argues that suicide is a sin for which one cannot repent. He wrote: "Life is a gift made to man by God and it is subject to Him who is master of death and life." He stated that he who takes his own life is sinning against God. He goes on to say that it is unnatural in the sense that it goes against our instincts of self-preservation. He also reasons that by killing himself man is damaging the community of which he is a part. He adds that anyone who kills himself to avoid punishment is a coward and concludes that suicide is "completely wrong." Many civil and criminal punishments and laws were implemented to discourage suicide.

As a result of church sanction, the stigma attached to suicide reached boiling point during the Middle Ages. The bodies of suicides were dragged to the outskirts of the town where a stake was driven through the chest so that the ghost of the departed would be pinned down and unable to come back and haunt anyone. Whatever the victim owned was confiscated, leaving the family, not only ostracised, but penniless. Anyone who attempted suicide, and failed, was sentenced to death. This led to the use of a strange saying: "If you fail they call you a criminal, if you succeed they call you a lunatic." The coroner juries found the deceased guilty of insanity rather than 'felo de se', which is Latin for 'felon of himself' – namely suicide.

The Renaissance is well known for its reawakening in all areas of life, and though the stigma of suicide remained, it was beginning to be challenged. For example, Sir Thomas More allowed assisted suicide on the island of Utopia. The subject was also being re-examined in the theatre, art and literature. The most notable was in the works of Shakespeare, where suicide appears thirteen times. His views reflect the medieval view of shame and despair on the one hand, and on the other it is seen as a noble and courageous act: "Death before dishonour" was a motto at the heart of courtly ideals. His dramatization of suicide drew it out of the closet by reminding society that it was a fact of life.

The first modern defence of suicide came in 1608 when John Donne, an English poet, wrote a treatise called "Biathanatos" which remained unpublished till 1647. In it he drew on the laws of Nature, theological sources and classical and modern legal systems, to argue that Christians should have the right to choose death. He argued against St. Augustine saying that if it were contrary to our instincts for self-preservation, then all acts of denying oneself should also be unlawful. He posed the question that if the church permits other forms of killing in the form of martyrdom, capital punishment and killing during war, then why do they consider suicide a sin? He summed up by pointing out that Scripture does not have any clear condemnation of suicide.

The historian and philosopher, David Hume, wrote "Of Suicide" in 1783. In this essay he argues that traditional views are muddled and superstitious. He argues three points against the traditional attitude towards suicide held by the church. First he says that suicide does not break the sixth commandment "Thou shalt not commit murder." That law is prohibiting us from taking other people's lives, because we have no authority over them, but it is not referring to taking our own lives. He then argues against clerics who said that suicide is a coward's way out, by saying that one would need to look at individual cases to draw that conclusion. In reply to the argument that suicide is rebellion against God, because it disturbs the natural order of the world, Hume turns the tables on the clerics by saying: "It is a kind of blasphemy to imagine that any created being can disturb the order of the world, or invade the business of providence." Just as God allows us to divert rivers for irrigation, he permits us to divert blood from our veins.

Suicide was a topic of philosophical debate on both sides of the channel with some French philosophers saying that suicide is a personal right. John Wesley, co-founder of the Methodist church, in an effort to try to persuade the destitute to continue living, wrote that suicide caused "a poor wretch by sin he cannot repent of, to rush straight through death into hell." His opinions about suicide were shaped by his fundamental belief that our choices, good or bad, have serious consequences for us, both now and for eternity.

273

In 1897 Emile Durkheim looked at the causes of suicide and observed that they were to be found in social factors and not in individual personalities. Social stressors contribute to suicidal behaviour. He divided suicide into four categories: First, Egoistic Suicide, which occurs when the person feels detached from society when, for example, bonds like family, work and community are broken for some reason – through retirement, loss of a loved one or other disruptions. The second, Altruistic Suicide, happens when the person is under the control of those around them, as in a cult or political cause. These people are willing to die for their cause. The third, Anomic Suicide is where the person feels that their lives lack meaning. The last category, Fatalistic suicide, is where excessive social restraint is threatened, for example a fugitive killing himself before the police can take him to jail. Durkheim's ground-breaking work helped to change the way society views suicide and thus began to shatter the taboos associated with it.

Sigmund Freud further influenced our thinking by highlighting mental disorders as a medical condition. They were, he said, a result of natural and physical factors.

As a result of these and other studies many changes were brought into civil, criminal and religious laws. For example, the Catholic Church began to allow these burials in church cemeteries and many countries de-criminalised suicide.

The current belief of the Catholic Church is that suicide is a serious sin. They argue that our lives are the property of God and a gift to the world, and that to destroy life is to wrongly assert dominion over what is God's. In the Catechism it states: "Suicide is contrary to love for the living God...it is seriously contrary to justice, hope and charity." The 1997 Catechism of the Catholic Church indicated that the person who committed suicide may not always be in their right minds and are therefore not completely morally culpable: "Grave psychological disturbances, anguish, or grave fear of hardship, suffering or torture can diminish the responsibility of the one committing suicide." It encourages prayer for those who have committed suicide in the knowledge that they will be judged fairly and justly. It also encourages believers to pray for the loved ones of the deceased to receive the healing touch and comfort of our Lord.

The modern day Protestant Church (Evangelicals, Charismatics and Pentecostals) are divided on this subject. Most, however, argue that because suicide involves self-murder, then anyone who commits it is sinning. Some say that because Christ took the punishment for all the sins of the world onto himself at the cross, the sin of suicide is no exception and a person who dies by their own hand will go to Heaven as long as they have received Christ as their personal Saviour. Some liberal Protestant denominations see assisted suicide as morally acceptable.

Having scanned history, we are now in a position to ask the next question: Is Suicide a Sin?

The answer seems to hang on the sixth commandment: "You shall not murder,"[1] or "thou shalt not kill". However this latter translation is incorrect. It is important to distinguish between 'murder' and 'kill' because the incorrect translation has been used to support many causes, from animal rights and the abortion debate to capital punishment. The verb used in the original "ratsah," is generally translated as 'murder' and refers only to criminal acts of killing a human being – an unlawful act. Whereas the word "kill" generally refers to the taking of life for all classes of victims and for all reasons – this can be a lawful act, for example killing an animal. God is saying, in the sixth commandment, that we are not to take a life *unlawfully*.

Is suicide the unlawful killing of oneself? When we look elsewhere in the Bible for our answers we find Job, having just heard about the death of all his children, crying out to God: "The Lord gave and the Lord has taken away?"[2] In the face of great suffering, Job reacted correctly to God – he acknowledged God's sovereignty over everything, including life and death. He is in essence saying: "Life and death are God's to give and to take away."

In Genesis God explains to Noah why murder is so wrong: "Whoever sheds the blood of man, by man shall his blood be shed; for in the

---

[1] Exodus 20:13
[2] Job 1:21

image of God has God made man."[1] If we commit murder we are killing someone who is made in the image of God. Likewise if we commit suicide we are killing one made in God's image.[2] Suicide is the self-murder of someone created in God's image and is, as such, a sin. Having established that, we may ask ourselves: Is suicide an *unforgivable* sin?

This idea comes from the early teachings of Saint Augustine who taught that suicide is self-murder and as such warrants an eternity in hell. It was believed that since the person committing suicide had no chance to ask for forgiveness, because it cannot be asked for after death, this sin remained un-forgiven.

This view shows a misunderstanding of the security of the salvation that a person receives when they accept Jesus as their Saviour. All sins, from birth to death, are forgiven. God declares at that point that nothing will separate us from Him – not our sins, not ourselves, not others, not demons, not mental health problems, not even death...nothing: "For I am convinced that neither death nor life, neither angels nor demons, neither the present nor the future, nor any powers, neither height nor depth, nor anything else in all creation, will be able to separate us from the love of God that is in Christ Jesus our Lord."[3]

Salvation is a state of being, not a state of doing. We did nothing to earn this gift of salvation and we can do nothing to get it rescinded. God does not revoke salvation because of our behaviour. He is not surprised by our sin. He gave us this gift knowing that we would continue sinning.   So once we have accepted Jesus as our Saviour, eternal life is secure.

The only mention made of an unforgiveable sin in the Bible is made by Jesus: "And so I tell you, every sin and blasphemy will be forgiven men, but the blasphemy against the Spirit will not be forgiven."[4] The generally accepted view is that Jesus was speaking about the

---

[1] Genesis 9:6
[2] Genesis 1:27
[3] Romans 8:38
[4] Matthew 12:31

Pharisees who had just accused him of casting out demons with the power of Satan. Their sin was their refusal to acknowledge the power of God in Christ. It has nothing to do with suicide and therefore suicide is not the unforgiveable sin.

But was St. Augustine right in believing that suicide cannot be forgiven because the person has no chance to repent? The Bible clearly forgives murderers, for example, Moses and David, but they had opportunities to ask for forgiveness. People who commit suicide don't.

To answer this argument we need to look at the reason why Jesus died on the cross: He died so that *all* sin could be forgiven. If we say there is one sin that is not covered by the cross, then the complete work of the cross is undone. There were no exceptions to what Christ died for – all sins were forgiven. Another misconception in the 'lack of time' argument is that we are saved because we say sorry for what we did – this implies that repentance can buy salvation. Repentance comes from God.[1] The mere thought that we need to ask for forgiveness is enlightened and comes from God. Without His prompting we wouldn't even think we needed to repent. We repent because we are saved, we do not repent to get saved. If repentance brought salvation, then salvation would be the result of works, which it is not.

Now that we have answered the question about whether suicide is a sin, we are in a better position to look at a hot debate that rages today. Are there any extenuating circumstances where suicide is acceptable? The 'right to die debate' has been discussed and argued in many books solely devoted to the subject, so I will be touching on it from a biblical point of view.

We first need to understand the various terms used in this debate, however there are many conflicting views as to their exact meaning. The word euthanasia comes from the Greek words "eu" meaning good and thanatos" meaning "death". It can be separated into two categories: Passive euthanasia, where the consent of the patient is obtained and active euthanasia (or mercy killing) where the person

---

[1] 2 Timothy 2:25

is unable to ask for the procedure for some reason, for example, the doctor who gives the patient a lethal injection. This is in no way suicide because the person does not die as a result of their own action. In many jurisdictions, active euthanasia is considered murder or manslaughter, whereas passive euthanasia is accepted by professional medical societies and by the law under certain circumstances.

According to the 26th report of the British Social Attitudes Survey published in 2010, 71% of religious people and 92% of non-religious people believe that a doctor should be allowed to end the life of a patient with an incurable disease. Whether the people interviewed are being asked if they condone the doctor making this decision without the patient's consent, is left unclear. It is alarming that so many believe that a person's life may be taken, with or without their permission, on the say-so of a professional. Oddly, passive euthanasia is legal in many countries, whereas suicide is illegal.

I believe active euthanasia is murder because it is taking someone else's life without their permission. Some say it is an 'act of mercy', and perhaps it is, but I don't believe we are in a position to judge whether that specific instance is 'merciful' or not because we cannot see what is going on in another person's mind. What if those who are in a comatose state are lying there completely enthralled by the presence of God? What if they are having a deep spiritual experience sailing through the cosmos being entertained and loved by God? Perhaps they are able to indicate, or even say, that they want to die, but what if they change their mind a few seconds before the lethal dose is delivered? Tragically, they would not be in a position to stop their deaths. Even if they could indicate, right up to the point of death that they wish to die, should we rule out the possibility of a miracle, or the possibility that God has another plan for their lives?

While I am living with chronic, debilitating pain and so can relate in some fashion to what a bed-ridden person may be going through, I cannot understand the full extent of some debilitating illnesses. I do not wish to appear insensitive to the suffering of others or to the hardship a loved one must feel when having to watch the ravages of a chronic disease. These circumstances must be indescribably difficult. But maybe we should be the bastions of hope for those we love who are in pain? Maybe we should stand by them by searching deep in our reservoirs of compassion and love to help them persevere? Maybe this incredibly hard time will become a time of triumph? Euthanasia by-passes any hope of victory and, in my opinion, it violates the sixth commandment even if intentions are based on heart-felt love.

Assisted suicide refers to the practice of a person taking their own life having received information, guidance or medication provided by another. For example, if the doctor inserts the needle that will deliver the lethal dose and the patient simply needs to flick a switch. Another example of assisted suicide is when Saul asked his armour-bearer to end his life. This action was a sin because it is strictly forbidden by God for anyone to kill His anointed. It can be argued that we too, as God's anointed, should not kill ourselves. There is no sanction in the Bible for assisted suicide.

Another interesting dilemma was presented with the invention of life-support technology. People are being kept alive when, it can be argued that God may think it is their 'time to go'. There is a difference though between helping people to die, as with euthanasia and assisted suicide, and prolonging the act of dying, as with life-support systems. There is no clear-cut answer. With each unique situation, loved ones involved need to seek God's guidance and wisdom and listen to the promptings of the Holy Spirit.

People may query whether suicide is a sin when it occurs as a result of mental illness. If sin involves a conscious decision to reject God, then one could argue that people who are incapable of balanced thought are not responsible for their actions. I believe that God sees into the hearts of man with great compassion and mercy and as such His justice will be overflowing with love. We cannot say whether someone's decision to kill themselves was conscious or not; only God can see the motives of the heart.

The same argument applies in the case of someone who is being tortured. It can be argued that this person is not able to make a balanced decision and that they are therefore not responsible for their actions. Again, God sees the heart and is merciful, we can only pray that if we are ever in any of these situations our first and continued response will be to cry out to Him.

The old adage: "Suicide is a permanent solution to a temporary problem," may seem flippant to those who are going through the anguish of mental illness, the persistence of addiction or for those who have been told that they have a fatal illness. But the possibility of your situation being temporary can only be pushed to one side if you refuse to accept the words of Jesus: "With man this is impossible, but with God all things are possible."[1] There is nothing that you are going through today that God cannot change for the better.

Heal and deliver me Lord!
Give me the courage to ask others for help.
Take away all thoughts of suicide.
Help me to decide that no matter what happens I will choose life and not death.
Give me the strength to see this through.
Help me to see that this situation can change.
Thank you that 'all things are possible with you.'

---

[1] Matthew 19:26

Won't I Be Better Off In Heaven?

My Dearly Loved Child

Your help comes from me because I am the Maker of Heaven and earth. I am the shade at your right hand so the sun will not harm you by day, nor the moon by night and I will keep you from all harm.[1]

I will supply all your needs according to the riches of my Son, Jesus.[2]

I am the God of hope who will fill you with joy and peace through the power of the Holy Spirit.[3] *I will give you strength and bless you with peace that passes all understanding.*[4]

I watch over your coming and going both now and forevermore with unequivocal love.

God

There are two different and opposite ways for believers to think: Treadmill Thinking and Travelator Thinking.

As I entered the gym I read the sign above the door and groaned inwardly: "No pain, no gain." I knew what I was in for and the prospect didn't make me happy – a date with the treadmill. "Think about why you are doing this." I wondered again, trying to motivate myself. "I've got to look like thin, athletic, beautiful Cynthia." My thoughts trailed off as I reached the treadmill, squatting like some kind of medieval torture device amongst a sea of grotesque looking machines.

"Right!" I said under my breath as I stepped onto the machine, "I can do this." The machine whirred into action, unlike my body that felt

---

[1] Psalm 121
[2] Philippians 4:19
[3] Romans 15:13
[4] Psalm 29:11

as though it was determined to resist every step. I looked up at the wall of the gym, covered with more motivational posters: "You only get out what you put in," I read, as I decided that today I would go farther and do more than I had ever done before.

I began walking and, as the machine sped up, I ran. Minutes ticked by like hours, and feeling bored, I began to read some more of the prominent posters: "Good is not enough if better is possible." I felt ashamed of myself: "I always do things half-heartedly. I must try harder to be better." Walking faster I read another slogan: "If you're not first, you're last." It confirmed my goal – I wanted to be the best. I was tired of being second rate. "It's all or nothing for me from now on!" A poster quoting Arnold Schwarzenegger caught my eye: "We all have great inner power; the power is self-faith." It was true, I thought, "I can do it all with this enormous power I have inside me." The sweat was running down my back and I felt like I could run another hundred miles. But that only lasted a few minutes longer....

Suddenly I felt really low again. This was too hard. Everyone was right: "Everything I do fails." Defeated, I switched the treadmill off and stepped down. As I walked out of the gym despondent, I read another poster: "Play like a champion, train like an underdog." It felt like a confirmation for what I already knew about myself: "I am an underdog and I will never be a champion."

As I walked outside into the milling crowd, the brilliant sunshine almost blinded. My legs felt as heavy as my heart: "Oh God!" I shouted inwardly, "I can't do this anymore!" All of a sudden I noticed the moving sidewalk up ahead as if for the first time. I had stood on this travelator many times before, but it was as though I was seeing it for the first time. It stretched out like a giant treadmill along the sidewalk, and as I stood there I studied the people and noticed a few interesting differences between it and the treadmill.

As people walked up to it, a look of anticipation and relief came over their faces, unlike the trepidation and dread I had felt about the treadmill. Whereas I had to work hard to go nowhere on the treadmill, the people on the travelator were moving fast with little or no effort. It began to dawn on me that this was very similar to how we, as believers think. Some of us rely on ourselves by putting huge effort into getting nowhere and others rely on God's Power and then rest in Him as He carries them along. We have a choice: We can either struggle with Treadmill Thinking or we can be at ease with Travelator Thinking.

The table below shows the differences between the two ways of thinking:

	Treadmill Thinking	Travelator Thinking
Expectation	trepidation/dread	hopeful anticipation
Goal/Purpose	to achieve our own ends	to live in obedience to please God
Controlling Thought	condemnation	God's love for me determines my self-worth
Means	service in hope of reward	Surrender to Christ's control
Power Source	reliance on self	reliance on the power of the Holy Spirit
Results	depression, despondency, apathy, worthlessness, approval addiction	a balanced mind, security, peace, satisfaction, thankfulness and joy

Treadmill Thinkers find it incredibly difficult to accept the fact that they are saved by grace – that they didn't earn it and that there is nothing they can do to keep it. They choose to believe rather, that they have done something to warrant their salvation, and that they can work somehow to maintain it. This is a self-inflicted religion based on self-effort and pride and will result in frustration and exhaustion. Although the reasons why I wanted to kill myself varied each time I tried, they all had one thing in common - Treadmill Thinking.

Many believers are convinced they can work their way to righteousness. They try hard to attain some lofty spiritual goal that often has no basis in what God has planned for their lives. They diligently serve in the church hoping for a reward, feeling crushed when none comes. When they do not get the appreciation they crave, they give up on all service, saying things like: "No one notices anything I do, so I don't know why I bother." Their goals for service have been exposed because they were not working to give, they were working to receive.

These people usually understand that Grace saved them, but they continue thinking that there is some way that they can work themselves into God's favour. They run on the fumes of their own efforts that can only lead to burnout and eventual withdrawal. They have failed to realise the simplicity of the message of Christ: "If any man remains in me and I in him, he will bear much fruit; apart from me you can do nothing."[1] They have not grasped that we are simply called upon to abide in Him.

Treadmill Thinking is at the heart of every believer who gets to the end of their tether: the addict who tries to give up without the help of God, the depressed person who incessantly replays words of condemnation in their heads, the invalid who cries out against God and not to Him, the person who is trapped in trying to perform for God or others and those anxious souls who cannot be content with the provision of God.

At first, Travelator Thinking looks like the hard option but in the long run, it is the easy option. Life is incredibly tough for many of us and it is often more instantly gratifying to find an easy way out, rather than making the changes that bring lasting joy. For some that instant gratification is the promise of heaven. It is an alluring destination, offering complete freedom from all trouble: "He will wipe away every tear from their eye. There will be no more death or mourning or crying or pain."[2] The question that I have often asked is: "How come everyone isn't clamouring to get there?" Then during

---

[1] John 15:5
[2] Revelation 21:4

284

my darkest days, when suicide is on the agenda I have thought: "Won't I be better off in heaven?"

The answer is a resounding, "yes!" This does not apply only to those who are looking for a way out: no matter how much anyone who has ever lived has enjoyed their lives while they were here on earth, heaven will be better.

But the question that should rather be asked is: "Will I be better off in heaven *now*?"

The answer to this question is not as simple. All through the Bible God emphasises the importance of 'life.' If we look at His creation we can see a celebration of life and an avoidance of all things pertaining to death. So we can be certain that life is important to God and He wants us to remain alive. But why is it important?

James writes: "Blessed is the man who perseveres under trial, he will receive the crown of life that God has promised."[1] Why would we need to "run with perseverance the race marked out for us,"[2] if there was not some plan for us in eternity? There is. We are being prepared for something after death and taking our lives early means we will enter eternity unprepared.

This can be compared to going to university. God decided long before you were born, that you would be going to the University of Life...

You are nervous on induction day and wonder if you will ever fit in with all the other students who seem to know where they are going and what they are doing. When you receive the course material, you panic and wonder how you will ever be able to get through the enormous load. Paging through the heavy textbooks, you see words and concepts that make no sense to you. Relieved, you see the Dean wandering through the garden – Surely he will be able to answer your questions and make sense of it all?

---

[1] James 1:12
[2] Hebrews 12:1

Seeing your agitation he places his arm around you and motions for you to go join him on a bench. As you pour out your heart to him he reassures you that you are not expected to know everything now, but that if you continue to study diligently it will all become clear. As you get up to leave he smiles down at you and simply says: "Enjoy yourself now!"

You are delighted by his comfort and feel a great sense of freedom in his parting words and, as the term wears on, you think you have discovered exactly what he means by enjoying yourself. You do what you want to do, when you want to do it and how you want to do it. There are parties, dinners and dances every night that keep you up ... and get you down. By the end of term, when exam time arrives, you are completely unprepared. After taking the tests you are convinced that you are going to fail. But when you get your test results back, you are surprised and perplexed. Written on the cover of the exam, in bold red ink are the words: "Repeat!"

Grateful to have a second chance you knuckle down and get more balanced about university life. You still attend the parties, but you leave at a reasonable time so that you can get up early in the morning to attend lectures. The term is going well until one day you notice what you think is an injustice occurring on campus. Rallying up a crowd of other disgruntled people you begin picketing. This all takes a lot of time: persuading others to join you in your cause, making posters, lobbying the faculty for change and broadcasting on the campus radio station for your rights to be heard. Before you know it, exam time has arrived and, yet again, you are completely unprepared. This time, as you write the test, you realise you are better at questions than answers. Once again, written on the cover of the exam in bold red ink are the words: "Repeat!"

The following term is hard. You resist your old habits and avoid the partying crowd and the picketing bunch and settle down to the task at hand. This time when exam time arrives, you feel excited because you are prepared and when you receive your results this time you see written on the cover in bold red ink: "Passed!"

As you leave the exam room, feeling as though you would like to shout out your achievement to the entire campus, you become aware of the students who are wearing special blazers and ties. You know they are the Prefects and they all look happy. They seem to be involved in every aspect of campus life – helping others with their work, in the canteen, in the faculty lounge...everywhere you look they seem to be making a difference and in charge. You long to be a Prefect.

As you walk back to your dorm, you see the Dean walking in the garden and going over to him you ask: "Dean, how do I become a Prefect?" Smiling, and obviously pleased by your question, he replies: "If you do well with the small things that you are given to do, you will be given more authority and responsibility over bigger things." With that, he hugs you and congratulates you on your achievements to date: "You are doing well. Keep on."

Maybe you have spent your time so far at the University of Life being distracted by the things you think will make you happy or maybe you have spent your time complaining about your lot. Either way, if we are not learning the lessons that God has in mind for us, we are going to get to repeat them. God never fails us when we have not passed the tests; he simply gets us to take them again until we learn that particular lesson. Once we have, we move on to the next one.

In the Parable of the Talents[1] Jesus explains this further: it is not just important to get through your course, it is important that you do well. Those who are "faithful with a few things," for example, living a productive life on earth, will be "put in charge of many things." Jesus explains that he who can be trusted with 10 talents (which was currency in those days) will be given 10 cities. Everything we do on earth is the "small things" and the "big things" refer to whatever we will be given to do in heaven. This implies that we will be given authority and responsibility when we get there.

It is common knowledge that there are consequences for our actions, so too there are ramifications for the way we live our lives. What we do now, will have an effect on how we spend eternity. We need to be trained to be responsible so that we can be trusted with authority.

---

[1] Matthew 25:14

The implication then is that if we complete the course we may end up being responsible for, and having authority over, more in heaven.

University prepares you for life, whereas living prepares you for eternity.

I love to let my imagination roam wildly through the possibilities about what I will be given to do in heaven: compose songs for the angels to sing with instruments and notes that have never been seen or heard; design a new life form and the planet it inhabits or perhaps create a new kind of delicacy that no one has ever tasted. The possibilities are endless - but the size of our responsibility and the extent of our authority may depend on how we conduct ourselves here on earth. While it is enormously exciting to think that all this is in preparation for something wonderful in heaven, it would also be such a shame to get there and realise that we are unprepared.

If you commit suicide, you have given up all chance of getting prepared – you have flunked out of the University of Life. You will arrive in Heaven unprepared for eternity.

Besides going against a commandment, besides the fact that you will be murdering a chosen, anointed, child of God made in His image and besides the fact that you will be unprepared for eternity; there are many more reasons why you should not take your own life. Outlined below are a few more **Reasons Why You Should Not Take Your Life**:

- **Others will be hurt** by this action - It brings heartbreak that is very difficult to overcome to those around you and for generations to come. The grief left behind after a suicide is complex. Not only do survivors need to come to terms with the anger they feel, they also need to grieve your loss. Suicide often leaves behind people who are dependant, for example children or elderly parents. Even if you have no one relying on you now, suicide ends all possibility of you being there for loved ones in the future. God says we are to "love our neighbours as ourselves."[1]

---

[1] Matthew 22:39

- **The legacy is destructive** – Broken hearts and lives are left in the wake of suicide.
- **It is pride** – The person committing suicide is announcing to God that they can see that the future holds nothing good for them. They know better than God and see no hope. It is not the way Jesus said it should be, He said: "I will come back and take you to be with me."[1]
- **It is an expression of your lack of faith** - It is a clear indication to God that you do not trust Him to take care of your financial, emotional and physical needs. By taking your life you are saying that you either don't believe that He is capable of changing circumstances or healing your wounds, or that He does not care enough to do it, or that you don't trust the way *He* wants to do it (not the way *you* want Him to fix it). With this act, God is completely shut out from being able to work further in your life. By taking your life you are declaring that you no longer believe "all things are possible with Him."[2]
- **It shows your unbelief** - At the point of killing yourself, are you a hundred percent sure that you are about to be face to face with God? I think this reality is seldom in a suicide's mind. If you imagined God right there with you, explaining that He has plans for you, suicide would no longer be an option. But even if you cannot see Him, He is there with you. He says: "I will never leave nor forsake you."[3]
- **It shows that you place your security in yourself** - At the point of wanting to kill yourself you have been looking to yourself, things, or others to find your security. You have found them wanting e.g. you are embarrassed beyond endurance for what you have done or you cannot contemplate living without the life-style you and your dependants had become used to, or you cannot fathom living without that loved one in your life. All these indicate that your security has been in something or someone other than

---

[1] John 14:3
[2] Matthew 19:26
[3] Deuteronomy 31:6

God. The Bible says: "Let the beloved of the Lord rest secure in him."[1]

- **It presumes upon His Grace** – If you commit suicide knowing that it is a sin, you are 'taking advantage' of the fact that you are forgiven. The Bible teaches that 'where sin abounds, Grace abounds more.'[2] Basically, you can never out-sin God's Grace, which covers all. However, a person should never presume upon this Grace and sin knowingly. Any abuse of the Grace of God has dire consequences, and in the case of suicide, those consequences are eternal.

- **All potential for good deeds is over** - It is putting an end to the work that God is doing in you to help you to live more abundantly so that you will be able to achieve the purpose that He has in mind for you: "I know the plans I have for you..."[3]

- **It denies the work of the cross**: Ultimately, the most important reason why you should not take your own life is that Jesus died on the cross for you. He says: "The thief comes only to steal and kill and destroy; I have come that they may have life, and have it to the full."[4]

- **All chance of telling others about Jesus is over** – Paul wrote: "If I am to go on living in the body, this will mean fruitful labour for me."[5]

- **It is throwing the gift of life back at God** – He created the world for us to enjoy and through suicide you are refusing that gift: "For it is by grace you have been saved...it is the gift of God."[6]

- **It is an expression of self-hatred** – Killing yourself is the ultimate expression of hate towards yourself. If the Creator of the Universe loves you, why would you hate yourself? God loves you fully and completely: "For God so loved the world that He gave His one and only Son."[7]

---

[1] Deuteronomy 33:12
[2] Romans 5:20
[3] Jeremiah 29:11
[4] John 10:10
[5] Philippians 1:22
[6] Ephesians 2:8
[7] John 3:16

- **It usurps the power that belongs only to God** – "The Lord gave and the Lord has taken away."[1]
- **Your body belongs to God** – It is His property because He made it, He paid for it and He lives in it: "Do you not know that your body is a temple of the Holy Spirit...you were bought at a price. Therefore honour God with your body."[2] We were bought with a price when Christ's death freed us from sin. We also do not have the right to do whatever we wish with our bodies because the Holy Spirit lives within us.
- **It is a bad witness to non-believers** – Non-believers look to us as an example of what it would be like if they came to know Christ as their Saviour. Suicide sends the wrong message and could cause non-believers to find an excuse not to come to know Jesus in their lives.

Maybe, after all these reasons, you are still crying out: "But you don't understand how hard my situation is!" No matter how much pain you are in, no matter how trapped, no matter how gripped you are by an addiction or habit, no matter how uncontrollable your thoughts, no matter how much debt you are in or how little money you have, no matter how ridiculed, pursued or persecuted you are and no matter what you are facing – God has the same question for you today, as he had for Abraham: "Is anything too hard for the Lord?"[3]

The Lord is my Shepherd, I shall not want.
He makes me to lie down in green pastures,
He leads me beside quiet waters,
He restores my soul.
He guides me in paths of righteousness
For his name's sake.
Even though I walk
Through the valley of the shadow of death,
I will fear no evil,
For you are with me;
Your rod and staff,

---

[1] Job 2:21
[2] 1 Corinthians 6:19
[3] Genesis 18:14

They comfort me.
You prepare a table before me
In the presence of my enemies.
You anoint my head with oil;
My cup overflows.
Surely goodness and love will follow me
All the days of my life,
And I will dwell in the house of the Lord
Forever.[1]

Amen.

---

[1] Psalm 23

References

Stanford Encyclopaedia of Philosophy website, "Suicide" (First published Tue May 18, 2004) http://plato.stanford.edu.

Caroline Leaf: "Who Switched off my Brain" (Nashville: Thomas Nelson, Inc.)

Crouch Foundation Website, "A History of Suicide" (created by Baton Rouge Crisis intervention Centre)

World Report on Violence and Health. World Health Organization; Geneva, Switzerland, 2002.

Random History website: Little known facts 2009. http://facts.randomhistory.com/2009/09/07_std.html.

Bertolote J.M, Fleischmann A. Suicidal Behaviour prevention: WHO perspectives on research. Am. J. Med. Genet. C. Semin. Med. Genet. 2005.

American Foundation for Suicide prevention website - CDC's National Center for Health Statistics for the year 2003.

Samaritans website: "Suicide facts and figures" 2013.

Institute for Health Metrics and Evaluation: "Global Burden of Disease," 2010.

Oliveira, MP; Silveira, DX; Silva, MT (2008 Jun). "Pathological gambling and its consequences for public health."

American Journal of Psychiatry, 2004.

Gary Vanderet, "The Skill of Handling Life's Troubles," Cultivating a Faith that Endures (Palo, Alto, CA: Discovery Publishing, April 27, 1986).

The Psychiatric Times: "The Link Between Substance Abuse, Violence, and Suicide," 2011.

"Suicide risk associated with drug and alcohol dependence" - Miller NS, Mahler JC, Gold MS (Cornell University Medical College).

Moss, Howard B. Chenb, Chiung M. and Yi, Hsiao-ye: "Subtypes of alcohol dependence in a nationally representative sample. Drug and Alcohol Dependence", (Retrieved 28 June 2007).

Kristin Neff, Ph.D - "The Power of Self-Compassion."

Will Bowen - "Complaint Free Relationships: Transforming Your Life One Relationship at a Time.".

National Institutes of Health – "Researchers Identify Alcoholism Subtypes." (June 28, 2007).

M. Scott Peck, "The Road Less Travelled" (New York: Simon & Shuster, 1978).

Witvliet, C.V.O., Ludwig, T. E., & Vander Laan, K. L. - "Granting forgiveness or harboring grudges" (2001) "Implications for emotions, physiology, and health" - Psychological Science, 12, 117-123.

John Wesley: Answer to Church's "Remarks"

Leahy A, Clayman C, Mason I, Lloyd G, Epstein - "Computerised biofeedback games: a new method for teaching stress management and its use in irritable bowel syndrome." (Department of Gastroenterology, Royal Free Hospital, London).

Lightning Source UK Ltd.
Milton Keynes UK
UKOW02f0638230816

281288UK00002B/34/P